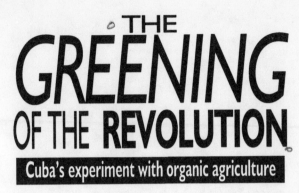

THE GREENING OF THE REVOLUTION

Cuba's experiment with organic agriculture

Edited by
Peter Rosset and Medea Benjamin

OCEAN

A project of Global Exchange

Cover design by David Spratt

ISBN 1-875284-80-X

First printed 1994

Printed in Australia

Published by Ocean Press,
GPO Box 3279, Melbourne, Victoria 3001, Australia

in association with Global Exchange,
2017 Mission Street, San Francisco, CA 94110, USA

Distributed in the United States by the Talman Company,
131 Spring Street, New York, NY 10012, USA
Distributed in Britain and Europe by Central Books,
99 Wallis Road, London E9 5LN, Britain
Distributed in Australia by Astam Books,
57-61 John Street, Leichhardt, NSW 2040, Australia
Distributed in Cuba and Latin America by Ocean Press,
Apartado 686, C.P. 11300, Havana, Cuba

CONTENTS

LIST OF TABLES

❧❧❧

Acknowledgements

Global Exchange was kind enough to organize the logistical aspects of our trip. We are greatly indebted to their staff, especially Rodrigo González and Medea Benjamin. We also thank the *Instituto Cubano de Amistad con los Pueblos* [Cuban Institute for Friendship Among the Peoples], as well as the Global Exchange associates in Cuba, Michele Frank and Leslie Balog. The staff of Marazul Travel in New York made many of the travel arrangements, for which we are grateful. Aaron Strain and Jane Lorenzo provided essential research and logistical assistance in the preparation of this report. Kevin Danaher was kind enough to proofread the manuscript. We thank all of the institutions and individuals in Cuba who welcomed us and gave us access to information and great hospitality. However, the authors and editors alone are responsible for the contents of this report.

Preface

This is the report of the *International Scientific Delegation and Fact-finding Mission on Low-input Sustainable Agriculture in Cuba*, organized by Global Exchange. The 20 members of this delegation (who are listed at the end of this document) traveled to Cuba from November 20 to 29 of 1992. The purpose of the mission was to report on changes that had taken place in Cuban agriculture since the 1990 collapse of that nation's trading relations with the socialist bloc. Word had filtered out into the international press that Cuba was in the process of a massive switch to organic farming because of a cut-off in imports of agrochemicals, and that there was a lot of exciting experimentation taking place. Accordingly, with the help of Global Exchange, I put together a blue-ribbon international scientific delegation to travel to Cuba and investigate these reports. This document represents the fruit of these efforts.

During our stay in Cuba we visited all major agricultural research centers located in the capital, as well as the major agricultural university, the office of the Food and Agriculture Organization (FAO) of the United Nations, a local non-governmental organization (NGO), and various urban gardens and private homes. We also traveled in Havana Province, which is distinct from the capital city, and in Pinar del Río Province, a major agricultural center. In the countryside we visited state farms, cooperatives and individual private farms, research stations, and other agricultural facilities. We conducted extensive interviews with government officials, farmers, farmworkers, farm administrators, researchers, professors, the representative of the FAO in Cuba and dozens of ordinary people.

The Ministry of Agriculture [MINAGRI] helped arrange our visits, but at no time did we feel restricted in our movements, nor were government officials present at many interviews. While the Ministry made many of the statistics in this report available to us, we were frustrated in our attempts to obtain certain types of figures, particularly those related to productivity, efficacy and yields. Some of the information is just not available, given this period of extreme economic chaos. Other information may be considered too sensitive to give to a foreign delegation. In any case, this lack of information inhibited our ability to draw certain conclusions in a definitive manner. Nevertheless, we felt we gained a great deal of insight into this very fascinating Cuban process, and present this information in the spirit of international scientific exchange.

Peter Rosset
Delegation leader
July 1993
Stanford, California

Introduction

Findings of the International Scientific Delegation and Fact-Finding Mission on Low-Input Sustainable Agriculture in Cuba

Cuba before and after the collapse of the socialist bloc

From the Cuban revolution in 1959 through the collapse of trading relations with the socialist bloc at the end of the 1980s, Cuba's economic development was characterized by rapid modernization, a high degree of social equity and welfare, and strong external dependency. While most physical quality of life indicators were in the high positive range, Cuba depended upon its socialist trading partners for petroleum, industrial equipment and supplies, agricultural inputs such as fertilizer and pesticides, and foodstuffs — possibly as much as 57 percent of the total calories consumed by the population. The U.S. trade embargo had directed Cuban trade toward the socialist bloc, while the favorable terms of trade which Cuba obtained there for sugar and its other exports made it cheaper to export sugar and import foodstuffs than to produce sufficient food domestically.

Cuban agriculture was based on large-scale, capital-intensive monoculture, more similar in many ways to the Central Valley of California than to the typical Latin American *minifundio*. Import coefficients of greater than 90 percent for fertilizers and pesticides give some idea of the degree of dependency exhibited by this style of farming, and the vulnerability of the island's economy to international market forces. When trade relations with the socialist bloc collapsed in 1990, pesticide imports dropped by more than 60 percent, fertilizers by

77 percent, and the availability of petroleum for agriculture dropped by a half. Food imports also fell by more than half. Suddenly, an agricultural system almost as modern and industrialized as that of California was faced with a dual challenge: the need to essentially double food production while more than halving inputs; and at the same time maintaining export crop production so as not to further erode the country's desperate foreign exchange position. The caloric and protein intake of the population began to drop alarmingly, and the first indicators seen in decades of possible malnutrition appeared. Food security had shown itself to be the Achilles' heel of the revolution.

Mobilizing science and technology to respond to the crisis

In some ways Cuba was uniquely prepared to face this challenge. With only 2 percent of Latin America's population but 11 percent of its scientists and a well-developed research infrastructure, the government was able to call for "knowledge-intensive" technological innovation to substitute for the now unavailable inputs. Luckily an "alternative agriculture" movement had taken hold among Cuban researchers as early as 1982, and many promising research results — which had previously remained relatively unused — were available for immediate and widespread implementation. Cuban scientists were also able to rapidly switch the bulk of their new research in the same new directions.

The Alternative Model versus the Classical Model

Planning authorities within the Agriculture Ministry have now officially declared that all new development of agriculture be based on what they call the "Alternative Model," which they contrast with the "Classical Model" of conventional modern agriculture. They now say that the Classical Model was always inappropriate for Cuban conditions, having been imposed by socialist bloc technicians. In this conceptual framework, the Classical Model is based on extensive monoculture of foreign crop species, primarily for export. It is highly mechanized, and requires a continuous supply of imported technology and inputs. It promotes dependence on international markets and, through mech-anization, drives migration of people from rural areas to the city. Finally, it rapidly degrades the basis for continued productivity, through the erosion, compaction and salinization of soils, and the development of pesticide resistance among insect pests and crop diseases.

The Alternative Model, on the other hand, is based on the Low Input Sustainable Agriculture paradigm, known as LISA in the United States. It seeks to promote the ecological sustainability of production by replacing the dependence on heavy farm machinery and chemical inputs with animal traction, crop and pasture rotations, soil conservation, organic soil amendments, biological pest control, and what the Cubans call *biofertilizers* and *biopesticides* — microbial formulations that are non-toxic to humans. The Alternative Model requires the reincorporation of rural populations into agriculture, through both their labor as well as their knowledge of traditional farming techniques and their active participation in the generation of new, more appropriate technologies. This model is designed to stem the rural-urban flood of migrants, and to provide food security for the nation's population.

Conversion from conventional agriculture to organic farming

Cuba today is undergoing what is essentially the largest conversion from conventional agriculture to organic or semi-organic farming that the world has ever known. Empirical evidence from the United States and elsewhere demonstrates that it can take anywhere from three to five years from the initiation of the conversion process to achieve the levels of productivity that prevailed beforehand. That is because it takes time to restore lost soil fertility and to re-establish natural controls of insect and disease populations. Yet Cuba does not have three to five years — its population must be fed in the short term. Clearly Cuban scientists and planners hope to shorten this process by bringing sophisticated, "cutting edge" biotechnology[1] to bear on the development of new organic farming practices. If this attempt is successful, the Cuban version of LISA would have significant implications both for other developing nations, as well as for the United States and Europe.

Elements of the Alternative Model

During our stay in Cuba we were able to document the development and implementation of alternatives in the areas of pest and soil management, labor mobilization, and participatory methods for generating new technology:

---

[1] As far as we were able to ascertain, Cuba has not liberated genetically engineered organisms into the environment. Instead, the biotechnology being used in agriculture is based on such non-controversial techniques as fermentation, tissue culture and serological testing.

• Management of insect pests, plant diseases and weeds

Integrated pest management, or IPM, is the basis for crop protection under Cuba's new model. It is built upon the most comprehensive large-scale pest monitoring system outside of the former socialist countries of Europe. Among the alternative tactics being integrated to offer insect control, the most important are conventional biological control based on mass releases of parasitic and predatory insects, and the use of biopesticides. In the latter area, Cuba is substantially more advanced than other Latin American countries and compares favorably to the United States. They produce formulations of bacterial and fungal diseases of insect pests which are applied to crops in lieu of chemical insecticides. A total of 218 local centers located on agricultural cooperatives and state farms produce these products of biotechnology for local use, while industrial production will soon be underway to supply high end markets on the larger farming operations that produce for export. Cuba is also the only country in the hemisphere to make large-scale use of microbial antagonists to combat soilborne plant diseases. New directions in weed management in Cuba are based on the scientific design of crop rotations to suppress particular weed species.

• Soil management

Cuba has made substantial progress in recent years toward arresting salinization and reversing soil erosion and the depletion of organic matter. Conventional agronomic techniques form the backbone of the soil conservation program, while organic soil amendments and innovative biofertilizers are in widespread use to restore soil fertility. The organic soil amendments come from livestock manures, the incorporation of green manure crops as part of crop rotations, composting of municipal garbage and other waste products, and most impressively, industrial-scale production of high quality humus using earthworms as composting agents. Furthermore, Cuban use of biofertilizers in commercial agriculture is unrivaled in the world, including not only standard *Rhizobium* inoculants for luguminous crops, but also free-living bacteria that make atmospheric nitrogen available for other crops. Perhaps of greatest importance for other developing countries, Cubans are mass producing solubilizing bacteria which make phosphorous — which on many tropical soils is bound to crop particles — available for uptake by crop plants. Finally, they are converting their dairy operations nationwide to the low-input Voisin Rational Grazing Management system made popular in New Zealand.

• Labor mobilization

The Alternative Model poses a dilemma for Cuban planners. While Cuban society is highly urbanized, currently available technologies for organic farming require more labor than the conventional practices they replace. Nowhere is this more obvious than in the national substitution of oxen for tractors, though other practices are more labor intensive as well. The short-term strategies in place to counter this problem include short (two weeks) and medium-term (two years) voluntary service mobilizations of urban workers to provide supplementary farm labor, and experimentation with both moral and financial incentives tied to productivity. They also have a new program designed to promote the re-creation of a more intimate relationship between farm laborers and the land they work. Longer term efforts are geared toward the creation of attractive new communities in the countryside, which offer better housing than in the cities. It is hoped that these new communities will at least stabilize rural populations, if not actually reverse the trend toward rural-urban migration. In the meantime, urban food production, reminiscent of "victory gardens," is being promoted.

• Generation and recuperation of knowledge

A pivotal component of the shift toward the new model is a recuperation of the knowledge that Cuban peasants have of traditional farming techniques, as well as their active participation (together with state farm technicians and managers) in the generation and dissemination of newer technologies. Towards this end, the Ministry of Agriculture sponsors farmer-to-farmer and farmer/extensionist/scientist workshops throughout the countryside, where farmers and scientists from different regions discuss the similar problems they confront and exchange ideas and solutions. These efforts in Cuba lag somewhat behind non-governmental organizations (NGOs) in other developing countries, where these NGOs are in the vanguard of the movement for popular participation in development. Yet if one considers that in these other countries NGOs must fill the vacuum left by disinterested governments, then the active role of the Agriculture Ministry in promoting this sort of participation in Cuba is all the more impressive.

Conclusions:
An experiment that the world should be watching

It is unclear whether the widespread implementation of an alternative model of agricultural development will, in conjunction with other government policies, allow Cuba to emerge from the crisis wrought by the collapse of the socialist bloc. On this point Cuban officials that we interviewed seemed fond of pointing out that, "though they said we were a satellite of the Soviets, our planet has disappeared and we're still here circling around." Yet they themselves acknowledge that Cuba, in the end, proved to be as dependent as the rest of Latin America.

It is beyond the scope of our expertise to predict whether such an economy can ever overcome, on its own, the loss of trade relations with the country or bloc on which it depended. As agricultural scientists and environmentalists, however, we *can* say that the experiment in agricultural alternatives currently underway in Cuba is unprecedented, with potentially enormous implications for other countries suffering from the declining sustainability of conventional agricultural production. We therefore call on the international scientific and agricultural communities to support the efforts of Cuban farmers, scientists and planners to remake their agriculture in a more independent and sustainable fashion, and to pay close attention to the lessons we may learn from both successes and failures in Cuba. While the present economic crisis in Cuba may be equivalent to "two steps back" for the island's population, the implementation of the Alternative Model may one day prove to have truly been a step forward, albeit taken under extreme adversity.

◆ 1 ◆

Economic development and agriculture in Cuba

After the 1959 revolution and before the 1990 collapse of trading relations with the socialist bloc, economic development in Cuba was molded by two external forces. One was the U.S. trade embargo, with its associated efforts to isolate the island economically and politically. The other was Cuba's insertion into the socialist bloc's international trade alliance with relatively favorable terms of trade. The .S. embargo had essentially forced Cuba to turn to the socialist bloc, while the terms of trade offered by the latter opened the possibility of more rapid development and accumulation on the island than in the rest of Latin America and the Caribbean.

Thus Cuba was able to achieve a more complete and rapid modernization than most other developing countries. In the 1980s it ranked number one in the contribution of industry to its economy and it had a more mechanized agricultural sector than any other Latin American country (see Table 1 for figures). Nevertheless, the same contradictions that modernization produced in other Third World countries were apparent in Cuba, with Cuba's development model proving ultimately to be of the dependent variety (Pastor, 1992). Agriculture was defined by extensive monocrop production of agroexports and a heavy dependence on imported agrochemicals, hybrid

TABLE 1: Comparative statistics on Cuba before the collapse of the Socialist Bloc

CATEGORY	Cuba 1965	Cuba 1988-9	Latin America 1988-9	USA 1989	Cuba: Rank in Lat.Am.
GENERAL:					
Population (1992)		10.6 mill			
Area (sq. km)		110,861			
Agricultural land (ha)		6,677,450			
Population: percent urban	55%	69%		74%	5
FOOD AND HEALTH					
Daily calorie intake, per capita	2,500	2,898	2,674	3,676	2
Daily protein intake, per capita	66 gm	77 gm	64 gm	110 gm	4
Per capita milk consumption		110 kg/yr		122 kg/yr	4
Life expectancy	55	73	67	75	2
Infant mortality/1000	44	13.6	20	10	1 (lowest)
Population per doctor		333		438	1 (most doctors)
Housing: rooms per family		4.1		5.1	1
EDUCATION					
Adult literacy		92.4%		95.7%	3
Secondary school enrollment		85%		99%	1
Teacher:pupil ratio		21:1		24:1	1
% university students: women		54%		50%	2
ECONOMY					
GNP per capita		$2,000		$19,840	3
Industry as percent of economy		45%		31%	1
AGRICULTURE					
Increase in per capita food production during 1980s		8%		-3%	1
Population per tractor in use		146		52	1 (most tractors)
Cultivated land per tractor (ha)		125		88	1 (most tractors)
Irrigation: % of cultivated land		26%		10%	4
Grain yield (MT/ha)		2.7	2.1	4.5	2
SCIENCE					
Pop. per scientist or engineer		830*		253	1 (most scientists)
CULTURE					
Movie attendance per person/yr		8.5		4.5	1
Theater attendance/person/yr		2.6		0.2	1 (in world)
Museum attendance/person/yr		0.8		1.5	1
Newspaper circulation/1000pop		140		259	1
QUALITY OF LIFE INDEX					
Physical Quality of Life Index (Overseas Develop't Council)		98/100		98/100	1 (11th in world, USA 15th)
Average Rank of Health & Education Indicators (Pastor, 1992)		1st in Latin Am			1

* It is likely that this figure underestimates the number of scientists and engineers. In Cuba we were given figures of 50 for scientists and 8 for technicians employed in science, which are probably overestimates. Deere (1992) quotes figures that 1.2 percent of the population (1 in 80) are technical personnel employed in agriculture or agricultural science, of which more than a third have university of higher degrees (1 in 215 people in the population at large)

SOURCES: New Book of World Rankings; WRI Environmental Almanac; FAO Yearbook; WHO Yearbook; UNESCO Yearbook; World Bank Development Report; MINAGRI; Pastor, 1992.

seeds, machinery and petroleum. While industrialization was substantial by regional standards, Cuban industry had a very high imported component consisting of inputs and capital goods (Pastor, 1992).

The Cuban economy as a whole was thus characterized by a contradictory dualism between its relative modernity and its function in the socialist bloc's division of labor as a supplier of raw agricultural commodities and minerals, and net importer of both manufactured goods and foodstuffs. In contrast to the situation faced by most Third World countries, this international division of labor actually brought significant benefits to the Cuban people. This is evident by comparing basic statistics on pre-1989 Cuba to those of other Latin American countries (Table 1). Prior to the collapse of the socialist bloc, Cuba had achieved high marks for per capita GNP[2], nutrition, life expectancy and women in higher education, and was ranked first in Latin America for the availability of doctors, low infant mortality, housing, secondary school enrollment, and attendance by the population at cultural events. In fact, Cuba ranked first in Latin America and eleventh in the world in the Overseas Development Council's Physical Quality of Life Index (which includes infant mortality, literacy and life expectancy), while the USA ranked fifteenth.

The Cuban achievements were made possible by a combination of the government's commitment to social equity and the fact that Cuba received far more favorable terms of trade for its exports than did the hemisphere's other developing nations. During the 1980s Cuba received from the Soviet Union an average price for its sugar exports that was 5.4 times higher than the world price (Pastor, 1992). Cuba also was able to obtain Soviet petroleum in return, part of which was re-exported to earn convertible currency. Because of the favorable terms of trade for sugar, its production far outweighed that of food crops.

About three times as much land was devoted to sugar in 1989 as was used for food crops (exclusive of cattle; see Table 2). In Table 3 we present data which demonstrates the importance of imported foodstuffs in making up the Cuban diet prior to 1990. Though the two sets of data presented differ slightly,[3] they clearly point to a pattern of food

---

[2] Gross National Product.

[3] Pastor (1992) provides a short bibliography on the reliability of Cuban data sources. Virtually all data reported in the literature, including in this report, was ultimately supplied by Cuban authorities. This is of course true for most national statistics from anywhere in the world. In accepting Cuban data one

dependency, with as much as 57 percent of the total calories in the Cuban diet coming from imports.

TABLE 2:   Distribution of agricultural land by category of use in 1989

Crop	% of agricultural land
Perennial crops	**38.0**
Sugar cane	29.7
Citrus	2.2
Coffee	2.2
Banana & plantain	1.7
Fruit trees	1.4
Cacao	0.1
Henequen	0.1
Minor perennials	0.4
Annual crops	**11.6**
Row crops	6.8
Rice	3.1
Tobacco	0.9
Forage crops	0.3
Other	0.5
Livestock	**44.0**
Managed pasture	16.2
Natural pasture	27.8
Idle	**6.5**
TOTAL	**100%**

Source: Ministry of Agriculture (MINAGRI)

Given that Cuba could provide a greater quantity and variety of foodstuffs to its population by exporting sugar and importing food with the proceeds, the strategy can be deemed to have been a rational and effective one. Because of the relatively favorable terms of trade, the Cuban economy was not "mined" by foreign interests to the extent that the region's other economies were, and the island was able to achieve a

---

must assume that the Cuban government is not more likely to distort figures than are other developing world governments.

partial escape from the "development of underdevelopment" trap in which the North's development is seen as a direct consequence of, *and* a direct cause of, the underdevelopment of the South. Furthermore, the revolutionary government's commitment to social equity, human capital formation and infrastructure development, together with its relative lack of corruption, allowed the island's population and economy to benefit from the greater opportunities for accumulation offered by its favorable insertion into international trade.

Nevertheless, when trade collapsed with the socialist bloc, the degree to which Cuba exhibited an essentially monocrop agriculture proved to be a major weakness. Thus it is useful for us to review Cuban agricultural history.

TABLES 3a and 3b: Dependence on imported foodstuffs

Food item	% imported
Cereals	79
Sugar	0
Beans	99
Meat	21
Fish	44
Milk & dairy products	38
Oil & lard	94
Roots & tubers (*viandas*)	0
Fruit	1
Vegetables	2

Source: MINAGRI data, 1989

Food item	% imported
Wheat	100
Beans	90
Canned meat	39
Poultry	33
Rice	50
Oil & lard	68
Butter	64
Total calories in diet	57
Animal feed	36

Source: Data from Deere, 1992

The origins of Cuban agriculture

Pre-Columbian Cuba was inhabited by two different peoples: the pre-agricultural Ciboneys and the agricultural Arawak. The Ciboney arrived on the island about 6,000 years ago and were primarily fishers and gatherers. The Arawak, who arrived later (1,500 years ago), not only gathered and fished, but also produced a great deal of their food themselves.

The staples of the Arawak diet were cassava and maize, which were roasted as well as processed into a fine flour (Sauer, 1966). Other crops included squash and beans which, when eaten with corn, provided balanced protein. Other protein sources included marine and fresh water fish, and shellfish. Arawak agriculture was quite advanced in ecological terms, relying on a sophisticated knowledge of resource management principles. Assemblages of species with different growth patterns, canopies and root structures minimized competition for soil and moisture resources. Peanuts and other nitrogen-fixing legumes were grown to enhance soil fertility and periodic burning of secondary forest released nitrogen and phosphorus, as well as exchangeable calcium and magnesium.

The "low-input" Arawak agriculture in the Greater Antilles produced high yields, a fact that was recognized by the Spaniards when they arrived in the late 15th century. In fact, it was Arawak food sources that kept the Spaniards alive for many years after their arrival. This agricultural system was soon erased, however, as the Spaniards sought to impose the plantation system of production.

The Spaniards and plantation agriculture

Sugarcane was introduced to Cuba on Columbus' second voyage but did not become the island's most important crop until the beginning of the 19th century. After a successful slave rebellion in neighboring Haiti, sugar production dropped drastically in that ex-French colony, leaving the Spaniards to fill the gap. Large tracts of fertile land in Cuba were converted to sugar production, and a new labor regime of African slaves was introduced.

The decimation of the indigenous Arawak people and their locally-adapted food system shaped the island's future food production systems. The Arawak diet and farming systems were replaced by the patterns of the Spanish and their African slaves. The Spaniards brought Old World crops such as wheat and citrus, as well as cattle, sheep, goats, and pigs. African crops grown on slave provision gardens included pigeon peas and yams from West Africa. Rice was introduced by the Spaniards, though it is likely that it was also grown as a slave crop.[4]

The imposition of the sugar monocrop essentially channeled the Cuban economy in ways from which it has not been able to escape to this day. On the eve of the 1959 revolution, Cuba was producing roughly 6 million tons of sugar per year and sugarcane was planted on over half the total area under cultivation. Beef, tobacco and pineapple were the other principal export crops. Land holdings were extremely concentrated, with the largest 9 percent of all farm owners owning 62 percent of the land (MINAGRI figures).

The revolutionary period: 1959-1989

The revolutionary government thus inherited an agricultural production system strongly focused on export crops grown on highly concentrated land. The first agrarian reform of 1959 converted most of the large cattle ranches and sugarcane plantations into state farms. Under the second agrarian reform in 1962, the state was able to take control of 63 percent of all cultivated land (Benjamin *et al.*, 1987).

Readers who are familiar with Latin America's typical patterns of *latifundio-minifundio* style countryside, where peasants eke out an existence in the interstices between giant haciendas, must discard these images when thinking of Cuba. Even before the revolution, individual peasant producers were relatively scarce. The rural economy was dominated by export plantations, and the population highly urbanized. That pattern was intensified in subsequent years, and by the late 1980s fully 69 percent of the island's population lived in urban settings (Table 1). Some 80 percent of the nation's agricultural land consists of the relatively large state farms, which correspond to the expropriated plantation holdings of the pre-revolutionary era. Only 20 percent of the agricultural land is in the hands of peasant producers, split almost equally among individual holders and cooperatives (MINAGRI figures), though they are very important in food production (see Table 4).

---

[4] A significant number of slaves imported to the West Indies were from West Africa. These slaves brought sophisticated rice planting techniques which they adapted to New World conditions. (Carney 1993, forthcoming).

TABLE 4:   Percent of selected agricultural items produced by the private sector (individual farmers and cooperatives), 1989

Item	% of total sales to the state
Viandas (roots & tubers)	36
Vegetables	69
Corn	63
Beans	64
Tobacco	75
Coffee	48
Rice	13
Citrus	12
Other fruit	58
Dairy	8
Beef cattle	25
Swine	19

Source: MINAGRI

The state farm sector and a substantial portion of the cooperatives are highly modernized, with large extensions of monocrops worked under heavy mechanization, fertilizer and pesticide use, and large-scale irrigation. For this sector the mental image that the reader should use is that of California's Central Valley, or "Soviet-style state farms," rather than that of El Salvador, say, or the Andes. The principal difference between California and Cuba would be the crop mix. In 1989 fully 60 percent of Cuban land planted to crops (as opposed to pasture) was in sugarcane, accounting for 7.4 percent of the volume of world sugar trade (MINAGRI data). The importance of sugarcane declined slightly during the early 1980s, but sugar and its derivatives still accounted for 75 percent of Cuban export earnings (see Table 5).

Continued reliance on sugar

While our delegation focused on food production, the sugar issue was frequently raised. One question delegation members repeatedly posed was the reason for Cuba's continued reliance on sugar for foreign exchange earnings, given its low commodity price. Benjamin in *No Free Lunch* (1986) cites a German economist's study which argues the unviability of sugar production when the world price falls below 11 cents per pound, as it usually does. Furthermore, demand for sugar is decreasing due to competition from other sweeteners and greater nutritional awareness. EEC competition, based on beets as well as state subsidies, augurs poorly for Cuba's longer term dependence on sugar. These points consequently call into question Cuba's continued reliance on sugar.

TABLE 5: Share of sugar and sugar derivatives in value of Cuban exports

Year	% of total value of exports
1980	84
1985	75
1988	75

Sources: MINAGRI; Pastor, 1992

Yet sugar still remains king in Cuba, and it is being planted on some of the country's most fertile soils, areas that could be used for food or other valuable cash crops (e.g. citrus). Continued reliance on sugar in the context of the current period could hitch the expenditure of critical imported inputs to a crop of decreasing worth in the international market. There is also some evidence that sugarcane production costs in Cuba are above world averages (Preeg, 1993).

Cubans respond that while sugar prices are low, prices for sugar byproducts are not. Thus they focus their development plans on linking sugar production with industry so that they can export products with values much higher than that of the original raw sugar. In fact, much research has gone into how to make the best use of all the byproducts of both production and processing of sugar. And in many sugar mills the bagasse produced during processing is used as biomass which is burned to generate electricity for the machinery.[5]

Shifting commodity prices, changes in exchange rates for currencies, and uncertain availability of food and feed on world markets all coalesce to make decision making on the proper balance between exports and food extremely difficult. Moreover, once decisions are made, they

---

[5] As of 1992, 60 of Cuba's 156 sugar mills actually produced excess energy which was pumped into the power grid (MINAGRI figures).

cannot be easily reversed in the short term. Cuba never quite managed to achieve an adequate balance, and given the present economic crisis that now greatly increases the demand for both food and hard currency, the dilemma will undoubtedly remain.

Dependence on imported inputs

Another dilemma that plagues the island is the fact that the agricultural sector has been so highly dependent on imports. In Tables 6a, b, and c, we present data on the structure of this dependence. According to Deere (1992), in the late 1980s, 48 percent of fertilizers and 82 percent of pesticides were imported. Data on the "import coefficients" of these inputs reveals even stronger dependency (Pastor, 1992). That is because the 52 percent of fertilizer that was made in Cuba was produced largely with imported raw materials. Thus the overall import coefficient for all fertilizer used in Cuba was actually 94 percent. The figures for herbicide and animal feed were 98 percent and 97 percent, respectively. The animal feed figures are so high because the balanced feeds were largely based on corn and other cereals, the bulk of which were imported. While Cuba's climate does permit the cultivation of corn, it has not been pursued extensively by the government (Deere, 1992). The other cereal crops are mostly inappropriate for Cuban agricultural conditions.

In summary then, the Cuban agricultural sector through 1989 was characterized by a high degree of modernization, the dominance of export monocultures over food crops, and a heavy dependence on imported inputs and raw materials. This agriculture was productive in terms of yields (see grain yield figures in Table 1), but it was highly susceptible to international market forces. Until the mid-1980s this was not a severe problem, as favorable trade agreements with the socialist bloc guaranteed the profitability of sugar exports, the availability of agrochemicals and fuel for agriculture, and an adequate supply of food for the Cuban population at reasonable prices. The fall of the socialist bloc changed all that.

TABLES 6a, b, c: Some aspects of the structure of external dependence of the Cuban economy

TABLE 6a: Import coefficients for agricultural products in Cuba, 1989. Percent of value added contributed by imports of final product and/or imported inputs used in its production.

Category	Import coefficient (%)
Foodstuffs	
Cereals	100
Beans	90
Rice	49
Raw Materials	
Fertilizer	94
Herbicide	98
Animal feedstocks	97

Source: Pastor, 1992

TABLE 6b: Dependence on imports of agricultural inputs, 1989

Item	% imported
Fertilizer	48
Insecticide, fungicide, herbicide	82

Source: Deere, 1992

TABLE 6c: Structure of Cuban foreign trade, 1988

Countries	Exports (%)	Imports (%)
USSR	66.7	70.8
Romania, Czechoslovakia, Bulgaria, Poland, East Germany, & Hungary	15.0	13.8
Rest of the world	19.3	15.4
TOTAL	100.00	100.00

Source: MINAGRI

◆ 2 ◆

The crisis and
the emergence of a new model

The outlook for the Cuban economy began to deteriorate in the late 1980s, as several Eastern European countries reneged on trade agreements and the Soviet Union increased its price for oil, leading to deteriorating terms of trade. According to estimates by Pastor (1992), the terms of trade faced by Cuba declined by nearly 30 percent during the decade. The immediate result was a rapid increase in the foreign debt, and what Pastor labels "socialist inflation." Since prices are fixed in Cuba, normal inflation cannot occur as a product of this type of macroeconomic situation. What happens instead is that a relative scarcity of consumer goods occurs compared to the aggregate purchasing power of the population. Thus while the average salary in real terms rose by nearly 20 percent in the decade, per capita personal consumption rose by less than 12 percent (Pastor, 1992).

In human terms this meant that average consumers perceived shortages — they could not find enough goods in the stores on which to spend their salary. People's savings rose rapidly (Pastor reports that perhaps as much as 40 percent of the disposable funds in circulation are in savings), providing fuel for a lively black market with soaring prices.

The collapse of trade with the Soviet Union

When trade relations with the Soviet Union crumbled in 1990, the situation turned desperate. In 1991 the government declared the "Special Period in Peacetime", which basically put the country on a "wartime economy" style of austerity program.

In Table 6 we presented the structure of Cuban trade until 1990. The Soviet Union accounted for about 70 percent of trade, and when the rest of the socialist bloc was added the total rose to 85 percent. That trade has since plummeted, plunging the dependent Cuban economy into crisis. To put this in perspective, it is worth noting how this compares in terms of impact with the U.S. trade embargo. The U.S. trade embargo, imposed in 1962, prohibits U.S. companies from trading with Cuba. The Cuba Democracy Act passed in November 1992 tightened the restrictions by barring subsidiaries of U.S. companies overseas from trading with Cuba.

Cuban officials have likened the swift cut-off of trade with the socialist bloc to a second, more severe embargo. Noting that by 1989 the U.S. embargo really only affected the price that Cuba needed to pay for convertible currency imports from the West, Carlos Lage, Secretary of the Executive Committee of the Council of Ministers, stated that,

> The [U.S.] blockade has always been present, but without a doubt our relations with the Soviet Union and the socialist bloc helped ameliorate its effects on our country's economy. A blockade that affects 15 percent of the economy is not the same as one the affects 100 percent of the economy.[6]

The "100 percent blockade" of course refers to the cut-off of eastern bloc trade. The Cuban economy has been hammered in many ways. The 53 percent reduction in oil imports shown in Table 7 has not only affected fuel availability for the economy, but has also reduced to zero the foreign exchange that Cuba used to obtain via the re-export of petroleum. Imports of wheat and other grains for human consumption have dropped by more than 50 percent (Deere, 1992), while other foodstuffs — with the exception of powdered milk — have declined even more. Cuban agriculture has been faced with a drop of more than 80 percent in the availability of fertilizers and pesticides (decline in direct imports plus the loss of raw materials for domestic production), and

---

[6] Interview on Cuban television, November 6, 1992. Reprinted in *Granma*.

more than 50 percent in fuel and other energy sources produced by burning petroleum.

TABLE 7: Comparison of selected Cuban imports in 1989 and 1992

Item	1989 imports	1992 imports	% change
Petroleum	13,000,000 MT	6,100,000 MT	- 53%
Fertilizer	1,300,000 MT	300,000 MT	-77%
Pesticides	US$80,000,000	less than US$30,000,000	at least - 62.5%
Animal feeds	1,600,000 MT	475,000 MT	- 70%
Powdered milk	36,000 MT	36,000 MT	0%

Source: Carlos Lage interview on Cuban television, November 6, 1992.

Suddenly, a country with an agricultural sector technologically similar to California found itself almost without chemical inputs, and with sharply reduced access to fuel and irrigation. This same country, which had depended on imports for almost 60 percent of its food, suddenly saw those imports drop by more than half. Average daily caloric and protein intake by the Cuban population may have fallen by as much as 30 percent from the levels achieved during the 1980s.[7] That would put Cuba 25 percent below the Latin American average for calories, and 16 percent below that for protein, still as good or better than 5 countries in terms of protein, but better only than Haiti and Bolivia for calories.[8]

Clearly Cuba is facing a food crisis, though far from the proportions of that faced by a country like Somalia. In fact it is amazing that the health of the Cuban people is as good as it is given this crisis, thanks to the equitable way in which the available food is distributed. We saw no children with distended bellies or other outward signs of hunger, and infant mortality has not increased.[9] Yet virtually all Cubans commented that they felt at least relative deprivation. Several spoke of

---

[7] Unofficial worst-case scenario figure provided to us by Cuban Agriculture Ministry officials.

[8] FAO Yearbook.

[9] Carlos Lage, interview on Cuban television, November 6, 1992. Reprinted in *Granma*.

the development of "food neuroses," as the particular items available from which to make up one's diet vary on an almost daily basis and getting access to that food is a daily chore.

The Cuban diet

The present day dietary problems have pre-1990 origins in both the colonial legacy described in Chapter 1, and in the promotion since 1959 of a "modern" or "western" diet that is neither well-suited to Cuban agriculture nor particularly healthy. The Special Period has therefore brought to the fore some historical and cultural problems that must now be seriously addressed.

At the time of the revolution, the diet of the Cuban people, as in the rest of Latin America, depended on what social class they belonged to. The majority of the population subsisted on a diet of rice, beans, and root crops called *viandas*, with an average caloric intake of only 1,200-1,300 calories per day. The upper classes, many of whom fled after the revolution, ate more meat and dairy products, as well as imported wheat in the form of white bread, crackers and pastas.

A key goal of the revolution was to guarantee everyone an adequate diet. To the leadership this meant not only a diet that was nutritionally adequate — but also a socially acceptable diet, aimed at replicating the diet of the rich. Food surveys in Cuba consistently show that what Cubans want for both lunch and dinner, every day, is rice, beans, a high-protein food (such as beef, poultry, pork, fish or eggs), *viandas* (which in order of preference are plantains, taro, potatoes, cassava, and sweet potato) and bread (Pérez and Muñoz, 1991). Everything is cooked with large quantities of lard or cooking oil. Unfortunately, this "culturally acceptable" diet is one that is both unhealthy (high-calorie, high-fat, high cholesterol, low-fiber) and expensive to obtain, in that much of the food and the materials to produce it must be imported.[10]

The nutritional goals set by the Cuban government in terms of calories and proteins have been very ambitious. With target values set consistently higher than UN standards, the national nutrition campaigns met with high rates of success up until the Special Period (see nutritional data in Table 1). While these national averages are not very meaningful in most countries because of large differences in consumption between

---

[10] It is widely known that Cuba is one of the few developing countries to have passed the "epidemiological transition" from a pattern of illness and mortality in which infectious diseases predominate to one based on obesity, heart disease and cancer, much like the United States.

social classes, this is not the case in Cuba. The rationing system and the wage policy (there is a 5:1 spread between the highest and lowest salaries) ensure that food is very evenly distributed.

While for 30 years Cuba was the only country in Latin America that had eliminated hunger, today's severe economic crisis is reversing this remarkable achievement. An inadequate nutritional intake has been reported among children between 6-12 months old, and many pregnant women are found to be anemic. In addition, a mysterious neurological disease which affected some 40,000 Cubans in 1992-1993 was thought to be related to a B vitamin deficiency.

Changing production and consumption patterns

The Cuban diet as promoted by the revolution until the present economic crisis was one based on massive imports of wheat and rice for human consumption, and corn and soybeans for animal feed. The government must now stem this reliance on imported goods and make the country more self-reliant. This means changing consumption and production patterns.

With cuts in animal feed imports and the urgent need to increase the supply of oxen to replace tractors, beef production has plummeted and red meat is now rarely available. There are also severe problems with the supply of milk and other dairy products. Before 1990, Cuba received some 23,000 tons of powdered milk annually from the Soviet Union and East Germany. Together with domestic production, this allowed the Cuban government to guarantee — through the ration system — one liter of milk per day to all Cubans under 13, as well as to seniors and people with chronic illnesses. Milk was also available off the ration card at a higher price, as were other dairy products such as cheese, butter, yogurt and ice cream. But by 1991, milk could only be guaranteed to those under 7, and no milk was available off the ration.[11] There was also virtually no cheese, butter or yogurt anymore. The result has been a decrease in the availability of animal protein in the diet.

Production increases of beef and dairy do not seem to be a likely solution to the animal protein situation, as cattle production is heavily dependent on imported animal feeds. Cuba's dairy herd is composed of 'modern' breeds that have been unable to adjust quickly to changes in

---

[11] The drop in milk availability is due to lower domestic production as a consequence of the cutback in feed imports. As Table 6 shows, powdered milk imports have been maintained, although milk is now purchased at international prices. (Lage, op. cit.).

diet from imported animal feed to pasture. Perhaps the best prospect is pork, since pigs easily change from balanced feeds to eating municipal garbage, sugarcane by-products and other alternative food sources. It is also a type of meat that is well liked by Cubans, and during this time when the lack of animal protein is causing discontent among the population, pig production has become a government priority.

Another source of animal protein that has become relatively scarce is chicken. In the 1980s, chicken was not only a mainstay of the food ration, but it was available on the open market at a cafeteria chain known as Pio Pio (similar to Kentucky Fried Chicken). Although Cuba's own chicken production increased significantly through the late 1980s, a substantial number of chickens and starter chicks were imported, as was most all of the feed. So by the early 1990s, chicken was in short supply. Eggs, once so abundant they were not even rationed, have been cut way back since commercial egg production is dependent on imported feed as well. An innovative way that the government has responded to the chicken and egg shortage is to give baby chicks out to the population to raise in their homes, since home-grown chickens can feed on household scraps.

Cuts in imported wheat from Russia have forced the government to reduce the bread ration to one roll per person per day, and to experiment with substituting sweet potato, rice and other flours for a portion of the wheat. At the same time, breads and pastas are more and more being replaced by traditional *viandas*, which grow well under Cuba's soil and climatic conditions and are popular with the Cuban population.

Before the Special Period there was a shortage of *viandas* relative to supply. The government's response to the "vianda question" was that they were "secondary crops" and thus could be left in the hands of small private farmers and cooperatives rather than be grown on state farms. But in reality Cubans don't consider *viandas* "secondary" but rather essential to their diet, and the small farmers and co-ops never produced enough to satisfy demand (Pérez and Muñoz, 1991). The state is now taking *viandas* seriously, and increasing their production is a top priority. The government is trying to get people to substitute *viandas* and vegetables for wheat and rice, and to substitute vegetable for animal protein.

The Cuban government is in a stronger position than most governments to alter consumption patterns, because it controls the food supply through the ration system and it controls the media for educational campaigns. But this has always been a very delicate political issue (Benjamin *et al.*, 1987). Cubans, like most people, have firmly set dietary tastes and preferences, and it is virtually impossible to get people to voluntarily change their habits, even if they are living under conditions of scarcity. It is easy for health conscious U.S. citizens to voluntarily cut or even eliminate meat consumption, because food is abundant for them and they have many choices. But in Cuba since the revolution, meat has always been in short supply and any effort by the government to encourage people to eat less meat for health reasons could have been viewed as an excuse to disguise supply problems.

In short, food is now the Achilles' heel of the revolution. It is the population's number one complaint. While Cubans have always complained about the lack of variety in their diet (Benjamin *et al.*, 1987), they are now complaining about the lack of enough food — period. For a long time to come, Cuba will be paying dearly for the dependence it developed on the socialist bloc for much of its food supply.

To address this dependency, the government launched an ambitious National Food Program in 1989. This program was conceived before the collapse of Soviet trade relations, for in the mid-1980s there was a realization that the heavy economic reliance on the Soviets was unhealthy. The main focus of this food program was to quickly increase the production of *viandas* and vegetables. Another priority was to make the area around Havana as self-sufficient as possible, given that the city and province of Havana account for some 30 percent of the nation's population and have traditionally been reliant on other parts of the country for most of their food needs (Deere, 1992).

Substituting local for imported technology

While the National Food Program called for a reorientation of agricultural production toward foodstuffs so as to make up for the import deficit, during the Special Period the country also needs to maintain or increase export crop levels in order to avoid further exacerbating the foreign exchange crisis. And we should remember that these two goals must be pursued virtually without chemical inputs, and with far less tractor power and irrigation than before.[12] It is a formidable task.

---

[12] Cuban officials told us that under their previous agricultural model, the goal had been to have level food production throughout the year, regardless of climatic conditions. They said they now realize this was a luxury made possible by cheap fuel imports to run irrigation equipment, and that they are now

Fortunately, Cuba was not totally unprepared to face the critical situation that arose after 1989. It had, over the years, emphasized the building up of human resources, and therefore had a cadre of scientists and researchers who could come forward with innovative ideas to confront the crisis.

In the early 1980s, Cuba's leaders had become increasingly disillusioned with the island's insertion into the international socialist division of labor.[13] They felt, as did many thinkers in other Latin American countries, that there was a distinct limit to the level of development that could be achieved on the basis of light industry and the export of raw agricultural commodities. Cuban leaders decided that technological expertise was going to be the world's most valuable commodity in the future, especially with the growth of high-tech, information-intensive industries.[14]

Accordingly, they invested the equivalent of an estimated $12 billion over the remainder of the decade in developing human capital and infrastructure in biotechnology, health sciences, computer hardware and software, and robotics.[15] The long term plan was to change Cuba's role in the world economy to that of purveyor of high technology, scientific consulting and quality health services.

At the same time, younger scientists in the Agriculture Ministry and the universities, influenced by the ecology movement, developed a critique of modern agriculture (Levins, 1991). They criticized the Cuban model of agricultural development for its dependence on foreign inputs and its tendency to produce environmental degradation, such as pesticide resistance and soil erosion. They began to reorient their research toward alternatives, such as biological control of insect pests.

In 1982 official research policy began to favor this tendency. At a conference on pest management held in Havana in 1987, the vast majority of the 185 papers presented focused on such alternatives.[16] One member of our delegation who was present at that conference had the opportunity at that time to speak with many of the Cuban researchers.

---

thinking more in terms of programming production to take advantage of natural rainfall patterns, with corresponding investment in food storage facilities.

[13] Interview with Juan Antonio Blanco, Havana, Cuba.

[14] This foreshadowed the analysis put forth by the present U.S. Secretary of Labor, Robert Reich, in his influential 1991 book, *The work of nations*.

[15] Interview with Juan Antonio Blanco, Havana, Cuba.

[16] Resumenes. Seminario Científico Internacional de Sanidad Vegetal. La Habana, 22-25 Septiembre, 1987.

There was clearly a division within the research establishment between younger scientists, low on the hierarchical totem pole, who favored alternatives, and many of the older ones, mainly in leadership positions, who believed strongly in the pesticide model.

Young scientists presented impressive research results at the 1987 meeting, on alternatives such as the use of ants and *Trichogramma* wasps for biological pest control. Some of these methods were already used in commercial crops. Nevertheless, the researchers complained that their approach was not taken seriously enough to be implemented on a broad scale, and they expressed frustration at ministry officials who favored pesticide imports.

While neither the expensive scientific investments in advanced technology nor the research into agricultural alternatives by young scientists had paid great dividends by 1989 (Pastor, 1992), they provided Cuba with crucial resources that are now being mobilized to face the agriculture challenge in the 1990s. As we show below, the Cuban leadership has put forth a "knowledge intensive" strategy based on local technology in order to reshape Cuban agriculture and make it more independent. Expertise in biotechnology has been combined with the alternative agriculture focus of many agricultural scientists to produce innovative responses to the crisis situation. Cuba is very well-positioned for a transition based on science and technology: while it has only 2 percent of the population of Latin America, it has almost 11 percent of the scientists.[17]

The Classical versus the Alternative Model

Critiques of conventional input-intensive agriculture abound in the United States and other developed countries (Altieri, 1987; National Research Council, 1989; Soule and Piper, 1992; Carroll et al., 1990; etc.), and the First World critics would be very comfortable with the official critique that has now been made the basis for policy in Cuba. This critique, as outlined in a chart [Table 8] circulated to Ministry of Agriculture personnel, counterposes what is called the "Alternative Model" to what is called the "Classical Model" of agricultural production.

The Classical Model represents conventional modern agriculture, as developed in California, the Soviet Union and Cuba, among other places. It relies on intensive use of chemical fertilizers, pesticides, mechanization, feedlots, petroleum and petroleum by-products, hybrid

---

[17] UNESCO Statistical Yearbook.

crop varieties and capital in the form of credit. It is based on crop monocultures planted on large holdings to take advantage of economies of scale. It has led to soil erosion, compaction, salinization and waterlogging, environmental contamination, pest resistance to pesticides and uncontrollable pest outbreaks. It has also led to an exodus of the population from rural areas as mechanization replaces human labor. It is also a model that has become increasingly expensive as input prices rise and farmers use increasing quantities to compensate for eroding soil fertility and the loss of natural pest controls. For developing countries it is even worse, because it creates a dependence on imports that use up scarce foreign exchange.

The Alternative Model, as put forth in Cuba, promotes crop diversity rather than monoculture, organic fertilizers and "biofertilizers" instead of chemical ones, and biological control and "biopesticides" instead of synthetic pesticides. Furthermore, animal traction is substituted for tractors, and planting is planned to take advantage of seasonal rainfall patterns in order to reduce reliance on irrigation. Local communities are to be more intimately involved in the production process, hopefully putting brakes on the exodus to the cities. Because a significant amount of foodstuffs is produced by the Cuban private sector — individual peasant farmers and cooperative members, as opposed to state farms — the Alternative Model and the National Food Program focus heavily on promoting their activities (see Table 4). In essence, this is a return to the importance of the family farmer.[18] As a proposal, the Alternative Model is very similar to that put forth for developing countries (Altieri and Hecht, 1990), as well as for the United States (USDA, 1980; National Research Council, 1989). In the United States, we call this Low Input Sustainable Agriculture, or LISA.

The key difference between Cuba and other countries, then, is not the analysis of the problem or the general outline of the alternative proposal. The difference is that in Cuba the Alternative Model has become official government policy, while elsewhere there are only

---

[18] The Cuban government has a checkered history of relations with peasant farmers. Various forms of farmers markets were tried in the 70s and 80s as incentives for peasant production, but were later abandoned (Benjamin *et al.*, 1987; Deere *et al.*, 1992; Deere and Meurs, 1992). Nevertheless, the National Food Program targets this sector for technical assistance, credit, and various forms of participation (Deere, 1992; our interviews with farmers and officials). A related point is that a large percentage of peasant food production probably finds its way to the black market.

isolated individual examples and widespread implementation remains a dream.

The vast majority of Cuban agricultural scientists and Agriculture Ministry officials whom we interviewed concurred on an important point. They say that the Classical Model of conventional agriculture that developed during the first 30 years of the revolution was a model imposed from outside. They express resentment toward Soviet and other socialist bloc advisers who were responsible for technology transfer to Cuba, and they are self-critical for having had a "colonized mentality." They believe that while the conventional model might be appropriate for Europe — where all of the expensive inputs are produced within each nation — for a developing country like Cuba it makes little sense because of the extreme dependency and external vulnerability that it promotes. The consensus position seems to be that this is a change that is long overdue, and the Special Period provides the only pretext and the motivation.

TABLE 8: Strategy for the development of specific projects: most relevant considerations to keep in mind.

(Ministry of Agriculture chart circulated to planning staff)

Classical Model vs	Alternative Model
(originating fundamentally in developed countries)	Maximum advantage taken of:
External dependence	• the land
• of the country on other countries	• human resources of the zone or locality
• of the provinces on the country	• broad community participation
• of localities on the province and the country	• cutting edge technology, but appropriate to zone where used
	• organic fertilizers & crop rotation
Cutting edge technology	• biological control of pests
• imported raw materials for animal feed	• biological cycles and seasonality of crops and animals
• widespread utilization of chemical pesticides and fertilizers	• natural energy sources (hydro, wind, solar, slopes, biomass etc.)
• utilization of modern irrigation systems	• animal traction
• consumption of fuel & lubricants	• rational use of pastures and forage for both grazing and feedlots, search for locally supplied animal nutrition

Classical Model (cont'd)	*Alternative Model (cont'd)*
Tight relationship between bank credit and production; high interest rates	Diversification of crops and autochthonous production systems based on accumulated knowledge
Priority given to mechanization as a production technology	Introduction of scientific practices that correspond to the particulars of each zone; new varieties of crops and animals, planting densities, seed treatments, post-harvest storage, etc.
Introduction of new crops at the expense of autochthonous crops and production systems	
Search for efficiency through intensification and mechanization	Preservation of the environment and the ecosystem
Real possibility of investing in production and commercialization	Need for systematic training (management, nutritional, technical)
Accelerated rural exodus	
Satisfying ever-increasing needs has ever more ecological or environmental consequences, such as soil erosion, salinization, waterlogging, etc.	Systematic technical assistance
	Promote cooperation among producers, within and between communities
	Obstacles to overcome: • difficulties in the commercialization of agricultural products because of the number of intermediaries • control over the market • poverty among the peasantry • distances to markets and urban centers (lack of sufficient roads and means of transport) • illiteracy

Remarks by President Fidel Castro to agricultural scientists in 1991 underscore this point. He stated that once the Special Period has ended, animal traction will still be an essential part of Cuban agriculture, indicating that the changes are not temporary but systemic.[19] He emphasized the centrality of the strategy of substituting scientific knowledge and expertise for imported technology and dependency, saying that,

> [Cuban] scientists will create resources that will one day be more valuable than the sugarcane.... Now more than ever the phrase 'economic independence' has meaning. We will achieve it through miracles of intelligence....

Conversion from conventional agriculture to organic farming

Conversion is the term commonly used in the United States to denote the fairly lengthy process of restoring soil fertility and natural pest controls in a farm that has previously made conventional use of chemical fertilizers and pesticides, both of which degrade the natural productive capacity of the soil over time. Conventional farmers compensate for this degradation by increasing chemical doses, putting them on a chemical treadmill with ever-increasing production costs needed to maintain productivity levels (Carroll et al., 1991; Altieri, 1983). The study of conversion to organics — the biological and physical processes that it entails, the management options open to the farmer, the microeconomics of the changeover — has become a sub-discipline within agronomy in the United States (USDA, 1980; National Research Council, 1989).

Empirical evidence from dozens of studies has shown that it generally takes from three to five years for a farmer switching to organics to equal the levels of productivity and profitability obtained in the final years of conventional production. After that time, organic production often becomes more profitable than the earlier system, as consumers pay a price premium for organic produce. During this three to five year period, however, the farmer must take positive steps to build up soil structure and organic matter, and establish pest natural enemies and groundcovers.

---

[19] Oxen are less damaging to the soil than tractors, and are more appropriate for small scale producers.

Remarks by Fidel Castro to the 5th Congress of the National System of Agricultural and Forestry Technicians, 1991

- "The food question has the number one priority."

- "We should not permit any lack of calories and protein, even if the proportions change between animal and vegetable sources."

- "We must produce more food without feedstocks and without fertilizers. We must plan 1992 as though we had none available. The little fertilizer that has been available has been dedicated to rice, plantains, *viandas* [roots and tubers] and vegetables: those foodstuffs that are produced directly in the countryside. Keep one idea clear: the country is without feedstocks and fertilizers."

- "Our problems must be resolved without feedstocks, fertilizers or fuel. All plans based on fuel availability must be cut practically in half; half of what the country consumed in normal circumstances."

- "We have bred 100,000 new oxen; we are breeding 100,000 more, hundreds of thousands of oxen. Even if we have to subsist on vegetable protein, we cannot eat the oxen because we need them to cultivate the land. The ox does not just save fuel: the ox can perform tasks that would be impossible for a tractor, raising the productivity of human labor. *Even when the Special Period ends, the role of the ox in Cuban agriculture will not be totally over.*"

- "We must convert farming into one of the most honored, promoted and appreciated professions."

- "We will achieve miracles with intelligence and sweat. *Scientists will create resources that will one day be more valuable than sugar cane;* they are developing bacteria that capture nitrogen from the air. Already many crops are produced with *azotobacter*; next year we will produce 8, 10, 15 million, whatever is necessary. A brewer's yeast factory can be converted into an *azotobacter* factory — it's only a question of packaging and distribution. We now have 200 CREE [Centers for the Reproduction of Entomophages and Entomopathogens] in the country; in 1992 we will be able to produce millions of liters."

- "*Now more than ever, the phrase 'economic independence' has meaning. We will achieve it through miracles of intelligence, sweat, heart, and the consciousness of humankind.*"

Source: MINAGRI   (Emphasis added)

Conversion in the United States has been limited to individual farms, while in Cuba it is virtually nationwide. In their efforts to implement the Alternative Model, Cubans are essentially attempting the largest scale conversion from conventional agriculture to organic or semi-organic farming in history. The only other case in modern history of widespread adoption of what we might call alternative practices was in the People's Republic of China during the 1970s. That experience was qualitatively different from the Cuban case in that the transition was from traditional low-input peasant practices to modified peasant practices, incorporating some scientific advances. Thus it does not represent a conversion from conventional modern agriculture. Furthermore, agrochemicals and mechanization have now become commonplace in China as part of the liberalization of the Chinese economy. Thus Cuba offers a unique opportunity for agricultural scientists the world over to study the process of large-scale conversion.

Whether Cuba's National Food Program and the Alternative Model of agricultural production will be sufficiently successful to allow the present Cuban economic and political system to survive its present crisis is an open question (see Pastor, 1992 and Preeg, 1993). But as an experiment in much-needed alternative practices, it is, we feel, a once in a lifetime opportunity. In the remainder of the report we present our findings on various aspects of both research for and implementation of the Alternative Model.

◆ 3 ◆

Management of insect pests, plant diseases and weeds

One of the keys to the Alternative Model of agriculture is to find ways to reduce chemicals used for management of plant diseases, insect pests, and weeds. This process began during the 1980s, but has taken on more urgency during the Special Period.

Agrochemicals were introduced in Cuba in the 1940s, and eventually became a cornerstone of Cuban agriculture. Like many other developing nations, Cuba was dependent on multinational corporations for its supply of these products. In its efforts to increase production of both exports and locally consumed crops, the government promoted the ever-increasing use of pesticides. However, rising import costs as well as the development of resistance, pest resurgence and secondary pest outbreaks, put the brakes to this trend well before the crisis of 1990.[20]

By 1982 Cuba was shifting toward an integrated pest management (IPM) paradigm. IPM, which the Clinton administration declared

---

[20] Resistance refers to the tendency of target populations to evolve tolerance to pesticides after repeated exposure. Pest resurgence after pesticide applications occurs because the natural enemies of the pests have been wiped out. Secondary pest outbreaks occur when previously insignificant organisms become pests after their natural controls have been eliminated.

official U.S. policy in June 1993,[21] refers to the integrated use of a variety of alternative pest, disease and weed control tactics, in order to reduce reliance on chemical pesticides. Pest populations must be carefully monitored, in order to program management interventions. A key component of IPM in Cuba is biological control, in which natural predators, parasites, diseases and antagonists of pests are deployed in order to manage their populations.

Cuba has a tradition of biological control that dates to the 1930s, when the parasitic fly *Lixophaga diatraeae* was introduced by North American researchers to control the sugarcane borer. However, more formal national research programs on biological control did not begin until the 1970s. In 1985, after many years of research, those efforts were transformed into a major campaign and biological control began to replace pesticides as the conceptual basis for pest management (Rego *et al.*, 1986).

These efforts did achieve a reduction in pesticide use, but when the Special Period was declared in 1991, Cuba was still importing $80 million in pesticides per year. With the adjustments that came with the Special Period, these imports were reduced to $30 million (MINAGRI figures). Fortunately, 20 years of increasingly intensive research into biological control and other alternatives had prepared Cuba for the undertaking of one of the most ambitious enterprises in integrated pest management in the history of any country.

The plant protection system of the Ministry of Agriculture consists of the National Service of Plant Protection, the Institute of Plant Protection, the Central Research Laboratory, 14 regional laboratories, more than 60 plant protection territorial stations distributed throughout the country, 27 frontier posts with diagnostic laboratories, and 218 Centers for the Reproduction of Entomophages and Entomopathogens (CREEs). In addition, there are other agencies specialized in a variety of crops that conduct research into plant protection.

The areas that have received the most attention in the last few years have been the development and mass production of bioinsecticides based on insect pathogens, and the mass production of insect natural enemies (mainly parasitic wasps and flies). The Cubans have also pioneered the use of ants for the control of sweet potato and banana pests. Most recently they have been working on techniques based on mass release of sterile males to suppress pest populations, but this work is still in the research stage. The development of natural pesticides based on plant

---

[21] *New York Times*, June 27, 1993, page 1.

extracts is another area that has grown in recent years, with particular interest in the neem tree. Finally, research and use of chemical pesticides still continues, but to a limited degree. The pesticide department at the Institute of Plant Protection is the smallest program of all.

The Special Period provided the opportunity for the focus on integrated pest management in Cuba to flourish in unprecedented ways. By the end of 1991, an estimated 56 percent of Cuban crop land was treated with biological controls, representing a savings, after costs, of US$15.6 million per year (MINAGRI figures).

Pest and disease monitoring

Cuba has in place a pest and disease monitoring system that is unrivaled in the developing world, and probably only matched in some formerly socialist developed countries. This is important, for example, when a pathogen or pest develops resistance to the pesticide used against it. It can be very time-consuming and expensive to find alternative methods of control. To prevent such resistance from developing, each local research center in Cuba maintains small plots of that area's important crops. As soon as resistance to a pesticide is detected in a pest or pathogen, the pesticide in question is temporarily retired and replaced with a battery of other control measures. Because of these tactics, for example, Cuba is the only country in the world still able to use the systemic fungicide Ridomil[r] against tobacco blue mold.

Each monitor plot is a representative site planted with the important crops and varieties of that region. A weather station records ambient climatic conditions. Periodically, someone records crop phenology, pest phenology, disease onset and development, and at the end of the season, crop yield data. In addition to the monitor plots, 1-3 representative fields of each important crop are sampled for the presence of diseases and pests. Reports are sent to the provincial lab where they are analyzed. If critical climatic conditions are present that are known to be conducive to outbreaks of certain pests or pathogens, the farms in the region are warned.

In the early 1970s, these plots were set up in Cuba with the help of Soviet scientists. Before that time, pesticides were sprayed on a regular schedule, but increased costs and danger to the environment made it necessary to reduce pesticide use. Such "rational pesticide management" systems worked in the Soviet Union, but Cuba's situation was more complicated because crops could be grown all year long and the crops required different sampling techniques and economic threshold calculations. These problems were solved by the Cubans, and today more than 90 percent of Cuban agriculture uses some kind of pest and disease monitoring. However, the monitor system has not been modified for use with biological control techniques; a farm is warned of the possibility of a pest or pathogen outbreak, but the means of controlling the outbreak depends largely on what is available in that area.

The disease and pest loss data is not in a computer database and does not appear to have been well-exploited for epidemiological modeling. This is unfortunate as it represents a unique long-term data set on tropical organisms. It was difficult to determine how successful the monitoring system has been. Researchers at the Institute of Plant Health said that the disease loss data was collected, but not fully utilized, and that some diseases causing significant losses were not receiving the attention they deserved. Researchers at the Plant Protection Institute said that some data collected over the last 10 years was very good, but other data, especially for soilborne diseases, was poor.

Biological control programs based on mass release of entomophagous insects

Entomophages are insects that eat or parasitize other insects, and thus can be released to achieve biological control of pests. The longest running biological control program in Cuba involves the parasitic fly *Lixophaga diatraeae* (Tachinidae) that we mentioned earlier. Since 1968 it has been reared and released in a massive program which now covers 100 percent of the area under sugarcane "seed" production, as well as a substantial part of the areas under general sugarcane production.

The other major effort in mass rearing and release of entomophagous insects is with tiny wasps of the genus *Trichogramma*, which parasitize the eggs of insect pests, thus controlling them. The *Trichogramma* are reared on host eggs of either *Corcyra cephalonica* or *Sitotroga cerealella*, both pests of stored products such as flour and grains. Parasitized host eggs are kept at ambient temperatures and transferred to small vials. The vials are placed in the field when approximately 50 percent of the adult *Trichogramma* have emerged from the host eggs. The source of the genetic stock of the *Trichogramma* is obtained by rearing adults from parasitized eggs of the target insect pests collected in the local area, from the crop plants where they will later be released.

In many cases the Cubans do not know which species of *Trichogramma* they have. Nevertheless, this practice of collecting local *Trichogramma* biotypes from the target host's eggs is an excellent method upon which to base a rearing and release program. Local biotypes of *Trichogramma* are used to combat the cassava horn worm, the tobacco budworm, various caterpillars that attack improved pasture grasses, and other common pest species. Though perhaps more widespread than in other Latin American countries, the use of *Trichogramma* and *Lixophaga* is not restricted to Cuba.

The use of entomopathogens
Entomopathogens are diseases of insects — bacteria, fungi and viruses — that can also be used for biological control. As they are not human disease organisms, they offer the possibility of non-toxic pest control. It is in the production and use of entomopathogens that Cuba has a substantial lead over most countries in the world, developing or developed. Here the Cuban investment in biotechnology is beginning to pay off for agriculture.

Research and development efforts in Cuba have led to techniques for the production, harvesting, formulation, application, and quality control of numerous bacteria and fungi, including *Bacillus thuringiensis, Beauvaria bassiana, Metarhizium anisopliae* and *Verticillium lecanii*.

Quality control and monitoring are carried out by three mechanisms: standardizing field dose rates; direct tests of pathogen virulence; and monitoring field effectiveness by collection and observation of exposed pests.

For each bacterial or fungal formulation, 2 percent of the harvested material is sampled and the concentration of spores or organisms is recorded. The application rate is determined by calculating the number of spores or organisms per unit volume and adjusting the volume applied to standardize the number of spores or organisms applied to a given area. Virulence is tested by exposing target pests to field rates of entomopathogens and recording the rate and severity of infection. Pests are also collected from fields where entomopathogens have recently been applied to record incidence and severity of infections. Specific application rates have been developed for each of the entomopathogens. Information on the production method, application rates, and target pests for the entomopathogens can be found in Table 9.

TABLE 9: Production methods, application rates, and target pests for entomopathogens in Cuba

Bacillus thuringiensis

B. thuringiensis strains collected from endemic populations in Cuba are being cultured on static medium made from a rice-based product with the addition of juice from locally available sources, including citrus, tomato or cucumber juice. Application rates are between 10^8 - 10^9 bacteria per hectare. *B. thuringiensis* is applied to control the following insect pests: *Plutella xylostella* (diamond-back moth), *Erinnyis ello*, *Heliothis virescens*, *Mocis sp.*, and several other important lepidopteran pests.

Beauvaria bassiana

B. bassiana is cultured on static medium and applied to control the following pests: *Cosmopolites sordidus* (banana weevil) in banana and plantain, *Cylas formicarius* (sweet potato weevil) in sweet potato, *Lissorhoptrus brevirostris* in rice, and *D. saccharalis* in sugarcane. The application rate is $1-3 \times 10^9$ spores per hectare in 10 to 40 liters/hectare of liquid formulation.

Verticillium lecanii

V. lecanii is being produced specifically for the control of *Bemisia tabaci* (sweet potato white fly) attacking a wide range of crops. The application rate is 10^{11} - 10^{12} spores/hectare applied as a liquid preparation.

Metarhizium anisopliae

M. anisopliae is a fungus that is produced on static medium. The spores are harvested and applied for the control of *C. sordidus*, *L. brevirostris*, several *Mocis sp.*, *P. xylostella*, *D. saccharalis*, and *Galleria mellonella* (greater wax moth) in bee hives. Application rates are 10^{11} - 10^{12} spores/hectare.

Production of biological control agents

For our delegation, the most interesting aspect of contemporary insect pest management efforts in Cuba were the Centers for the Production of Entomophages and Entomopathogens (CREEs) where decentralized, "artesanal" production of biocontrol agents takes place. The construction of these facilities had been approved by the government prior to 1988, however few had been built before the beginning of the economic crisis. The government has since invested its limited capital in the construction and operation of these centers. By the end of 1992, 218 CREEs had been built throughout Cuba to provide services to state, cooperative, and private farm operations.

The centers produce a number of entomopathogens, as well as one or more species of *Trichogramma* spp., depending on the crops grown in each area. They are maintained and operated by local technicians with college degrees, two years of post-high school vocational training, or high school diplomas. The CREE our delegation visited produced the following entomopathogens: *Bacillus thuringiensis*, *Beauvaria bassiana*, *Metarhizium anisopliae* and *Verticillium lecanni*. One *Trichogramma* species for the control of *Erinnyis ello* was also being reared and released.

The Center employed four technicians with college degrees, four mid-level technicians, and seven high school graduates. All were children of members of the cooperative where it was located. According to what they told us, the cooperative received a 10 year loan from the bank to construct and equip the Center — a medium-sized house filled with sterile microbiology-type lab rooms and about 20 small fermentation tanks. According to the director, the Center provided their products free of charge to the cooperative, at the same time selling them to neighboring farmers, state farms and co-ops. He said that the sales were sufficient for them to break even — covering the cost of their salaries, the loan payments, and supplying the pest control needs of the entire cooperative. It would be no exaggeration to say that the CREE was the single most impressive thing we saw on our visit. It was exciting to see the sons and daughters of *campesinos* producing products of modern biotechnology on a local scale. To our knowledge nowhere else in the world do such things exist.

The CREEs are part of a two-pronged strategy for production of biopesticides. The CREEs are considered to be "artesanal production" — though they are certainly high tech by most standards. Meanwhile, the country has a network of over 30 brewers yeast factories which use large scale fermentation technology. These normally function for only four days per month making yeast. The remainder of the time they were idle, but they are now being converted to use the idle days to mass produce biopesticides on an industrial scale. Thus there will be a "commercial" product with high standards of quality control for the high end market — state farms and large co-ops that produce for export — while the network of CREEs will continue producing a lower priced product for local use.

Additional research programs in insect pest management

Cuban scientists are actively involved in several other lines of research in developing alternatives to conventional insecticides. The research areas include work on parasitic nematodes and plant derived pesticides.

A program to develop reliable and cost-effective methods for the production and field application of several species of nematodes that attack insects is underway. The Cubans have been working with *Neoplactana sp.*, *Heterohabditis sp.*, and *Steinerneema sp.* Mass production of these nematodes is still in the developmental stages.

Cuban scientists are screening a large number of plants for insecticidal, fungicidal, bactericidal, and herbicidal qualities. In addition to these screening efforts looking for new plant species with promising traits, applied work on the cultivation and production of two species of plants with known insecticidal qualities, neem and *Melia*, has been initiated. Small plantations of neem and *Melia* have been started and research on formulations and application methods is advancing.

Biological control using ants

Based on an old practice of peasant farmers, Cuban researchers studied and further developed an elaborate and unique system of biological control of *Cylas formicarius*, the sweet potato weevil, using the predatory ant, *Pheidole megacephala*.

banana ant

The management system includes the establishment of reservoir areas where the ant is naturally abundant. In these areas, usually forested patches or areas with perennial crops, all pesticide application is prohibited. *P. megacephala* colonies are transported from the reservoirs to the fields where sweet potatoes are planted. Colony transfer occurs in a variety of ways. A common one, requiring high labor input, is the use of banana stems. Banana stems are cut into several pieces, which are placed on the ground in the reservoir area. Stems are baited with honey or a sugar solution and covered with a wet cloth or with banana leaves. The honey and humidity attract the ants which proceed to move their colonies to the stems. Colonized stems are then transferred to sweet potato fields where they are exposed to the sun, causing the stems to dry out and forcing the ants to relocate and construct their nests in the ground. Once there, *P. megacephala* prey on *C. formicarius* larvae.

This method has provided close to 99 percent control of the sweet potato borer in the Pinar del Río Province, with lower production costs and higher yields per hectare (Castiñeiras *et al.*, 1982). So successful has the method been that the Ministry of Agriculture prohibited the use of any chemical insecticide in sweet potato fields where this method is being employed. Where applications of pesticides for other pests are necessary, special permission is required from the Ministry. In the last few years, these applications have consisted of biological insecticides such as *Bacillus thuringiensis* or *Beauveria bassiana*. The same control method is being employed in plantain production for the control of the black plantain weevil *(Cosmopolites sordidus)*, using *P. megacephala* and *Tetramorium guineense*.

Management of plant diseases

Early Cuban research on plant pathogens centered on the etiology of poorly understood diseases. Now, however, most important diseases have been studied and the emphasis is on methods of diagnosis and disease reduction in major crops. In potato, serious diseases include early blight, caused by *Alternaria solani*, and late blight, caused by *Phytophthora infestans*. Major diseases in tomato are early blight, late blight, *Fusarium* diseases and gray leaf spot, caused by *Stemphyllium solani*. Research is also being conducted on bacterial spot of sweet pepper caused by *Xanthomonas campestris*, on yellow and black sigatoka disease of banana caused by *Mycosphaerella musicola*, on blue mold (*Peronospora tabacina*) and black shank (*Phytophthora nicotianae* var. *nicotianae*) of tobacco, and on coffee rust (*Hemeliea vastatrix*).

Until recently, disease diagnoses could not be performed at local research centers because the tests did not exist. Now the National Animal and Plant Health Center (CENSA) has adapted techniques from Cuban veterinary and human health research for use in diagnosis of plant bacteria and viruses. Techniques such as electron microscopy, serological tests (ELISA), immunofluorescence, and dot blot tests are now used to detect quarantined pathogens and to certify seeds, as well as to diagnose diseases in the field. In fact, Cuba now produces and exports ELISA kits for detecting plant pathogens of worldwide importance. Their strategy is to produce cheaper kits, undercutting sales by developed country companies. The sophistication of plant protection research and application in Cuba is rapidly approaching the level they have achieved in human and veterinary medicine, which already has worldwide recognition.

Since 1989, the cost of fungicides has become prohibitive. Fungicides are used only for foliar diseases of potato (i.e., *Phytophthora infestans* and *Alternaria solani*), *Alternaria* leaf blights of onion and garlic, and some sugarcane diseases, while alternatives are stressed for other pathogens.

A major disease of banana in Cuba is yellow sigatoka disease, caused by *Mycosphaerella musicola*. This fungus kills banana leaves, which reduces subsequent fruit yield. Incidence is highly influenced by rainfall and humidity, and a strong relationship exists between disease incidence and yield reduction. To determine the rate of disease development in Cuba, observations are made on the number of infected leaves and the position of the youngest leaf infected. Sigatoka-tolerant cultivars are planted, but if disease appears anyway and is detected, affected leaves are removed so they won't serve as sources of further dissemination. Leaves are also sprayed with mineral oil, which appears to inhibit infection or lesion development.

Biological control of plant pathogens

A relatively new research direction in Cuba is the biological control of plant diseases using microbial antagonists. In a short period, Cuba has advanced further than other countires toward large-scale implementation of this sort of biological control. Research in this area is scattered among several institutes, including the Institute of Sugar and the National Academy of Science. At the Institute for Basic Research on Tropical Agriculture, research is done on such projects as the biocontrol of *Sclerotium rolfsii* in peanuts and beans using the fungus *Trichoderma* as the antagonist. At the Plant Protection Institute, research is performed on a number of specific biocontrol projects, such as biocontrol of tobacco root diseases and biocontrol of nematodes. Technical research is also conducted on mass production of inoculum, formulations, and storage of biocontrol products. The National Animal and Plant Health Center also studies mass production of biocontrol agents.

One of the main obstacles to be overcome in biocontrol research is the lack of taxonomic knowledge of the fungi involved. Cuban researchers try to use native strains of fungi in biological control, because fungi from other sources would not necessarily be adapted to Cuban crops, climate, and soil. However, identification is sometimes a problem, due to the lack of reference books and the equipment needed for modern taxonomy. *Trichoderma*, for example, is an extremely difficult genus to study. A species such as *Trichoderma viride* turns out to be a complex of many closely related taxa. Much of the current taxonomic literature involves identifications based on serological or DNA hybridization techniques unavailable at most laboratories.

Another obstacle is the need for strict quality control. First the inoculum produced at the CREEs has to be free of major contamination. Then it must be tested periodically for vigor and virulence. Finally, the methods of application of biocontrol agents must be more precise than with pesticides. Cuban scientists said that farmers distrusted biocontrol techniques and therefore one "bad" batch of inoculum could unjustly prejudice them against a technique that was effective when properly prepared and applied.

Screening biocontrol agents is a time-consuming process, and evaluations in the lab to find antagonists effective in the field is difficult. An example of the procedure involved was described by researchers at the Institute of Plant Protection. They had been interested in biological control for years but mainly out of curiosity. Then, in 1990, they began to work in earnest. First, they decided to pick a "model system" on which to base all subsequent biocontrol work: they needed to choose an important crop with a serious disease, and the disease had to be caused by a pathogen that could readily be attacked by an antagonistic fungus. They reviewed the existing literature, evaluated the resources they had, and chose tobacco as the crop, and its complex of root disease-causing pathogens (*Phythophthora nicotianae*, *Rhizoctonia solani*, *Fusarium*, spp., and *Pythium*, spp.) as the targets.

In addition to its economic importance, tobacco had the advantage of being a transplant crop whose seedlings are started in small beds. It would be very difficult to establish a soilborne biocontrol agent in a large field, but relatively easy to add one to a small seed bed. These biocontrol agents would be expected to persist in the soil of the beds and control seedling diseases. In addition, they might also colonize the seedling root and persist once the seedling had been transplanted, therefore continuing to protect the seedling in the field.

Having chosen their model, the researchers set out to collect their antagonists. They visited diseased tobacco fields to collect soil samples. They chose the most severely diseased areas of the affected fields, and then collected soil from the rhizospheres of healthy plants growing among the diseased ones. They made isolations and selected 25 colonies of *Trichoderma*. These were evaluated in paired *in vitro* tests with the target pathogens.

The researchers noted the relative growth rates of the paired fungi and any evidence of parasitism by the antagonist toward the target pathogen. Based on these results, the candidates were narrowed to eight. These isolates were used in greenhouse tests with tobacco seedlings grown in trays of diseased or sterile soil. The candidates were then further narrowed to four, and tested in larger trays of severely infested soil with different concentrations of biocontrol agent added. At the same time, research began into the mass production of *Trichoderma* inoculum. In the end, one isolate was selected for tobacco that worked very well against *Phytophthora* and *Rhizoctonia*, while also exhibiting fair control of *Fusarium* and *Pythium*. This isolate is now used in almost all tobacco seed beds in the tobacco-producing province of Pinar del Río, and according to the researchers we spoke with, the results are good. Tobacco growers have eliminated the use of Ridomil and methyl bromide against fungi in tobacco seed beds.

Another isolate of *Trichoderma* from the four finalists was selected for use with sweet pepper; this isolate proved to be the best seed colonizer, staying on the seed during storage while retaining virulence. It is now being tested in one state farm.

Each biocontrol agent must pass safety regulations based on those of the FDA and of the European Economic Community. It has to be observed and tested for efficacy at a quarantine lab and to undergo toxicological testing in order to be registered for use.

Little work has been done on post-harvest use of biocontrol agents, although such work is recognized as necessary, especially with potato. One project at the Plant Protection Institute, now in its initial stages, is a study of fluorescent *Pseudomonas* bacteria as potential antagonists of soft rot bacteria of potato and banana.

Another goal is to integrate biocontrol with soil improvement research, in particular to study the interaction of mycorrhizal fungi, rhizosphere bacteria and biocontrol organisms. This is important since mycorrhizae, which stimulate plant growth, sometimes influence disease development and conversely, some biocontrol agents influence plant growth.

Nematodes

Nematicides are expensive and, in Cuba's experience, not terribly effective. The soil flora in continuously cropped fields appears to deactivate nematicides. At first, research was oriented towards cultural control measures, such as planting in nematode-free seedbeds, reducing populations of weed hosts, and using crop rotation and tillage practices detrimental to nematodes. Biocontrol measures were meant to be one part of such a program.

The fungus *Paecilomyces lilacinus* is a parasite of nematodes, especially *Meloidogyne, spp.* A strain from the International Potato Center in Peru is currently being used in banana culture to control *Radopholus similis.* The fungus is grown on rice husks and added to banana plantlets from tissue culture. The fungus is also added to potting soil and seedling beds in coffee and guava nurseries to protect seedlings with the intention of transmitting this protection to the field. The fungus must be used in conjunction with other methods such as reduced nematicide doses and crop rotation, since it is not as effective at controlling nematodes at high densities. Future work will include searching for local strains of fungi antagonistic to nematodes, experimenting with different methods of mass production, and researching the use of *Pasteuria penetrans*, a bacterium that is an obligate parasite of nematodes.

Biotechnology
The final type of plant disease control employed in Cuba is the use of biotechnology[22] to produce seedlings of bananas, plantains and timber species that are free of viruses and other plant diseases. This is important as many diseases are passed on from parent plant to the cuttings or seeds that are used for reproduction. To avoid this, tiny seedlings are produced in test tubes by culturing tissue from healthy growing tips or meristems. Though tissue culture is used in many countries, Cuba is perhaps the most advanced Latin American country in this field.

Weeds
Integrated weed management has been a major field of study in the United States for the last 15-20 years. However, weed management in

---

[22] As far as we were able to determine, there are no plans in Cuba to release genetically engineered organisms into the environment. The biopesticides and biofertilizers are naturally occurring strains that have been isolated in Cuba, and are mass produced and then reintroduced to the environments where they occur. Nor are the disease-free seedlings produced by tissue culture genetically engineered. The only genetic engineering used in relation to agriculture is in the development of diagnostic kits for plant viruses, a technique in common use in many parts of the world. Other than that, there is substantial work underway in the biomedical sector for development of vaccines, diagnostics and new medicines.

Cuba before the Special Period had been mostly dependent on the use of agrochemicals.

The fall of the Eastern Bloc left Cuba without a cheap source for the herbicides on which it had become dependent. Furthermore, traditional methods of weed management had nearly been lost with "high technology" emphasis on herbicide usage. During the last couple of years, since the beginning of the Special Period, an effort has been made to rediscover the traditional methods used by *campesinos,* and furthermore to look for the scientific basis for the success of their methods. Research focused on four major areas:

1) a monitoring technique which can predict weed pressures and community composition a year in advance;

2) systems of rotations based upon a prediction model based on the monitoring;

3) very selective use of herbicides in combination with the above methods; and

4) tillage methods, including design of new farm implements.

Techniques for monitoring weed populations have been studied by scientists in many countries, but have generally not been explored under commercial conditions. Yet the Cubans are actually using their systems on about 16 state-owned farms across the country — three in Havana province and one farm in each of the other 13 provinces. The techniques combine into a mathematical model data such as the previous years' weed species and densities; a determination of the seed bank and seed viability; the type of crop to be planted and how well it will compete with those weeds; the effectiveness of herbicides on those weeds; and how similar the growth habit of the weeds is to the desired crop. With this data, the scientists have been able to determine with a very high degree of accuracy what the weed problems will be, and devise suitable responses. This provides the opportunity to plan what crops will be planted one year in advance.

Also very important is crop rotation. Crops can be selected which can better outcompete the weed community. For example, corn can be used in rotation with beans because it can shade out lower growing weeds. A corn rotation may be used in conjunction with a selective herbicide to kill broadleaf weeds which could not be used in a bean crop. For severe weed problems, a crop with a very dense cover such as sweet potato is planted, which effectively smothers virtually all weeds. Table 10 outlines some of the recommended rotations.

TABLE 10: Rotations to control different weed species
(adapted from Institute of Plant Protection pamphlet)

To control annual grasses and certain other perennial grasses such as Johnson grass (*Sorghum halepense*), rotations such as the following combinations with sweet potato are recommended:

Sweet potato → potato → peas → beans
Sweet potato →potato → sweet potato → potato
Sweet potato → beans → sweet potato → potato
Sweet potato → potato → sweet potato → potato
Sweet potato → beans → sweet potato → beans
Sweet potato → potato → peanuts → potato
Sweet potato → peanuts → sweet potato → peanuts

Against Nutgrass (*Cyperus rotundus*) the following rotation is suggested to reduce populations:

Corn → potato → sweet potato → beans
Corn → peas → sweet potato → beans
Corn → beans → sweet potato → potato
Corn → sweet potato → potato → beans
Sorghum → peanuts or velvet beans → sweet potato → beans

To control Feverfew or Mugwort (*Parthenium hysterophorus*) and other Dicotyledonous annual weeds, adequate results can be obtained with a system which includes:

Corn or sorghum → potato → corn or sorghum

In all cases, this pamphlet stresses, selective herbicides must be used, but not relied upon as the only control method.

The last important method in use involves cultivation and soil preparation. Major objectives are to arrange tillage operations based on the weed community while attempting to minimize the number of passes in a field. Rototillers are rarely used; instead, more commonly found are discs, rotating discs, and what is called the multi-plow. This was designed by Cuban agricultural engineers to open the soil, and do some subsoil cultivation, but not turn the soil, thereby not exposing more seed to germination. It essentially lifts and drops the soil, breaking weeds from their roots. This type of implement is best used when soils are free from pathogens such as nematodes, where turning over of the soil by disc may be desired.

Little work has been done with biotechnology in relation to weed suppression, and the use of grazing animals to feed on weeds has received little attention. There are a few examples of geese used to control a parasitic plant of tobacco, though there have been problems with the management of the geese. Sheep are used in some areas to graze in citrus orchards with good success.

In summary, we might say that Cuba has made very impressive advances toward monitoring and biological control of insect pests and diseases. In these areas they are certainly among the world's leaders. Weed management has been slower to develop in Cuba as it has been elsewhere — nevertheless they are closer than most countries to widespread implementation of weed monitoring and scientifically designed rotation schemes.

♦ 4 ♦

Soil management:
A key to the new model

S oil is the most important resource for agriculture, and its conservation and improvement are key to a successful conversion from conventional to organic farming. Soil management practices in Cuba prior to the Special Period seem to have been like those of most other countries during the age of industrialized agriculture. Practices were production-oriented, based on high-energy inputs, and expended the soil as if it were just another input used in the production of crops. Little was done to protect the soils from erosion, loss of fertility, salinization, and other forms of degradation.

This is no longer the case. There is now great concern for implementing a sound and effective soil management program that includes minimum tillage, rational use of fertilizers, the use of soil amendments, crop rotations and crop covers. This is principally a result of the fact that increasing the dosages of fertilizers and pesticides to compensate for soil degradation is no longer an option.

Classifying the nation's soils
As a first step toward implementing an effective soil management program, Cuban researchers launched an ambitious project to reclassify,

evaluate, and map the country's soils in great detail, and to interpret the maps for sustainable management.

The soils have been mapped at a scale of 1:250,000, and this is being followed by very detailed soil maps at a 1:25,000 scale, and careful evaluations of soil fertility. This will be done in a plot by plot and farm by farm basis.

Of the agricultural lands, 8.0 percent have been rated as having soils with very high potential productivity; 26.2 percent high; 44.4 percent low; and 21.4 percent very low. There are great variations in soil productivity among the 14 provinces (see Table 11). Six of the provinces have soils of high to moderate productivity, while six have soils of moderate to low productivity, and two have soils of relatively low potential agricultural productivity. Cuba is not blessed with particularly fertile soils, though they do have a favorable ratio of population to arable land (see Table 1). With nearly 66 percent of the agricultural lands having soils with low or very low potential, the concentration of soil fertility building efforts on these poorer lands could pay relatively large dividends.

TABLE 11: Classification of potential soil productivity by province (*Percentage of soils*)

Province	Very high	High	Low	Very low
Pinar del Río	5.3	32.6	47.3	14.8
La Habana	27.8	23.2	32.5	16.5
Matanzas	21.6	24.6	23.8	30.0
Villa Clara	3.1	23.8	48.1	25.0
Cienfuegos	7.8	30.0	47.2	15.0
Sancti Spiritus	5.6	39.6	39.4	15.4
Ciego de Avila	27.5	28.1	39.2	5.2
Camaguey	1.8	33.4	38.2	26.6
Las Tunas	3.8	27.9	43.9	24.4
Holguín	—	12.4	56.2	31.4
Granma	0.2	7.2	84.9	7.7
Santiago de Cuba	1.4	35.1	24.2	39.3
Guantánamo	1.8	16.8	51.2	30.2
Isla de la Juventud	0.8	36.5	41.1	21.6

Source: MINAGRI

TABLE 12: Organic matter applied to soils in Cuba
(MT/year)

Type	1989	1990
Total applied	2,973.7	2,822.8
Cattle manure	2,217.5	2,413.5
Pig manure	15.5	9.4
Poultry manure	161.6	128.2
Cachaza	289.8	207.8
Turba	49.8	50.0
Other	239.8	13.9
Equivalent in N-P-K		
N	35.4	33.6
P_2O_5	14.6	13.8
K_2O	26.8	25.4

Source: MINAGRI

Use of soil amendments

Due to excessive cultivation and heavy use of fertilizers and pesticides most of Cuba's agricultural soils suffer from the depletion of organic matter, with resulting loss of fertility. Over the past three years, efforts to maintain and improve soil fertility have been based primarily on organic amendments and biofertilizers. Table 12 shows the amounts of organic materials applied to the soils and the equivalent amounts of nutrients contained in them, and gives an idea of the extent of this massive fertility management program.

Crushed zeolite rock, mined locally in a number of places, is used as a part of this program. Composting of crop residues is now also common. They are also working on the collection, processing, and utilization of urban garbage.

Cubans have greatly expanded the use of green manures, mostly inoculated legumes, and mostly in crop rotation combinations. The new program involves the search for rotation schemes which will both improve the soils as well as improve crop yields. By increasing the productivity of the soils through crop rotations and other management practices, they believe that they can achieve sustainable production. Velvet beans, cowpeas, soybeans, sorghum, and *Sesbania* (a nitrogen fixer which is salt tolerant) are some of the green manures used in rotation programs with some of the main target crops.

One interesting and effective way that eroded lands have been reclaimed is by filling gullies with soil and organic matter removed from lowlands and carted up by wagons pulled by either animals or tractors. This is essentially a revival of a very old practice which some of the small farmers had never stopped using. In general, the most rapid adoption of soil conservation techniques has come in parts of the country where the farmers had been most severely impacted by soil erosion in the past.

Reducing tillage

A key component of this soil management program is to reduce or even eliminate tillage to prevent erosion. The Cubans have been trying to reduce tillage since 1968, but this process has been greatly accelerated since 1989. By 1992, tillage operations had been reduced from a national average of 10 to 12 per season to only three to five (MINAGRI figures). Minimum or zero tillage is better for the soil in every way except weed control, because tillage kills weeds. In the United States, minimum tillage is accompanied by increased herbicide use, whereas Cuba is trying to achieve it with alternative weed management technologies such as crop rotations (see weed section in previous chapter).

Because of the petroleum shortage many if not most tractors are idle. Everywhere we saw tractors parked and ox teams plowing fields. By our own observations and according to what we were told by Cuban officials, animal traction is replacing tractor use on a wide scale. Animal traction cuts down on soil erosion and has a positive effect in reducing degradation of hillsides, and is feasible during the rainy season when tractors would bog down in the mud. The down side, of course, is that it is very labor intensive. Nevertheless, Cubans emphasize the benefits and see it as part of the Alternative Model. Other low impact strategies in field preparation are being implemented as well. For example, in rice cultivation, a system where large new dikes had to be rebuilt by heavy equipment every year is being scrapped for a design that will not require annual machine use. Another part of the effort to eliminate tillage is the locally made ox-drawn multi-plow that slices under the soil surface, cutting off weed roots without turning the soil over.

Salinization and acidity

Cuba is a long and narrow island, and Cuban agronomists say that as a result, there is severe salt stress on about 800,000 hectares of farmland, particularly in the eastern and southern parts of the country. In addition to salt accumulations, the eastern region has also been affected by drought, rising water tables, mine tailings, and poor management of forest lands. This region has therefore been targeted for special emphasis in the nation's sustainable agriculture program.

To provide organic matter under conditions of salt stress, many rice farmers are now using *Sesbania* in their rotations. And the Institute of Soil Science is searching hard for other salt-tolerant plants. So far 40 species (grasses, legumes, roots and tubers, vegetables, *Amaranthus*, etc.) have been studied and rated for degree of salt tolerance.

At this point, they claim to have generally arrested further salinization throughout the country. As Table 13 shows, however, very little progress has yet been made in actually rehabilitating or ameliorating the saline soils.

TABLE 13: Rehabilitation of degraded soils
(Percentage Rehabilitated or Improved)

Type	Affected (ha)	1989	1990
Erosion	3,681	86.5	86.1*
Salinization	780	0.1	0.1
Acidity	1,133	27.0	26.5
Poor drainage	100	4.0	6.7
Little organic matter	3,000	86.5	94.1

Source: MINAGRI

* Principally via agronomic methods of erosion control (contour ploughing, etc.)

As of 1990, approximately 27 percent of soils affected by excess acidity have been ameliorated, primarily through the application of high-calcium materials such as crushed limestone, which is abundant in Cuba. They are currently making rapid progress in ameliorating the remaining soils which have this problem.

In contrast, little progress had been made by 1990 in draining excessively wet agricultural soils. They have since started a drainage program to reclaim soils that have been degraded through over-irrigation in the past, as well as soils, mainly in low-lying coastal areas, which are naturally wet.

Fertilizers

From being a country highly dependent on inorganic fertilizers for growing food and export crops, there is now a comprehensive transformation to alternatives to obtain plant nutrients from organic sources available locally. Research in this area is being conducted by the Institute for Research into Soils and Fertilizers, the Institute for Research on Ecology and Taxonomy, and the "Bioagriculture Front" created by the National Academy of Sciences in order to find solutions to the problem of food production during the Special Period.

Since 1989, fertilizer availability has plummeted by 80 percent. Cuba has responded with a biofertilizer program that by 1992 was making up 30 percent of the deficit (MINAGRI figures). Recycled organic waste along with other biofertilizers like nitrogen-fixing bacteria and earthworm humus, quarried minerals, and peat have helped close the gap.

One factor that has mitigated the effects of this dramatic decline is the previous years of research that had been carried out on biofertilizers. With the present crisis, this accumulated research as well as new research results have immediate application in the field. Since 1985 there had been a great push to increase bioproduction, but this push has been intensified since 1989. Some biotechnologies developed elsewhere are also applied, often with little testing by local institutions. Today there is almost no gap between research results and field application.

The starting point for developing the low-input fertilizer strategy is to determine, for each combination of crop and soil, the minimum quantity of plant nutrients needed to produce the crop. They have already obtained results of fertility trials for all major crops.

Biofertilizers

Nitrogen-fixing microorganisms, such as *Azospirillium*, are being used to increase the availability of this nutrient to crops. Bacteria from the genus *Rhizobium* are being used for legumes; *Azotobacter* is being used for non-symbiotic N-fixation in grasses, including sugarcane.

The Institute for Research into Soils and Fertilizers has a laboratory in Havana where they produce enough *Rhizobium* inoculum for the whole nation, providing up to 80 percent of the nitrogen required by leguminous crops. *Rhizobium* inoculant is commonly used in other countries as well. More unique to Cuba is the commercial use of the free-living nitrogen-fixer *Azotobacter*.

By 1991 the Institute for Research into Soils and Fertilizers was producing 5 million liters of liquid *Azotobacter*, which is applied to leaves or to the soil. The use of *Azotobacter* has provided 40-50 percent of the nitrogen needs of non-leguminous plants (MINAGRI figures). Another benefit of *Azotobacter* that Cuban scientists have discovered is that it shortens crop production cycles by 7-12 days in nurseries and 20-21 days in the field. Also, a reduction in blossom drop has been associated with the use of *Azotobacter* due to the production of giberellins, citokinins and autines by the bacteria. The Cubans claim they have achieved a 30-40 percent increase in yield for maize, cassava, rice and other vegetables.

A second area unique to Cuba has been the widespread use of bacteria of the genus *Bacillus* to promote the solubilization of phosphorus from Oxisols and Ultisolsoils. In tropical and subtropical areas there is an abundance of soils with high contents of aluminum and iron oxides. These minerals form insoluble complexes with PO_4, making it unavailable to plants. The "phospho-solubilizing" bacteria, as these bacteria are called, make this PO_4 available to plants.

The Institute for Research on Ecology and Taxonomy is now studying *Vesicular Arbuscular Micorrhizae* (VAM), fungi that penetrate roots and help with uptake of phosphorus and other nutrients, as a way of increasing plant uptake of mineral nutrients. VAM, by increasing the root's effective area of absorption, increases the amount of nutrients available to plants.

The Institute has identified 53 species of VAM in Cuba, and is planning to introduce VAM nationwide for coffee plantations. It also plans to create a system of "biofactories" for crops produced by tissue culture, such as plantains, sugarcane and potatoes, and fruit trees such as mango, guava, papaya, and avocado. The Cuban government is planning to produce 18 tons of VAM material for commercial purposes next year, making it the first country in our knowledge to do so.

Green manures and crop rotations

As a way of increasing the amount of available nutrients to plants, Cuban scientists have been using several combinations of crops with grasses and legumes. For the case of rice mentioned earlier, they are using a rotation system that consists of planting rice for 2 or 3 years and then rotating with the legume *Sesbania*. This legume is able to incorporate up to 60 tons of green manure in 45 days, providing up to 75 percent of the nitrogen needed by the next rice crop. *Sesbania* is used due to its tolerance to high levels of soil salinity. Sorghum is being used in tobacco as a green manure. Other legumes, like beans, are being used in crop rotations and as green manures.

Intercropping

Intercropping refers to the growing of two or more crop species together in the same field. Traditionally, the Cuban small farmer has routinely intercropped a variety of crops: corn with beans, corn with cassava, coffee with plantains, and a variety of other combinations. During the years of modernization little thought was given to this traditional technique since the Classical Model was based on intensive chemically-based and mechanically-harvested production. With the exception of traditional production of coffee under shade trees and/or plantains, no intercropping systems were used in commercial-scale production.

Intercropping has seen something of a resurgence in the context of the Alternative Model. Three general areas in which the technique is either being used in production or under strong consideration for development are 1) soybeans and common beans intercropped with sugarcane, 2) green manure crops interplanted with a variety of crops, and 3) a variety of combinations being considered in conjunction with the new weed management system. Additionally, it is quite obvious from casual observations that the intercropping of a variety of crops (e.g. corn/cassava, plantains/cassava, coffee/taro, corn/taro) remains common in the home gardens of small producers, cooperative members, state farm workers and even city dwellers.

Perhaps the most significant development in the technique has been interplanting soybeans with sugarcane. As described elsewhere in this report, a substantial portion of animal feed had come from imported soybeans and corn before 1989. Among other programs aimed at making up this 30 percent shortfall is an extensive program of interplanting soybeans with sugarcane. While we were not able to obtain exact production figures, technical experts claimed that the technique was not only working to help make up for losses in imported soybeans, but also has helped reduce the nitrogen fertilizer use in sugarcane.

A second major use of intercropping is now beginning to emerge in conjunction with soil fertility and conservation. As noted in Table 11, approximately 45 percent of the cultivable land in Cuba has problems with erosion. Among the strategies developed to cope with this problem, a major thrust has been crop rotations in an attempt to maintain crop cover all year around. Many legumes were chosen as rotation crops to help with fertility while protecting the soil surface. It is thus a small step from planting alfalfa, for example, as a rotation crop, to planting some other crop into the alfalfa, to interplanting alfalfa with the crop. Indeed, according to some soil scientists, the talk is shifting to crop *succession* rather than rotation. The Cuban concept of crop succession seems to incorporate aspects of both crop rotation and intercropping.

As with the programs for weed management, intercropping is a technique that is currently contemplated, but is not under very widespread implementation.

Earthworm humus

Cuban scientists have been able to develop a full technology for the production of humus from earthworms, also known as vermicomposting or vermiculture. By using California Red hybrids they have been able to provide 2 percent of soil nitrogen with each application of 4 tons/ha of earthworm humus (MINAGRI figures).

Cuba's vermicomposting program started in 1986 with two small boxes of redworms, *Eisenia foetida* and *Lumbricus rubellus*. Today there are 172 vermicompost centers that in 1992 produced 93,000 tons of worm humus (see Graph 1).

GRAPH 1: Yearly production of worm humus in Cuba
(Metric tons)

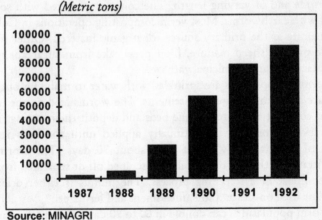

Source: MINAGRI

Several different institutions and companies are involved in vermiculture operations. Research is conducted primarily by the Institute of Soils and Fertilizers and the National Institute of Agricultural Sciences. At the Soil Institute plans exist for a vermiculture research facility, but construction has not started. The Institute is presently spearheading efforts to market and sell worm humus in 40 kg, 1 kg, and 1/2 kg bags under the trade name *Midas*. A 40 kg bag of Cuban worm humus can sell for as much as US$80-100 on the international market, though humus production has not reached levels that permit significant exports. Income generating schemes have focused on joint production ventures and the sale of technical assistance for start-up vermiculture programs outside Cuba.

The humus that is produced in vermicomposting provides binding sites for plant nutrients, improves soil permeability, helps control diseases that attack plants, and stimulates plant growth. Cuban researchers have found that nitrogen concentrations are higher in the vermicompost than static compost piles. For instance, four tons of vermicompost can replace forty tons of cow manure per hectare of tobacco and in one test plot, has resulted in a 36 percent improvement in yield (MINAGRI figures).

The production of vermicompost requires a mixture of worm castings, organic material, and bedding in various stages of decomposition. First, manure is composted for approximately 30 days in a static pile process, then transferred to open vermicompost beds approximately 5 feet wide and of varying length. The compost is mixed with soil and seeded with earthworms. Most vermicomposting operations in Cuba use cow manure as the primary source for organic material. Other sources include pig and sheep manure, filter press cake from sugarcane, coffee pulp, plantains, and municipal garbage.

Vermicompost beds are sprinkled with water to maintain optimum moisture and temperature requirements. The worms feed on the freshly applied compost at the top of the beds and deposit their castings in the lower levels. Compost is continually applied until the beds reach a height of approximately 3 feet after about 90 days. The worms are concentrated in the top of the pile and scraped off or separated from the vermicompost in a screening process. The humus is either dried and bagged or used on-site as a soil amendment and fertilizer.

Worm populations can double in 60 to 90 days. Worms that are not used to seed new compost piles are dried and used as a supplemental protein for animal feed. New plans include the production of earthworm excrement to be used as substrate for bacteria, which in turn will be used as biofertilizer, and as high-protein food supplements for shrimp and chickens. (See Table 14 for the approximate composition of Cuban earthworm humus.)

TABLE 14: Chemical composition of Cuban worm humus

Element	Content
Nitrogen	1.5 - 2.2%
Phosphorus	1.8 - 2.2%
Potassium	1.0 - 1.5%
C/N Ratio	10-11
Humic Acids	3.5 - 4.0%
Organic Matter	65 - 70%
Bacterial Flora	40x10* Col/g

Source: MINAGRI   *exponent missing in original

Five experimental stations located in different parts of the country have responsibility for training new worm growers in their regions. Information is exchanged among worm growers at an annual national conference on vermicomposting and vermiculture. National television programs and newspaper articles are used to help educate farmers, school children, and the general public about vermicomposting. Recommendations for garden application and for potted plants are made on television and in the press, but home worm composting is not commonly practiced and commercial vermicompost is not available for home use.

Waste recycling

As a result of Cuba's dramatic shift from classical to low-input agriculture since 1989, resource recovery and recycling programs are being implemented on a countrywide scale. Cuban scientists are converting "waste" products into animal food, energy, and fertilizer. Organic by-products from sugarcane processing, cattle ranches, sheep ranches, poultry and pig farms, coffee harvests, crops and foodstuffs are being collected and processed into biofertilizers (see above).

Resource recovery programs include waste recycling from the following primary sources:

- cows, pigs, sheep, and poultry
- garbage (food waste)
- crop residue (green manure)
- sugarcane processing

Processing methods include:
- vermiculture/vermicomposting
- static pile (aerobic) composting
- anaerobic digesters
- mechanized, on-site recycling of industrial waste

In addition to the impressive vermiculture program previously discussed, several recycling programs stand out as examples of innovative solutions to production and pollution problems.

1. Sugarcane

Sugarcane production is virtually organic in Cuba, which really is not new. What is new is the maximum utilization of cane and cane processing by-products to produce energy, fertilizer, animal food supplements, and irrigation water. Waste water, filter press cake, and bagasse are three by-products that have been effectively recycled. Waste water from 152 sugarcane processing plants is used to irrigate cane fields. Filter press cake, a processing by-product that is high in phosphorus, potassium, and calcium, is used as fertilizer. And bagasse, a dry pulp, is used as animal feed and biomass for energy production.

2. Swine production

In the 1950s, large-scale swine production did not exist in Cuba. Today, 14 farms with approximately 2,000 pigs at each installation complement small, private pig farm production. There is a concerted effort among institutions to promote pork as the principal source of protein in Cuban households and provide sufficient quantities to meet those needs.

The recycling goal at the large pig farms is zero waste discharge. Liquid and solid waste at the large installations is treated and used for a series of applications, including vermicompost, energy (biogas), and feed supplement. Recycling at the state pig farms focuses on:

A. Processing food scraps from work places, restaurants and schools for pig feed supplement. Since 1989, 1,200,000 tons of supplementary animal food was produced from garbage, equal to 70,000 ha. of soy cultivation or 200,000 ha. of corn.

B. Researching the use of cane by-products as a high yield biomass for feed.

C. Growing water hyacinths in processed waste water from pig farms for use as protein rich animal food supplement.

D. Fermenting and drying solid waste from pig farms as organic material for vermicomposting.

E. Using nutrient-rich waste water for aquaculture.

F. Producing energy from swine excrement using biogas plants to meet on-site energy needs.

G. Using processed slaughterhouse waste as protein supplement in feed.

Alternative, supplemental feeds have helped alleviate a 30 percent feed supplement deficit that has resulted from the unavailability of corn and soy imports. Other efforts to find replacements for imports, like a project that utilizes treated molasses from sugarcane processing as a nutritious feed supplement, have been stymied by high capital and energy requirements for processing.

3. Cattle

In 1990, in response to the severe shortages of imported animal feed, Cuba began to experiment with a new system of cattle management called Voisin Rational Pasture Management, named after the French agronomist who proposed this technique in the 1960s (it is also called rotational or rational grazing). The basic technique involves using movable electric fencing to confine cattle to small pasture areas, where their manure refertilizes the forage plants. The enclosures are moved around the fields on a tight schedule.

Environmental pollution is reduced as fewer pesticides and fertilizers are used to produce feed, and manure is distributed to benefit pasture plants and soil rather than concentrated where it can become a pollution problem.

In New Zealand, farmers using this technique are able to equal U.S. dairy production levels, without using any of the balanced animal feeds that U.S. cattlemen depend on, in an area only the size of Wisconsin. They also raise seven more times sheep than the United States, also without grain supplements. Data like this has influenced the Cuban Institute of Animal Science to seriously study Voisin grazing management.

Voisin Pasture Management has been implemented on a wide scale since May 1991. Today over 300,000 hectares (450 units of 600-700 ha. each) are under the Voisin system. The principle idea behind Voisin Management is that if pasture plants and soil are taken care of, they will in turn take care of the grazing animals.

However, researchers at the Cuban Animal Institute admit they have much more research to do before they can call their Voisin program a success. Details on pasture ecology, pasture nutrition, paddock layout and fencing, feed planning, economics, recovery periods, stock rate, and forage allowances are presently unavailable. Furthermore, competing demands for cattle manure are already evident. Vermiculture operators want manure as a primary source for their compost systems while Voisin pasture managers want to keep it on their fields.

4. Biogas

Anaerobic biogas digesters are used on a small, experimental scale to produce energy and fertilizer from animal excrement. Plans exist to expand the use of biogas digesters but information about the scope of such plans was not obtained.

5. Human manure

Compost from aerobic digesters is a potential new source of bio-fertilizer, harvested either directly from composting toilets or transferred from composting toilets to vermicompost operations. A pilot compost project is presently underway at the "José Antonio Echeverria" Institute of Higher Education.

Studies are also being conducted by the Institute of Soils and Fertilizers on the feasibility of using waste water and sludge from central sewage treatment for irrigation and fertilizer, respectively.

An important piece of the new Cuban agriculture model is thus the recycling of organic waste. Cuban researchers have evaluated minimum fertilizer input needs and have coordinated inter-institutional efforts to produce fertilizers, in Cuba, to meet those needs. Though in its nascent stage, the recycling program is demonstrating how "waste" products can be harvested and used to reduce dependency on fertilizer imports, improve soil fertility, and address serious pollution problems.

Reforestation

A key component of soil management involves care of Cuba's forests. Trees cover more of the island now than in 1959 — something few countries in the world can boast.

When the Spanish first arrived in Cuba, some 80 percent of the island was covered by forests. By the time of the revolution in 1959, forests covered only 17 percent of the land. Several reasons accounted for that deforestation. Trees were cut to establish settlements and get raw materials for construction. They were also used as sources of fuel and charcoal for cooking. Perhaps the most important cause of deforestation was for the development of sugarcane plantations during the 17th, 18th and 19th centuries. Forests were razed to plant sugarcane, and much firewood was needed for the process of sugar manufacturing.

After the Cuban revolution, attention was given to the severe problem of deforestation and land erosion. Starting in the 1970s, a program for the development of community nurseries or *viveros populares* was created nationwide. The objective was to collect seed, raise seedlings in the community nurseries and plant them in the countryside. Under the name of *Plan Manati*, the Cuban government has continued the reforestation of degraded areas and the reclamation of areas affected by mining activities. The plan consists in providing plastic bags and seeds to interested people, who later on will use them for the reforestation of degraded areas. (See Table 15 for recent figures on the provision of seedlings for reforestation.)

In 1989-1990, over 200,000 hectares were reforested. In terms of total forested area, in 1990 two million hectares were forested, 1.7 million of them natural forests and 332,000 hectares of plantations. Today 18 percent of Cuba is covered with forests — a net *increase* since 1959. Meanwhile, net *de*forestation plagues the rest of Latin America.

TABLE 15: Numbers of trees planted of the most important tree species used for reforestation
(Thousands of seedlings)

Year	Pine	Casuarina	Mahogany	Ocaje
1989	2546.6	174.5	174.5	2435.3
1990	3237.3	767.9	1004.2	4411.3

Source: Boletín estadístico de Cuba. Enero-Junio 1990. Comité Estatal de Estadística

♦ 5 ♦

Mobilizing labor

Under the Classical Model, great attention was given to mechanization, as much because of the already high degree of urbanization of the Cuban population as for any other reason. Thus, a great deal of Cuban agriculture had been mechanized prior to the 1989 crisis (see Tables 17a and 17b).

This high degree of mechanization created the conditions for a labor crisis in the Special Period. Much of the extant mechanized activities had to be curtailed due to a shortfall in petroleum resources, thus requiring a reversion to animal traction. Exacerbating this, the new low-input sustainable techniques required significant additional amounts of hand labor.

This second point merits considerable reflection. Cuba's first agricultural model was largely derivative, copying the basic forms of technologies developed elsewhere. A major part of those technologies had been developed in capitalist and socialist countries where an industrial workforce was not particularly keen on returning to rural areas to work in the fields. Thus the trajectory which had evolved outside of Cuba was simply transferred. The techniques of mechanization were effectively worked out elsewhere and transferred directly to Cuba.

The new model of low-input sustainable agriculture (LISA) does not have this advantage. Most of its paradigms have been developed in small and/or marginalized units both in Cuba and the developed world. So the problems of large-scale implementation have never been faced. In this sense Cuba is certainly in the vanguard.

But the lack of mechanization technology for LISA means that the pattern followed in the old model is simply not available for the new one. Bulgarian implements have not been developed for packaging vermiculture humus and John Deere has never developed a machine that can harvest a sugarcane/soybean intercrop. Consequently, as long as such technology is in its developmental stage, the large-scale implementation of LISA requires a massive mobilization of a new agricultural workforce. Cuba has responded to this need in several ways.

TABLE 16a: Labor force per sector of the economy

Sector	1988 (1000s)	percent
Total civilian sector	3,740.6	100
State sector	3,531.3	94.4
Private agriculture	167.9	4.5
Small farmers	101.9	2.7
Cooperative members	66.0	1.8
Salaried private sector	17.8	0.3
Self-employed workers	28.8	0.8
AVERAGE PRODUCTIVITY:	8,464 pesos / yr	
AVERAGE SALARY:	2,242 pesos / yr	

Source: MINAGRI

Throughout the countryside temporary labor camps have been built to house urban workers who "volunteer"[23] their labor for anywhere from two weeks to two years. Short-term workers leave their jobs or their studies for 15 days at a time to volunteer in the countryside, living in dormitories at the agricultural camps. In 1991, the first year of these two-week mobilizations, some 146,000 residents of Havana participated (MINAGRI figures).

---

[23] "Volunteers" in Cuba receive at least their normal salaries during the volunteer work period. There are also a variety of social factors that influence an individuals decision to volunteer or not.

TABLE 16b: Agriculture Ministry labor force by type of production

TOTAL	1989 (1000s)
Ministry of Agriculture	581.2
Farming and livestock	429.4
Crop production*	222.7
Cattle	159.5
Swine	12.1
Poultry	30.6
Other animals	2.4
Agricultural services	2.1
Silviculture	30.6
Agroindustry	51.0
Tobacco	34.1
Animal feeds	4.6
Construction	10.8
Transport	3.1
Distribution & marketing	54.6
Other activities / projects	1.7
AVERAGE PRODUCTIVITY:	5,451 pesos/year
AVERAGE SALARY:	2,054 pesos/year

Source: MINAGRI   *Sugar production is under the purview of the Sugar Ministry

The two-year volunteers are organized in work brigades called *contingentes*, or contingents, where they work long hours (often 12-hour days) but receive higher pay and above-average living conditions. To convince workers to stay on after their two-year stints are up, the government is building attractive agricultural communities near state farms, with family units modeled on the attractive housing design created for the Pan-American Games, medical facilities, sports and recreation facilities, etc. In fact, the only new housing being built in Cuba during the Special Period is in these agricultural communities.

Incentives to volunteer for both the short-term and long-term stints seem to be largely moral, although some material incentives either creep into the system or are actively being experimented with (in the case of those making a two-year commitment). As an example of the former, one 18-year-old member we spoke with in the *Las Marias* camp outside of Havana told us that he liked the camp better than his Havana job because he got three days off every two weeks, rather than just two. An older woman told us that she made more money in the camp than in her job in Havana. Another said that the field work was easier than his Havana job. Others said that with the food situation in Havana so bad, working in agriculture meant they could eat better.

An experimental way to entice workers to stay on the land has been to maintain the same workforce on the same piece of land over the entire agricultural cycle. Previously, work teams on large centrally managed farms might plant one plot, and never return to it. They might weed and harvest plots that other teams had planted. The goal now is to re-create a more traditional relationship of the producer with the land. State farms are being broken up into smaller management units and work crews are given responsibility for a given piece of land. Furthermore, a bonus system is being established in which the base pay is augmented according to the production (quantity and quality) on that parcel, thus adding another material incentive to the system. Workers we interviewed at *Las Marias* said these bonuses had doubled their pay in the last year. They also claimed that yields had doubled since the system had been implemented. Cuba is presently testing this system in the plantain and citrus sectors, according to Ministry of Agriculture officials.

But despite such examples, the vast majority of people with whom we spoke claimed to be living in the camps as a service to their country, and most expressed a commitment to sign up for another two-year stint when their current one ended. It thus seems that this impressively large mobilization of the workforce has been accomplished largely through the double vehicle of material incentives (ensuring that *at least* the material conditions of one's normal job would be realized) coupled with moral incentives (in a time of crisis your country needs you to work in the field), with a seemingly large component attributable to the latter.

According to officials, these temporary measures are meeting current special labor requirements. But there are serious questions about quality of work, and about the cost in transportation, housing, food, etc., especially for the short-term volunteers. While the two-year volunteers are a better solution, it remains to be seen if these long-term volunteers will continue to come forward in sufficient numbers. Currently it does not appear likely that workers idled in Havana due to lack of materials and energy supplies will indeed take advantage of the housing incentives and amenities being offered in rural areas.

Another approach to the increased labor demands of the Special Period is known as the *Turquino* plan[24], which makes agricultural work mandatory for young men completing their military service. A voluntary female component is also included in this plan. The hope is that many of these young people will find rural life attractive enough to make a permanent move to the countryside once their duty is up.

Community gardens

Another way that labor has been mobilized to help grow food is through a "victory garden" type of program to promote urban gardens. Before the Special Period, Cuban cities were dependent on the rural areas for their food, as a result of a lack of agricultural land near cities, cultural urban bias, and urban opportunities for career advancement away from agriculture. This agricultural dependence on the rural areas necessitated an intricate refrigeration, transportation, storage, and distribution system which required petroleum at all of its stages. The Special Period has had an extremely detrimental effect on the availability of petroleum, causing a severe reduction in food supply in the cities. This effect has been most strongly felt in Havana, where about one-fifth of the population resides.

Urban gardens can do much to reduce the pressures of the national food shortage in Cuba due to the Special Period. Localized production alleviates the problems of transportation and post harvest storage. Small-scale production relies on human resources, as opposed to heavy machinery and other energy-taxing inputs. With the Cuban diet quite low in vitamins and minerals, produce from urban gardens can help alleviate these deficiencies. The crop diversification common to small-scale gardening also greatly reduces vulnerability to plant diseases and pests. Finally, through urban gardening, individuals are empowered as they work to resolve their problems of food availability, instead of looking to the state or the black market to supply their needs.

Urban gardens take on three basic levels of organization in Cuba: individual and family gardens on private land, organized groups of neighbors gardening on public land, and institutionally organized gardens.

The first type of garden is planted by an individual or family on their own private property. The produce from these gardens is for personal consumption, with all production inputs provided by the gardeners themselves. Seeds are cheap and are often available at shops

---

[24] This plan actually began before the Special Period on a trial basis.

called *agromercados*, where Cubans buy their produce, and at the national seed company in Havana.

Gardens organized by private groups on public land are informally structured by those involved. Land is obtained by contacting *Poder Popular* (People's Power), Cuba's elected governing body, or through mass organizations such as the Federation of Cuban Women or block committees (called Committees for the Defense of the Revolution). Once the land is approved for use, the group of gardeners decide for themselves what and when to plant, and they also provide their own supplies.

The third type of garden is organized by an institution, such as a school, workplace, or mass organization. Decisions concerning what is planted, work scheduling, and responsibilities are made as a group by the participants. The produce from the gardens is used to provide food for the institution's cafeteria or distributed to local day care centers, rehabilitation centers, hospitals, etc. In other cases, however, the participants are free to take the produce home to feed themselves and their families.

Knowledge about agriculture is not uncommon in the Cuban population, even among the urban dwellers, because the Cuban revolution has tried to keep people connected to agricultural work and the production of food. This goal stems from a fundamental philosophy of José Martí, Cuba's national hero, that everyone should know what is involved in the production of the goods that they consume. Thus, Cuban youth often attend junior high schools in the countryside, with agricultural work a daily part of their course work. In addition, many Cubans make an annual commitment to do two weeks voluntary agricultural work. Furthermore, knowledge regarding small-scale low-input gardening is presently being spread through a television show being aired twice a week. This method of mass extension via television is crucial during the Special Period, as paper shortages prevent mass printing of informational material.

Urban gardening has become very prevalent throughout Havana City, as well as in other areas of the country. Unfortunately, it is impossible to calculate the importance of urban gardens in terms of production. We were told that due to budget cutbacks no government office maintains such statistics.

Some members of our delegation felt that the urban gardening option was still underexploited. Though we saw many gardens, particularly in the famous new "greenbelt" around Havana, there still are many patches of urban land that are not being used. Why? Some

Cubans say it's not worth it because produce is stolen from the gardens. Others make what seem like excuses: the soil is not good, we don't have enough space, we have no tools or seeds, not enough time, etc. It may be that the government has not done sufficient promotion, or it may be that there is a mental block that many urbanites have; for decades, the revolution has told them it would take care of the food supply for them and growing your own food or getting your hands dirty was for people in "underdeveloped" countries, not for Cubans. A more widespread educational campaign to promote the "joy of gardening" would seem to be in order.

Nevertheless, through the development of new rural communities and the re-creation of the relationship between a farmworker and the land, the Alternative Model is geared toward the revitalization of rural life. At the same time the urban garden program, to the extent that it is working, is promoting the "greening" of the cities.

◆ 6 ◆

Generating and using knowledge

New systems of farm production and readjustments of rural-urban living patterns are at the heart of Cuba's short-term quest of a new model for food production. Of equal importance, however, especially for the long-term, is Cuba's recognition that a substantially revised knowledge base is needed if adequate yields are to be achieved in low-input agriculture. An impressive finding of our delegation's visit was the sense that the country has thoroughly embraced the challenge of creating a comprehensive and scientifically sophisticated knowledge base to support the new model. Indeed, the impression we received is that Cuba is now one of the most important places in the world for scientific research on LISA. In this section, we will sketch the first glimpses of Cuba's new knowledge-making process in terms of its origins, directions, and likelihood for success.

Since 1989, Cuba has fully accepted the policy to promote a new science of agriculture. From 1989-1992, they moved substantially to implement this policy at the levels of the research station, the extension services, and the farm producers. For a large country, such a rate of change in scientific research patterns would be unimaginable. Even in a small country, it is an achievement worth noting by students of politics and public administration. Furthermore, it is essential to remember that seeking a new science of agriculture marked the second major shift since the revolution in 1959. As noted earlier, Cuba's rapid march into research has been matched only by a few other historical examples.

Cuba possessed only a small capacity for agricultural science before 1959, and it was oriented to the production of export crops dominated by foreign interests. Research stations (and their dates of founding) were in citrus (1915), sugar (1924), tobacco (1937), silk culture (1938), and coffee (1939). In addition Cuba had the Experimental Agronomy Station of Santiago de las Vegas, founded in 1904 as the first agricultural station in all of Latin America. With the exceptions of some of the research at the Agronomy Station and of the citrus research station, however, virtually all other agricultural research efforts were on non-food crops. Before the revolution of 1959, therefore, Cuba had limited facilities for research and little of it was aimed at helping to improve the farming and diets of most of the Cuban people.

After 1959, Cuba rapidly evolved a sophisticated network of crop and animal research institutes controlled by the Ministry of Agriculture, several research stations run by the Ministry of Higher Education, and the research facilities of the Ministry of Sugar Production. Not only did these stations encompass a wider variety of research problems, they were all linked to the political and social priorities of improving the Cuban diet and the health of the Cuban people. Very quickly Cuba's research enterprise moved Cuba into a high-input, high-yield producer of its traditional crops, especially sugar, which it sold in order to import its staples of wheat, rice, and beans as well as much of its animal feeds.

Now that the ability to trade sugar for staples is vastly diminished, Cuba is again transforming its agricultural science, but this time the political priorities are aimed at enabling Cuba to maintain its production levels of export crops with vastly lowered inputs, most of which will be made in Cuba, rather than imported.

What is remarkably new and interesting about Cuba's new research directions are their heavy emphases on understanding and exploiting the subtle yet powerful abilities of biological organisms to perform many of the tasks previously done by synthetic chemicals, which typically have little subtlety of biological knowledge incorporated in their design. Biologically-based or -derived fertilizers and biological control of pests, as described earlier, are at the heart of this new quest for biologically sophisticated manipulations of agroecosystems.

Two points of paramount interest stand out from our under-standing of the new Cuban research directions. First, as we outlined in Chapter 1, the movement toward the new research programs predated the start of the Special Period in 1989. Numerous researchers told us that they had raised their voices about the needs for lower-input agriculture in the mid-1980s. They reported that administrative and political leadership within the government was decidedly not interested at the time and that they felt their analyses and proposals fell on deaf ears. Similar to many complaints heard from scientists in other countries, Cuban scientists interested in low-input strategies felt marginalized and ignored.

A shift in their fortunes came after 1989 when Cuba's prior arrangements for high-input export-oriented agriculture collapsed. Suddenly these scientists found themselves at the top of political and administrative agendas. Their day in the sun had arrived, and they have subsequently moved to top priority for funding. The future prosperity and even security of Cuba is seen by all to be riding on the shoulders of the low-input agricultural scientists.

Second, the motivations of the low-input scientists, prior to 1989, were based on some of the same philosophical views about the environment that motivated scientists elsewhere. Heavy uses of mineral fertilizers and synthetic pesticides were seen as destroying nature and ruining the future prospects of the coming generations. These Cuban scientists felt it was not right to continue along the agricultural development lines they had mastered so well.

Our impressions, therefore, were that research programs in low-input agriculture resulted from a series of changes in global politics and a growing sense of ineffectiveness and immorality in existing research directions. As a result, administrative and political leaders have, for pragmatic reasons of protecting the national economy, embraced a group of scientists originally motivated by concerns over the fate of nature. Both parties have embraced their newly found common interests with gusto and enthusiasm.

While the enthusiasm for research to support the new model was unmistakable and of vast importance for the success of the research, we also recognized that the Cubans are still essentially working with the old organizational structure of agricultural research. Most institutes are heavily oriented to single commodities (e.g., tobacco, sugar, rice, pork). Sugar is the main agricultural crop, yet it is located in a different ministry from the rest of agriculture. Thus it appeared to us that bureaucratic divisions existed between research programs that dealt with biological phenomena that will not be confined to the organizational charts of ministers.

We raised questions about coordination and cooperation across bureaucratic lines at several times during our visit. Always we were assured that organizational problems had been surmounted and all appropriate research workers were collaborating. We have no reason to doubt the enthusiasm we saw will go far to promote these collaborative discussions. Nevertheless, we felt that the potential divisions remained.

Along similar lines of reasoning, we noted that one particular crop, beans, does not have a high priority identification within the Ministry of Agriculture's research institutes. Instead, research on beans is buried within INIVIT, which has a broad mandate in the starchy roots (cassava, sweet potatoes, and taro), starchy fruits (plantains and bananas) and vegetables of various sorts. Given the importance of beans as a source of high quality protein, we were concerned that the dietary importance of beans was not matched by a corresponding prominence in the research bureaucracies.

Similarly, we found a comparable invisibility of research on maize, a potential food crop that is not a part of the contemporary Cuban diet. Nevertheless, Cubans did consume corn historically. Furthermore, Cuba imports large quantities of corn for animal feed. Given the suitability of Cuba's climates and soils for maize and beans, and the potential benefits of them, we found the invisibility of these two plants within the research institutes to be puzzling. Perhaps it would be useful for the Cubans to revisit the potential worthiness of these two plants and to reconsider how they have organized their research on them.

Local knowledge and popular participation

A pivotal component of the Cuban research shift toward sustainable agriculture is an exploration of the knowledge base of Cuba's farmers. The Ministry of Agriculture has responded by placing an explicit emphasis on increasing the degree of local participation in decision-making and toward developing agricultural systems adapted to the local agroecological conditions.

At the community level, the Ministry has encouraged the recovery of former land use practices such as animal traction, intercropping, biological pest control techniques, crop rotations, agro-pastoral and agro-forestry systems. Farmers are also being asked to participate in the selection and dissemination of cultivated plants. At the time of the delegation's visit, the replacement of tractors by animal traction for land preparation in the food crops sector was well underway, as mentioned earlier. This rescue of one traditional technology is being promoted as a prototype for other forms of local knowledge that can facilitate the shift to a low-input sustainable system of agricultural production.

The policy objectives of the Special Period to achieve a low-input sustainable agriculture without a reduction in yields have required a major reorganization in the structure and flow of agricultural research and extension in Cuba. The de-emphasis of capital- and energy-intensive technologies requires new relationships between scientists, extension agents, and farmers. The pre-existing role of scientists as generators of innovative technological packages and extension agents as conduits of their delivery to farmers is clearly changing in favor of a partnership between the three in the development and dissemination of new approaches.

Towards this objective, the Ministry of Agriculture currently sponsors farmer-to-farmer and farmer-to-extensionist/scientist workshops in the provinces. Farmers from different regions facing similar problems are brought together for information exchange. The objective of this innovative form of exchange is to: (1) make locally adapted/developed technologies known to a broader audience; (2) facilitate farmer knowledge of techniques and practices successfully used in other regions with similar crop complexes; and (3) promote scientific research and development of promising low-input innovations.

Cuban scientists have become increasingly dependent on farmer innovation and experimentation for research directions that complement their efforts to develop promising organic farming practices, as well as adapt techniques developed outside the country. The new approaches are being implemented and can be grouped into two categories: (1) technologies recovered or developed at the local level that have widespread applicability, which extension agents and scientists disseminate over a broader region; and (2) low-input technologies utilized in other countries, which are promoted for local experimentation and adaptation.

One example where local knowledge from farmers proved the catalyst for technology generation is represented in the biological control program of the sweet potato weevil as described in Chapter 3. Some Cuban farmers began experimenting with collecting colonies of ants in banana orchards and transferring them to sweet potatoes. Cuban researchers investigated and refined the locally developed technique, which was subsequently disseminated by the Ministry of Agriculture to other regions.

The case of the decentralized biological control program also illustrates the importance of farmer-scientist collaboration in the transfer and adaptation of organic farming techniques to meet national needs. The Ministry of Agriculture has committed substantial capital investments to localized biological control efforts for insect pests and plant pathogens which involve the construction and operation of the CREES (the local Centers for the Production of Entomophagous and

Entomopathogens described in Chapter 3). Though much of the research on the ecology, production methods, and field use of the insects, fungi, and bacteria produced in these centers has been performed by scientists, the success of these programs depends on local participation for production, field monitoring, and application methods, as well as for refining the technologies to fit the local agroecological conditions. In this vein, we were struck by the remarkable fact that the CREE we visited was completely run by the grown children of local farmers.

The renewed emphasis on germplasm banks during the Special Period illustrates yet another area in which local knowledge and community participation is being incorporated into Cuba's sustainable research program. While founded over 10 years ago, germplasm reservoirs for national research are receiving greater emphasis today. The *Instituto Nacional de Investigaciones Fundamentales de la Agricultura Tropical* (INIFAT) is sponsoring a national program for the popular collection of crop varieties. Farmers are encouraged by INIFAT to collect currently utilized and promising varieties of food crops for evaluation and germplasm conservation. The conservation of genetic material is considered urgent by INIFAT researchers because genetic erosion has been accelerated by the adoption of green revolution technologies over the past decades.

Moreover, emphasis on labor-displacing mechanized agriculture resulted in the steady out-migration to cities of farmers with knowledge of local varieties. As these dramatic changes have occurred in less than one generation, considerable hope is being placed on the prospect for rescuing funds of local knowledge that might otherwise have vanished.

Despite the progress that has been made, and the apparently good intentions, one still has to say in terms of rescuing the knowledge of local farmers and promoting more participatory research, that Cuba lags behind the non-governmental organization (NGO) movement in other developing countries (see for example Chambers *et al.*, 1990; and Altieri and Hecht, 1990). Yet if one considers that in these other countries NGOs must fill the vacuum left by disinterested governments, then the active role of the Ministry of Agriculture in promoting change in Cuba is all the more impressive.

◆ 7 ◆

Conclusion

It is not easy for Cuba to overcome the ideology of developmentalism it inherited from both the West and from the socialist bloc (Levins, 1991). Developmentalism as ideology meant that everything more "modern" was better — that imported pesticides and mechanized monocultures were better than intercropping, animal traction and natural pest control. It also meant that bigger was better — large state farms and large cooperatives were better than individual farms or smaller cooperatives.

As has been the case for untold numbers of Third World countries, adopting this Classical Model of agricultural development has meant the hemorrhaging of scarce foreign exchange for the import of manufactured inputs, and a poor level of food security as a product of severe dependency upon international markets and vulnerability to their fluctuations. This model has also put the agricultural sectors of developing nations onto the same treadmill that the United States is on, one of ever-increasing costs and the declining sustainability of production. Soil is eroded, compacted and otherwise degraded, insects and diseases become resistant to pesticides, groundwater is contaminated, and farmers become ever more indebted.

Planning vs. management: failure of the Classical Model

The Alternative Model now under consideration in Cuba *does* represent a break with developmentalist thinking. To the extent that it is implemented in most or all of its aspects, it will also represent a clear break with developmentalist practice. The new model is clearly not without its opponents within the Cuban hierarchy, so to a certain extent the manner in which internal politics play themselves out over the next few years will determine what happens in this regard.

It is perhaps ironic that socialist bloc believers in central planning and their opposites in western agribusiness should have agreed on the Classical Model of agricultural production. Yet it seems to us that the failure of the old model is not a failure of planning *per se*, but rather a confusion of units — planning units versus management units (see Levins, 1991). If the unit of planning were not large, Cuba today might well be facing the sort of mass famine taking place in Somalia. Without the Cuban government's ability to implement a long-term plan to build human capital and scientific capability, it would not be possible to consider an alternative model today. Without the high degree of organization exhibited by Cuban society, scarce resources could not have been mobilized to counteract the sudden drop in food imports.

Few countries in the world could face the external shocks that have buffeted Cuba since 1989 without mass starvation. In this light it is perhaps remarkable that caloric intake has not dropped *more* than 30 percent, that we saw no children with distended bellies, and that other health indicators remain good.[25] This we believe, is a tribute to Cuba's planning and organization. And without a planned economy, it is unlikely that new agroecological research results could be implemented so rapidly.

Therefore, we believe that the failure of the Classical Model in Cuba to provide food and foreign exchange while preserving its productive capacity was not a product of large-scale planning. Rather we see it as the failure of a system built on overly large *management* units — the large-scale monocultures of export crops — as distinct from *planning* units. Such farming enterprises encourage the psychological and physical separation of administrators, farmers and farmworkers from the land, making detailed management of local knowledge of agronomic conditions impossible. The only way to administer a huge farm — either corporate owned in California, or a state farm in Cuba — is to prescribe treatments that can be applied to the entire area, such as pesticides and fertilizers. Careful husbandry of soil fertility and structure, which require different practices tailored to different parts of each field, are out of the question.

The Alternative Model addresses this issue. Many state farms have been broken into smaller management units, diversity between and

---

[25] In a noticeable change from pre-1990, we did encounter several children begging in Havana, though more often than not they requested pens and chiclets rather than food or money. We also observed an alarming increase in prostitution around tourist hotels.

within fields is being reintroduced, and production teams now work the same plot of land from planting through harvest. Much of this is experimental, however, and we feel that far more change is needed in this direction. The experiences of organic farmers in the United States have shown that this type of production requires that the farmer or manager be in far more intimate contact with the land than is necessary for conventional production. One must know each patch of soil — where organic matter is abundant, where soil structure is poor, which side of the field insects invade from, and where the ant nests are.

Thus we urge our Cuban colleagues to continue this process of decentralizing production by breaking up large production units into more manageable pieces.[26] But at the same time they should not abandon central planning, which is necessary in order to make efficient use of scarce resources. Research strategies must be worked out, the relationship between new sites of food production and transportation and storage facilities must be charted. Seasonal successions of crops with different rainfall requirements must be planned in advance. In sum, what should be made smaller is the unit of management and production, but strategic planning is a necessity to prevent chaos in a time of scarcity.

"Satellite without a planet"

It took the crisis of the Special Period to force needed changes on Cuban agriculture. While no one would wish such conditions on their own country, it left many of us wondering whether we did not need a Special Period ourselves, to force us to implement practices with greater long-term sustainability.[27] The economic crisis wrought by the collapse of trading relations with the socialist bloc does indeed represent two steps back for the Cuban people in that it has caused much suffering and scarcity. We can only hope that the rise of the Alternative Model for agriculture will truly come to represent a big step forward.

Cuban officials repeatedly told us, "The United States claimed we were a satellite of the Soviets, yet our planet has disappeared and we're still here!" While it would be unprecedented for a Latin American country to find a truly independent path to development, it will not be easy for Cuba to survive the present situation with its society intact.

---

[26] In this context we applaud the increased attention being paid to independent small farmers.

[27] Though we wonder if other countries would show the same political will and organization necessary to make such changes in the face of opposition from business interests.

Since we visited in November 1992, two severe storms have devastated Cuban agriculture. In March 1993 the same "storm of the century" that wreaked havoc along the eastern coast of the United States destroyed as much as half of the food crops that we saw planted, just before they were to be harvested. Another storm then hit while sugarcane was being trucked from the fields to the mills, causing such severe losses that Cuba had to default on major delivery commitments for the first time ever.

Under such conditions we join with Cuban intellectual Juan Antonio Blanco in calling for an end to the U.S. trade embargo on purely humanitarian grounds.[28] Yet like him, we wonder what would become of the Alternative Model if it were to be confronted with a flood of U.S. imports — the words of Fidel Castro that the "ox is here to stay in Cuba" notwithstanding.

The Cuban experiment

In the rest of the world an alternative model of agriculture exists in theory, but in practice it remains a dream. If the Cuban people have been shown to be anything during the past three decades it is audacious. Today, in the midst of the most severe crisis in their history, they are making a bold attempt to change the rules of the game. Though it is impossible to say if they will ultimately be successful, what they have already achieved under conditions of extreme adversity is impressive. We are left with images of the daughters and sons of peasant farmers producing cutting edge biotechnology, literally on the farm, and supplying their parents and neighbors with organic substitutes for toxic pesticides and chemical fertilizers. We remember the enthusiasm of young agricultural scientists and their determination, to quote Fidel Castro, to "achieve miracles with intelligence and sweat." And we can only hope that they do achieve miracles — not just for their hungry population, but for all of us whose countries also face a crisis in agriculture.

The Cuban experiment is the largest attempt at conversion from conventional agriculture to organic or semi-organic farming in human history. We must watch alertly for the lessons we can learn from Cuban successes as well as from Cuban errors. And it behooves us to support this experiment which is so potentially important for all of us.

---

[28] U.S. law prohibits the sale of food and medicines to Cuba, and requires that medical donations first receive a licence from the U.S. Treasury Department.

Literature cited

Altieri, Miguel A. 1987. *Agroecology: The Scientific Basis of Alternative Agriculture*. Boulder: Westview Press.

Altieri, Miguel A., and Susanna B. Hecht. 1990. *Agroecology and Small Farm Development*. Boca Raton: CRC Press.

Benjamin, Medea, Joseph Collins and Michael Scott. 1987. *No Free Lunch: Food & Revolution in Cuba Today*. San Francisco: Institute for Food & Development Policy.

Carney, Judith. From Hands to Tutors: African Expertise in the South Carolina Rice Economy. *Agricultural History* (forthcoming)

Carroll, C. Ronald, John H. Vandermeer and Peter M. Rosset. 1990. *Agroecology*. New York: McGraw-Hill.

Castiñeiras, A., Susana Caballero, G. Rego and Mirtha González. 1982. Efectividad técnico-económica del empleo de la hormiga leona *Pheidole megacephala* en el control del tetuán del boniato *Cylas formicarius elegantulus*. Cienc. Tec. Agric. (Cuba), suplemento, 103-109.

Chambers, Robert, Arnold Pacey and Lori Ann Thrupp. 1990. *Farmer First: Farmer Innovation and Agricultural Research*. London: Intermediate Technology Publications.

Deere, Carmen Diana. 1992. *Socialism on one island? Cuba's National Food Program and its prospects for food security*. Institute of Social Studies, The Hague, Working Paper Series No. 124.

Deere, Carmen Diana, and Mieke Meurs. 1992. Markets, markets everywhere? Understanding the Cuban anomaly. *World Development*, 20(6):825-839.

Deere, Carmen Diana, Mieke Meurs and Niurka Pérez. 1992. Toward a periodization of the Cuban collectivization process: Changing incentives and peasant response. *Cuban Studies*, 22:115-149.

Levins, Richard. 1991. *The Struggle for Ecological Agriculture in Cuba.* Boston: Red Balloon Collective Environmental Action Series Pamphlet No. 1.

National Research Council. 1989. *Alternative Agriculture.* Washington: National Academy Press.

Pastor, Manual, Jr. 1992. *External shocks and adjustment in contemporary Cuba.* The International & Public Affairs Center, Occidental College, Working Paper.

Pérez Marin, Enrique, and Eduardo Muñoz Baños. 1991. *Agricultura y Alimentación en Cuba.* Havana: Editorial de Ciencias Sociales.

Preeg, Ernest H. 1993. *Cuba and the New Caribbean Order.* Washington: Center for Strategic and International Studies.

Rego, G., D. Collazo and Amelia Borges. 1986. Eficacia técnico-económica de *Lixophaga diatraeae* basada en el índice poblacional de *Diatraea saccharilis.* Rev. Protección Vegetal (Cuba) 1:255-260.

Sauer, Carl O. 1966. *The Early Spanish Main.* Berkeley: UC Berkeley Press.

Soule, Judith D., and Jon. K. Piper. 1992. *Farming in Nature's Image: An Ecological Approach to Agriculture.* Washington: Island Press.

U.S. Department of Agriculture. 1980. *Report and Recommendations on Organic Farming.* Washington, DC.

International Scientific Delegation and Fact-Finding Mission on Low-Input Sustainable Agriculture in Cuba, November 1992

Peter Rosset, Delegation leader
Entomologist and Agricultural
Ecologist, Stanford Universty*

Nanda Berman
Environmentalist, Ecology Action

Larry Burkam
Horticulturalist, Bio-Integral
Resource Center

Judith Carney
Geographer, University of
California at Los Angeles

Orville Coil
Farmer, Fairborn, Ohio

Carl Davidson
Farmer, Sidney, Ohio

Jeffrey Dlott
Entomologist, University of
California at Berkeley

Paul Gersper
Soil Scientist, University of
California at Berkeley

Jeanne Haught
Geographer, University of
California at Los Angeles

Juan Martínez
Agricultural Economist, Mexico

John McConkey
Journalist, Ithaca, New York

Julio Monterrey
Entomologist, Managua, Nicaragua

César Morales
Agronomist, Oaxaca, Mexico

Catherine Murphy
Student activist, San Francisco

Ivette Perfecto
Agricultural Ecologist and
Entomologist, U of Michigan

John Perkins
Historian of Science, Evergreen
State College

Carmen Rodríguez-Barbosa
Ecologist, University of Michigan

Jeff Schatz
Environmentalist and Businessman,
Los Angeles, California

Nina Shishkoff
Plant Pathologist, U.S. Department
of Agriculture

John Vandermeer
Ecologist, University of Michigan

** Institutions listed for identification
purposes only*

Cuba Travel Seminars

Global Exchange organizes monthly educational seminars to Cuba examining topics such as public health, sustainable agriculture, women's issues, and the political and economic situation. These trips, which are usually 10 days long, give participants a rich understanding of both the negative and positive features of Cuba's revolution.

All trips spend some time in Havana and some time in other parts of the island. Another distinctive feature of our trips is personalized attention: in addition to daytime group activities, we try to accommodate individual requests in evening sessions that are mainly held in Cuban homes. Most trips are $1200: price includes roundtrip airfare from Miami, double accommodations, visas, all transportation in Cuba, breakfast and dinner each day, translation of all programs and reading materials.

If you are interesting in joining one of these tours, call us at (415)255-7296.

Sample themes include:

Agriculture & Sustainable Development

Cuba's Bicycle Revolution

Women's Delegation

The Cuban Economy at a Crossroads

Public Health in Cuba

Afro-Cuban Culture

Cuba in a Changing World

In addition to the monthly thematic tours listed above, Global Exchange can also organize tours to Cuba designed specifically for your organization.

Global Exchange, 2017 Mission St., Rm. 303, San Francisco, CA 94110
(415) 255-7296, FAX(415)255-7498, E-mail: globalexch@igc.org

Also published by Ocean Press

TOMORROW IS TOO LATE
Development and the environmental crisis in the Third World
by Fidel Castro
Comprising Castro's controversial and widely-discussed speech
and Cuba's main submission to the World Earth Summit in Río
in 1992, this book casts the international environmental crisis in a
new, important perspective.

AFROCUBA
An anthology of Cuban writing on race, politics and culture
by Pedro Pérez Sarduy and Jean Stubbs
What is it like to be Black in Cuba? Does racism still exist in a
revolutionary society which claims to have abolished it? How
does the legacy of slavery and segregation live on in today's
Cuba?

CUBA: TALKING ABOUT REVOLUTION
Conversations with Juan Antonio Blanco by Medea Benjamin
A frank discussion on the current situation in Cuba, this book
presents an all-too-rare opportunity to hear the voice of one of
the island's leading intellectuals.

FACE TO FACE WITH FIDEL CASTRO
A conversation with Tomás Borge
One of the most important books to emerge from Latin America
in the 1990s, this is a lively dialogue between two of the region's
most controversial political figures.

ZR RIFLE
The plot to kill Kennedy and Castro
by Claudia Furiati
Thirty years after the death of President Kennedy, Cuba has
opened its secret files on the assassination. These Cuban files
show how and why the CIA, through those responsible for its
anti-Cuba operations, along with the anti-Castro exiles and the
Mafia, planned and orchestrated the Kennedy assassination.

For a list of Ocean Press distributors, see the copyright page

THE LAST WILDERNESS

By Murray Morgan

THE LAST
WILDERNESS

University of Washington Press

Seattle and London

52201

The last chapter appeared in part in *The Saturday
Evening Post* under the title "Loneliest Spot in America."

Library of Congress Cataloging in Publication Data

Morgan, Murray Cromwell, 1916–
    The last wilderness.

    (Washington paperbacks; 81)
    Reprint of the ed. published by Viking Press, New York.
    1. Olympic Peninsula. 2. Morgan, Murray Cromwell,
1916–   I. Title.
[F897.05M67   1976]   979.7'94   76–41
ISBN 0-295-95319-5

This book is for

OTTO AND PHYLLIS GOLDSCHMID

Contents

Foreword

My first memories of childhood are of vacations spent on the Olympic Peninsula. I remember standing knee-deep in the icy water of the Lilliwaup. The salmon were running, and the great fish bumped my legs as they charged at the falls. There were Indians, real Indians, with dip nets and spears, and an Indian woman, brown as a teddy bear, speared a salmon and handed it to me, and I wrestled it ashore.

I remember too a beach resort on a lagoon somewhere along the canal. They were logging the east shore in those days, and there was a show on the bank across from the resort. The logs were dragged to a flume, which shot them over the cliff and into the canal. We would sit for hours watching the great brown logs appear on the flume, leap into space, and disappear in a white splash that had rainbows in it if the sun was right; then bob up, whale-big, as the thundering crash rolled across the water.

You couldn't have planned it better for kids.

So this is a love story. I have been in love with the Olympics for as long as I can remember.

I can't list all the people who have helped me with this book. There are some whose names I don't remember, people who told stories as we sat on docks down at Grays Harbor, or walked along trails by the Quinault, or paddled canoes down the Hoquiam.

But there are many others I have no trouble remembering. There is Stewart Holbrook, whose books so delight me, and who has written so much and so well about the peninsula. I must say thanks to him for permission to quote from his writings. And thanks too to Betty MacDonald, Angelo Pellegrini, James Stevens, Archie Binns, and the late Brandon Satterlee for permission to quote from their works.

I leaned on many library staffs in gathering material, and all proved most helpful: Tacoma Public Library, Seattle Public Library, University of Washington Library, Port Angeles Public Library, Hoquiam Public Library, Aberdeen Public Library, Washington State Historical Society Library, Washington State Library, British Columbia Legislative Library, and Vancouver Library.

I also used the files of the Grays Harbor *Washingtonian,* Aberdeen *World,* and the Seattle *Post-Intelligencer.* While I am mentioning newspapers, I must thank the Seattle *Times* for the excellence of its historical research, particularly that done by Lucile McDonald, whose reporting of regional history seems to me the best I have read in any newspaper.

Others who helped me gather material for this book include Dave James of Simpson Logging Company; Conrad Speidel of Weyerhaeuser Timber Company; Mrs. Lena Huelsdonk Fletcher; Mr. Fred J. Overly, superintendent, Olympic National Park; Charles and Minnie Peterson; Dr. Erna Gunther; Jim and Ann Faber; George P. Murphy of the United States Weather Bureau; Mrs. Mary Healey of the Seattle Chamber of Commerce; Lisa Wagner, Grays Harbor County Clerk; and Commander Ross Gilmore of the United States Coast and Geodetic Survey.

I must mention Mrs. Ross Gilmore; Mrs. Norm Barto, wife of the lighthouse-keeper on Tatoosh Island; and the camp cooks at Camp Grisdale, the South Olympic Tree Farm, and the LaPush Lifesaving Station, each of whom memorably kept me from starving at some stage in the preparation of this manuscript.

Malcolm Cowley and Helen Taylor offered encouragement and good advice. My wife, Rosa, battled valiantly against some extravagances I had thought to include.

None of these people are responsible for errors of fact or interpretation that may have crept into the work. I am to blame for the fact that throughout the term "rain forest" is used in the loosest possible sense—a forest where there is lots of rain—rather than in the precise sense of applying to an area in which the annual rainfall exceeds a hundred inches and there are climax conditions of forest growth.

I have included in this book two towns which, purists may argue, do not belong to the peninsula proper. They are Port Gamble, which is on the Kitsap Peninsula, an outgrowth of the Olympic Peninsula; and Home, on an outgrowth of the Kitsap Peninsula. I included Port Gamble because it is the economic big brother of Port Ludlow, a true peninsula town. I included Home because it fits in with the Olympic Peninsula more than with the rest of Puget Sound, and besides, it was simply too charming to leave out.

Murray Morgan

THE LAST WILDERNESS

1

In the Time
Before Everything Changed

i

"God made the universe," the saying went, "and when He finished He dumped everything left over onto the Olympic Peninsula."

Thus the pioneers explained the fist of land thrust north between Puget Sound and the Pacific Ocean, a wilderness area of six thousand square miles, as large as the state of Massachusetts, more rugged than the Rockies, its lowlands blanketed by a cool jungle of fir and pine and cedar, its peaks bearing hundreds of miles of living ice that gave rise to swift rivers alive with giant salmon; the first land in the Pacific Northwest to be reported by explorers, the last to be mapped —the last wilderness.

The Indians too were inclined to blame their gods for the excessive ruggedness of the peninsula. In the Time before Everything Changed, they said, this land by the ocean had been a low and rolling plain, deep with grass and rich with starchy camas bulbs—open land, where elk grazed placidly, an easy place to live. But even in the Time before Everything

3

Changed there were feuds among the People. Wolf and his folk were always trying to capture Wren, who lived in a cabin of grass mats down by the surfless sea. One day the Wolf folk surrounded Wren while he was gathering seeds; they were going to kill him, but Wren slipped by Wolf and fled along the beach. As he dropped the seeds he had gathered they sprouted into pinnacle rocks, which still stand like sentinels along the western shore from Tahola to Tatoosh. When he ran east, across the plain, he kicked the dirt into great heaps —the Olympics. Wren escaped. And to this day a wolf cannot catch a wren.

The professional storytellers who took over Paul Bunyan from the loggers naturally credit Paul with the creation of the mountains that grow America's greatest forest. They say that when Paul had finished logging and clearing North Dakota so the Swedes could go there ("Because," Paul explained, "everyone knows a Swede belongs in North Dakota"), his pet and helper, Babe, the Blue Ox, came down with the croup. Johnny Inkslinger, the first bureaucrat in American mythology, suggested that a million gallons of milk from the Western Whale might be good for what ailed the colossal critter. So Paul carried Babe to the Northwest and laid him gently on the plain that stretched from the Rockies to the sea. The rolling hills of the Palouse country are the imprint made by Babe's ribs; in his thirst he licked the Grand Coulee dry. Paul dug Coos Bay, down Oregon way, as a whale trap, but before a whale swam into the pen Babe grew so weak that the great logger despaired of saving him. So Paul dug a grave for Babe, a hundred miles long. As he worked he threw the dirt to his right, the rock to his left, the dirt making the smooth line of the Cascades and the rocks the rugged heap of the Olympics. Before Paul had scooped out the last of the rocks he heard a whale splashing in his trap. He stepped down Coos Bay way, milked the whale, and poured the green milk into the Blue Ox, who recovered. So Paul scooped out the Strait of Juan de Fuca and let the Pacific rush into the unneeded grave, thus forming Puget Sound and leaving the rock pile of the Olympics bordered west and north and east by deep salt water.

The geologists who undertake to explain the Olympic Peninsula admit that much of its past remains a mystery; but, with the Indians and the folklorists, they say that once upon a time this land was flat, a smooth plain lying under a shallow sea. From age to age molten rock bubbled up from below, only to be buried under the mud and sand drifting down from above. About 120 million years ago the bed of the ocean buckled, and the folded rocks were forced above the surface of the sea. Across the next hundred million years the mountains rose and fell to the pulse-beat of geology: three times they came up from the depths, and twice they subsided. They emerged for the last time twenty million years ago, bare and black, wet, shining, jumbled, a mass undominated by any single peak.

The forces that raised the Olympics are still at work. Most geologists believe that the mountains are even now being pushed higher. But other forces work to wear down the peaks —wind and rain and ice.

The rain falls steadily and heavily over the peninsula, slanting down in wind-snapped sheets during the winter storms, drizzling through the spring nights, settling in heavy dew on summer mornings. The western slope of the Olympics is the wettest place in the United States. Over a thirteen-year period the weather observer at Oxbow on the Wynooche River measured an average of 150.73 inches of precipitation annually, the national record. (Weather men estimate there may be spots in the mountains which get as much as 250 inches a year.) On January 21, 1935, the ranger stationed at

Quinault reported a twenty-four-hour rainfall of exactly one foot; the same day an observer at Spruce measured 11.59 inches.

This overwhelming moisture is carried in by the prevailing west winds. The air moving across the unbroken reaches of the Pacific is warm and watersoaked when it rises over the six-thousand-foot slopes of the mountains. Rising, it cools, and, cooling, it loses its capacity to hold moisture: the rain is squeezed out. Once across the summit, the air is warmed as it slides down the eastern slope; its capacity for holding water increases, and weather stations on the leeward side of the mountains report annual precipitation of less than twenty inches—one-sixth of the average figure at the windward stations. Sequim, which lies only sixty miles northeast of sodden Oxbow, averages only slightly more than sixteen inches a year; the farmlands there are irrigated, and the town, proud of its dryness, has put up a sunbleached sign with the slogan: SEQUIM—WHERE WATER IS WEALTH.

The water that falls on the western slopes means wealth too—the wealth of the rain forest. The Indians believed the forest was made from the bodies of those who lived on the land in the Time before Everything Changed. Once, they said, there was no wood in the land, nothing but grass and sand, so Those Who Changed Things decided the Indians would need fuel. They went about changing people. To one they said, "You are old and your heart is dry; you will make good kindling wood, for your grease has turned hard and will make pitch. Your name is Do-ho-dupt, and you shall be the spruce tree, which, when it grows old, will make dry wood always." To another: "Your name is Kla-ka-bupt, and you shall be the hemlock, with your sour smell." Those Who Changed Things knew the people would want some harder wood— so: "Kwahk-sa-bupt, you of the strong muscles and firm flesh, you shall be the alder. You, Kla-haik-tle-bupt, are tough and strong, and you shall be the yew tree, and the people will use you to make wedges for splitting logs. And the people will need soft wood for canoes, so you, Lla-ae-sook, the young-old man, shall be the cedar." To Dopt-ko-bupt they said, "You shall be the crab-apple, and since you have a bad temper you shall bear sour fruit." And the trees grew and endured.

The forest that covers the Olympic Peninsula is the thickest part of the evergreen jungle that extends from Northern California to the Alaska Peninsula. The trees push up two hundred feet and more above the spongy mat of the forest floor —push up so high that the murmur of the wind in the branches is indistinct, and the rays of the midday sun filter down like light into deep water. The women of the pioneers complained most of the silence of the rain forest. "It is seven months," says an early journal, "since I recall a songbird."

Most of the pioneers soon gave up and left the coastal forest to the Indians. To this day the shoreline between Grays Harbor on the Pacific and Port Angeles on the Strait is Indian country: the Quinaults, the Quillayutes, the Makahs, and the Clallams outnumber the whites in the rain forest.

Yet these Indians are not people of the forest, nor were they in the old days. They lived with their backs to the woods, their faces to the sea. They looked for their living to the sea and the beach and the steep-slanting, dangerous salmon-choked rivers. They seldom ventured into the deep jungle, almost never climbed through the tangled undergrowth to the flowered highlands above the trees, where the tawny-rumped elk sported in summer. In the legends of the coastal tribes the man who went into the forest was not called "Brave Hunter" or "Elk Stalker" or anything like that; he was called simply "the Fool."

Yet it was the sea, the supporting sea, that brought an end to the Indians' way of life, for they lived where the Northwest Passage was believed to debouch into the Pacific.

For two hundred years, beginning in the middle sixteenth century, the Northwest coast was one goal of adventurous captains who sought the legendary Strait of Anian, the non-existent shortcut to the Orient. In 1543 two Portuguese-born explorers, Juan Cabrillo and Bartolomé Ferrelo, sailing under the flag of Spain, came up the coast at least as far as the Umpqua River. A generation later Francis Drake appeared in the same waters in the *Golden Hind.* Neither the Portuguese nor the Englishman claimed to have found the Strait of Anian, but a few years later a Greek who called himself Juan de Fuca, and who appears to have been a most plausible liar, told of locating the long-sought passage.

While idling in Venice shortly after the turn of the seventeenth century, de Fuca met an English geographer and whiled away some hours spinning tall tales of exploration on the high and suitably distant seas. De Fuca claimed that in 1592, sailing out of Lower California for the Viceroy of Mexico, he had taken a ship up the West Coast until he came to a great channel leading east—undoubtedly the Strait of Anian. The geographer spread the tale, and for the next two centuries seamen of many countries searched for the passage.

There were others who were de Fuca's peers as prevaricators. Captain Lorenzo Ferrer de Maldonado claimed not only to have discovered the Strait of Anian but to have sailed through it in 1588, east to west, emerging, he said, under the shadow of a western mountain so abrupt that from the summit a man could push boulders onto the decks of ships in the channel. Another deep-sea liar, one of higher rank, Admiral Pedro Bartolomé de Fone, turned the strait into a river and populated it with cultured savages who lived in a great city on a lake in the interior plain; the admiral said he had been there in 1640, and he called his stream *Rio de los Reyes* —River of the Kings.

While the Spaniards were pushing up the coast from Mexico in pursuit of these fantasies, the Russians were working down from the Aleutians in search of furs. Their interest started on a day in 1701 when Atlasov, a merchant of Irkutsk, knelt before Peter the Great to present him with 3500 furs, tribute from the fierce tribes of the Kamchatka peninsula, who had adopted Atlasov as prince. Among the 3500 were ten pelts of a type never seen before in the court of the czars, a fur to rival sable and ermine, soft fur of darkest brown, with tips of white and sheen of silver—immediately, at first glance, the most wanted fur in the world.

Russian hunters pursued the sea otter along the shores of Kamchatka, and, when the herds thinned, the pursuers ventured to sea in strange sewn-together boats, discovered the Kurile Islands, and stole the furs from the backs of the hairy Ainus.

In 1741 Vitus Bering, a Dane in the service of the czar, sailed east from Siberia on a voyage of discovery, reached Alaska, coasted briefly along its wooded shores, and turned back, only to be shipwrecked on a lonely island west of the Aleutians, where he died. Many of his officers and crew survived, living through the winter on the flesh of island animals and making clothes from the pelts. In the spring they fashioned a boat from the wreckage of their ship, sailed back to Kamchatka, and appeared at Avatcha Bay, a fur-trading center, clad in coats of sea-otter fur.

The Siberian hunters soon were sailing to Bering Island in their sewn-up longboats. They quickly killed off the herd that bore the silvery pelts, and sailed again east to the Aleutians to find more islands and more fur. Decimating otters and Aleuts as they went, they pressed on, down the chain of islands to the Alaskan mainland, down the mainland toward Mexico. The retreat of the sea otter before the hunter mapped the North Pacific.

The Spaniards, aware of the Russian fur empire building in the north, sent new expeditions up along the coast. In 1774 Juan Pérez sighted a glittering mountain rising from the dark mainland and named it Sierra de Santa Rosalia, a name that has given way to Mount Olympus. Storms drove Pérez back south, but the next year two Spanish vessels, a ship and a schooner, under Bruno Heceta, made a landfall at Destruction Island. They landed and claimed the land for His Majesty the King, Don Carlos III. The next day a party was sent ashore on the mainland to fill the schooner's water kegs; the Indians ambushed them, killing or capturing all six. Desperately short-handed, the expedition returned to San Blas.

Then came the ubiquitous English. On February 2, 1778, His Majesty's Ships *Resolution* and *Discovery*, under James Cook, Post-Captain of the Royal Navy, Fellow of the Royal Society, stood away to the northward from the Hawaiian islands in search of the Northwest Passage. "Without meeting with anything memorable, on the 7th of March the long-looked for coast of New Albion was seen, extending from N. E. to S. E., distant ten or twelve leagues."

In the words "New Albion" sounded the clash of empires, for New Albion was what Francis Drake had christened this coast he briefly saw, and on the strength of that visit England claimed the Northwest coast, despite Spaniards to the south and Russians to the north.

"The land," Cook noted in his journal, "appeared to be of

moderate height, diversified with hills and valleys, and almost everywhere covered with wood."

The ships worked northward. They saw no harbor, much less any great passage. But finally Cook noticed a configuration that seemed promising—a low cape, ragged with evergreens, and off the cape a steep, bare island. "Between this island or rock, and the northern extreme of the land, there appeared to be a small opening which flattered us with the hopes of finding an harbour," he wrote. "These hopes lessened as we drew nearer; and at last we had some reason to think the opening was closed by low land."

The risk of entering the possible passage was too great for sailing ships. Cook ordered his vessels away from the dangerous shore, and on his chart he named the point of land Cape Flattery.

So it was that on a gray spring day the *Discovery* and *Resolution* crossed the western entrance of the Juan de Fuca Strait without knowing it, and found anchorage in the shadow of the rain forest, at Nootka Harbor on Vancouver Island.

With Cook was an American, John Ledyard. Eight years earlier Ledyard, then nineteen, had slipped away from Dartmouth college in a canoe, seeking adventure. Subsequently he shipped out, joined the British Army at Gibraltar, left the Rock on a mule boat bound for the Barbary Coast, found passage home, studied briefly for the ministry, and sailed before the mast to England. There, finding himself in London with sixpence to his name, he talked his way into a berth on the *Resolution*.

Gazing at the evergreen tangle of the Northwest coast, Ledyard was stirred by the thought that this was the back door to his homeland. "Though more than 2000 miles from the nearest part of New England," he wrote in his journal,

"I felt myself plainly affected. It soothed a homesick heart and rendered me very tolerably happy." Ledyard was deeply impressed by the animals at Nootka. "The light in which this country will appear most to advantage respects the variety of its animals and the richness of their fur." Captain Cook agreed. "Sea otters, which live mostly in the water, are found here," he noted. "The fur of these animals as mentioned in the Russian accounts, is certainly softer and finer than that of any others we know of, and therefore the discovery of this part of the continent of North America, where so valuable an article of commerce may be met with, cannot be a matter of indifference."

Nor was it. Cook sailed on to the north, where he probed the Arctic Ocean in search of the Northwest Passage before turning back and finding death in Hawaii. The expedition started home by way of the Orient. In the holds of the two ships lay the otter furs, shedding and mildewing in the tropic heat but, bedraggled though they were, still worth a hundred dollars apiece to the traders of China when the vessels paused there. A mutinous grumbling arose among the seamen when the *Discovery* and *Resolution* sailed on to England, rather than returning to the sea-otter grounds.

On their return to England the men of the expedition spread the word of the great wealth awaiting anyone who would risk a ship in the fur trade. Ledyard returned to the United States and preached the same gospel. Eventually trading ships were fitted out with cases of cheap whisky, boxes of chisels and knives, plates of copper—goods destined to change the way of life of the coastal tribes.

But along the shore of the Olympic Peninsula, all unsuspecting, the people went on hunting the otter as they always had.

ii

The sea otter is a lovable animal. Even the Siberian hunters who all but exterminated the species remarked on the otter's gentleness, playfulness, and fondness for its young—qualities the killers considered "almost human." Georg Wilhelm Steller, the scientist on the Bering expedition, wrote, not long before his death in Siberia, a classic description of the animal: [1]

> The sea otter is usually five feet long and three feet in cir-cumference at the breast bone, where the body is thickest. The largest weighed, with the entrails, seventy to eighty Russian pounds. . . . The skin, which lies as loose on the flesh as in dogs and shakes all over when the otter runs, so far surpasses in length, beauty, blackness and gloss of the hair that of all river beavers that the latter cannot be com-pared with it. . . . .
>
> Altogether, in life it is a beautiful and pleasing animal, cunning and amusing in its habits, and at the same time ingratiating and amorous. Seen when they are running, the gloss of their hair surpasses the blackest velvet. They pre-fer to lie together in families, the male with its mate, the half-grown young, . . . and the very young sucklings. . . . The male caresses the female by stroking her, using the fore feet as hands, and places himself over her; she, however, often pushes him away from her for fun and in simulated coyness, as it were, and plays with her offspring like the fondest mother. Their love for their young is so intense that for them they expose themselves to the most manifest dan-ger of death. When their young are taken away from them, they cry bitterly like a small child and grieve so much that, as we came to know on several occasions, after ten to four-teen days they grow as lean as a skeleton, become sick and feeble, and will not leave the shore.

[1] F. A. Golder, *Bering's Voyages* (New York: American Geographical So-ciety, 1922).

When frightened they take the suckling young in the mouth, but the grown-up ones they drive before them. If they have the luck to escape they begin, as soon as they are in the water, to mock their pursuers in such a manner that one cannot look on without particular pleasure. Now they stand upright in the water like a man and jump up and down with the waves and sometimes hold the fore foot over the eyes, as if they wanted to scrutinize you closely in the sun; now they throw themselves on their back and with the front feet rub the belly and pudenda as do monkeys; then they throw the young ones into the water and catch them again, etc. If a sea otter is attacked and nowhere sees any escape it blows and hisses like an angry cat. When struck it prepares itself for death by turning on the side, draws up the hind feet, and covers the eyes with the fore feet. When dead it lies like a dead person, with the front feet crossed over the breast.

Large numbers of sea otters lived in the kelp beds along the coast of the Olympic Peninsula. They were hunted by individuals all year long, but the big hunts, involving whole villages, started in September and continued until the winter storms made the ocean unsafe for the shallow hunting canoes.

There were three men to a canoe—a captain and two paddlers. Hunters preparing for the chase bathed and rubbed their bodies with hemlock sprigs morning and evening for four days; each captain stayed by himself in the woods, and his paddlers stayed together. The hunters slept apart from their wives on beds of hemlock and spruce, for they believed the fragrance of the boughs would help to rid them of human odor; they slept little, for they believed their own fatigue would enter the body of the otter and make it sleep. They ate little, and when they did eat, the captain would toss the first bite of food into the fire, asking help of the spirit of fire. They ate no fat, but sometimes a captain rubbed his body with fat taken from a corpse.

On the fourth morning, after dedicating themselves to the

hunt, they would come from the woods and assemble by the flotilla of canoes, which stood on blocks on the beach. The spears and clubs and bows and arrows and paddles were already in the canoes, under blankets of cedar. The hunters carried the black dugouts to the water and pushed out through the surf. Then the canoes pulled together in a hunting pack.

"Ya-ah!" someone shouted. And the others beat on the sides of the dugouts with their paddles and cried in unison, "We-ay!" Four times they uttered this ceremonial cry of the kill, and four times they sang an ancient song—not a song about the sea otter, but of Man and the Spirit. At the last phrase of the song the paddles dipped together, rose, and dipped again. The crews paddled desperately hard, seeking the privilege of leadership, which carried with it the right to the first shot, but, though racing, they remembered at each stroke to flip the spearlike paddle blade forward so the drip scattered thinly, almost soundlessly, over the gray-green waters.

When one of the canoes had taken the lead the others fell in behind in a flying V. From the cliffs the flotilla looked like a flock of geese spread out against the sky. The leader picked a kelp bed, where otters were known to sleep. When he saw an otter he raised a paddle, and behind him forty other captains raised theirs to show they had caught the signal.

The lead canoe waited while silently the others spread in a wide circle that encompassed the otter and the leader. Slowly the leader raised a short bow armed with a bone-tipped arrow. Then came the shot.

If struck, the otter would struggle on the surface, trying to dislodge the arrow. The leader waited. The other captains signaled for their men to paddle them in so they could spear the prize.

If the leader's first shot missed, the otter dived. The lead canoe moved closer, following the telltale bubbles, and the circle of black canoes moved over the waves, centered on the lead canoe. The hunters pounded on the sides of the dugouts to frighten the otter, and they beat the water with the flats of their paddles. When the leader saw large bubbles rising far apart he raised his paddle, signaling the others to be alert. The shiny black head broke the surface, the round eyes caught sight of the converging canoes, a shower of arrows splashed the water, and the otter, if unwounded, dived again before it could catch full breath. Up it came, sooner this time, and, if not struck then, it soon would be, for each dive was shorter and the dugouts bunched ever closer.

The skin belonged to the man whose arrow struck the animal; if more than one arrow found the mark it was shared. The leader, who got the first shot, had the best chance, but if his arrow missed he got nothing. Leadership lasted only through the day. On the next hunt there would be a new race for leadership.

As they paddled back to shore, each man who had killed an otter wore an arrow in his hair. The next day each man with a skin laid his otter on a fresh cedar mat, cut the skin downward from the throat, saying, "I have hit it." The fat flesh was kept for food.[2] The skin was suspended on a frame with a heavy stone attached to the flippers. Later it was stretched on a cedar frame, dampened, fleshed with a cockle-shell, and

[2] Steller spoke of the flesh of the otter as savory and delicious. His seems to have been a minority opinion, induced by the conditions of shipwreck. Captain H. J. Snow probably expressed the majority opinion in his book *In Forbidden Seas* (London, 1910): "There is no accounting for taste, of course. I have tried it on many occasions cooked in various ways, but a more disagreeable, ranker-tasting meat I have yet to find. Not a hunting season would pass without someone trying it. The sailors, both Chinese and Japanese, whom I had at different times, ate crow, shag, gull, fox, whale, and, of course, fur-seal and sea-lion, but they always gave otter-flesh the go-by."

stretched again. The standard size for a large skin was six feet, seven inches, by two feet, nine inches. The skins were used for ceremonial capes and for blankets to wrap around the noble dead.

iii

It was seven years after Captain Cook's departure that the next European vessel visited the Northwest coast. In 1785 there came, strictly for trade, a brig from China, under Captain James Hanna, who obtained for a small outlay in barter goods 560 sea-otter skins, which he sold for $20,600. After that the traffic grew steadily.

In 1787 five trading vessels visited Nootka, among them the *Imperial Eagle,* which had sailed from Ostend the year before under the flag of the Austrian East India Company. On a clear day in July the *Imperial Eagle* left Nootka on a trading run to the south. On the bridge was Captain Charles William Barkley and with him his eighteen-year-old bride, Jane, who recorded the events of the day in her diary:

> In the afternoon to our great astonishment we arrived off a large opening, extending to the eastward, the entrance of which appeared to be about four leagues wide and remained about that width as far as the eye could see, with a clear easterly horizon, which my husband immediately recognized as the long lost strait of Juan de Fuca, and to which he gave the name of the original discoverer, my husband placing it on his chart.

Captain Barkley, who had furs on his mind, didn't take time to explore the strait. He cruised on south and lost five men to an Indian ambush near the mouth of the Hoh. Even so, it was a successful trip: while on the Northwest coast the *Imperial Eagle* took aboard eight hundred sea-otter skins.

The following year another British trader, John Meares, visited the peninsula. Meares was an odd one—young, good-looking, impetuous, brave, a romantic with an eye for a quick pound, an imaginative man with a weakness for self-glorification and a cheery disregard for fact when distortion or prevarication offered more immediate rewards. The Indians called him Aita-aita Meares—"the lying Meares." He was an instrument of destiny.

When Cook's men returned to England, talking of fortunes to be made in the fur trade between the Northwest coast and China, Meares listened. He was no man to overlook the possibility of fast money, even though danger might be involved. Meares had been unemployed since the end of the American Revolution, when, at the age of twenty-seven, he retired from King George's Navy, a lieutenant. There was one big difficulty about entering the fur business: the trade in New World furs was in the hands of two royally chartered monopolies. Meares dodged this by going to India, organizing himself as a Portuguese trading company complete with dummy stockholders, and chartering two ships, which in 1786 sailed east under the green, scarlet, and gold colors of Portugal. One disappeared after selling a load of opium on the Malay Peninsula; the other reached Alaska, where, during a severe winter, twenty-three of its crew froze or starved before a rival vessel—one with a legitimate connection with the South Seas Company—showed up, gave necessary assistance, but shooed the interlopers out of the company trading preserve. The ship got back to India without pelts.

It says something for Meares' powers of persuasion that by 1788 he had two more ships, the *Felice,* which he captained, and the *Iphigenia,* Captain William Douglas. They departed for Nootka, where Meares proposed not only to barter for furs but to found a permanent colony made up of Chinese coolies and Hawaiian women—an experiment that never came to fruition.

On reaching Nootka, he bought (so he said) some land from the Indians (they said he neglected to pay, which sounds probable), and he set some of his men to building a boat. Then Meares went off exploring. He visited Neah Bay, where he encountered the formidable Makahs, of whom he wrote:

> About five o'clock we hove to off a small island. . . . In a very short time we were surrounded by canoes filled with people of a much more savage appearance than any we had hitherto seen. They were principally cloathed in sea otter skins, and had their faces grimly bedaubed with oil and black and red ochre. Their canoes were large, and held from twenty to thirty men, who were armed with bows, and arrows barbed with bone, that was ragged at the points, and with large spears pointed with muscle-shell. . . .
>
> The chief of this spot, whose name is Tatootche, did us the favour of a visit and so surly and forbidding a character we had not yet seen. His face had no variety of color on it, like the rest of his people, but was entirely black, and covered with a glittering sand, which added to the savage fierceness of his appearance.

Meares wrote of appearances. His first officer, Mr. Duffin, was sent in the longboat to explore the Strait of Juan de Fuca and barely survived to write of action:

> At 2 P.M. came to in a small cove in three and three quarters fathoms, close to the rocks. . . . The people here all claim Tatootche for their chief. They appeared to us to be a bold, daring set of fellows; but not being near any of their villages I was under no apprehensions. At seven A.M. came alongside of the boat several canoes, with a great number of men in each. Several of the people attempted to come into the boat; I, at the same time, desiring to keep them out, not

permitting any of them to come in. . . . One of the canoes put off a little from the boat; when one of the savages in her took up a spear pointed with muscle-shell, and fixed it to a staff with a cord made fast to it, at the same time putting himself in a posture of throwing it, and signifying, by his gestures, that he would kill me: I at the time took no notice of him, not thinking him serious. Upon inspecting, however, their canoes, I found them all armed with spears, bludgeons, and bows and arrows; I also perceived a number of armed people amongst the trees on shore, opposite the boat: I then found they meant to take the boat; upon which I ordered the people to get their arms ready, and be on their guard, and narrowly to watch the motions of the man with the spear, and if he attempted to heave it, to shoot him.

The words were scarce uttered, when I saw the spear just coming out of his hand at Robert Davidson, quarter-master and cockswain; on which I ordered them to fire,—which one person did, and killed the man with the spear on the spot, the ball going through his head. The rest of the people jumped overboard, and all the other canoes paddled away. We instantly had a shower of arrows poured on us from the shore; upon which a constant fire was kept on them, but with no effect, they sheltering themselves behind large trees. I was wounded in the head with an arrow immediately as the man fell.

We weighed anchor, and pulled out with two oars, keeping the rest of the people at the arms. We found the shore on both sides lined with people, armed with spears, stones, etc., so that it appeared plainly their intent was to take the boat. A great quantity of arrows and stones came into the boat, but fortunately none were wounded mortally. Peter Salatrass, an Italian, had an arrow sticking in his leg all the time till we got clear of them, not being able to pull it out without laying open the leg, the arrow being bearded, and with two prongs; I was obliged to cut his leg open to get it out, as it had penetrated three inches. The Chinaman was also wounded in the side, and another seaman received an arrow near his heart. As soon as we got clear of them, we made sail and turned out of the bay.

Meares made no more effort to explore the strait. This did not prevent him from showing on a chart he published later a great river, the Oregan, flowing into the eastern end of the strait. He really did see a snowcapped mountain, and he named it Olympus. The name replaced Sierra de Santa Rosalia, which Juan Pérez had applied fourteen years earlier. Meares sailed south and joined the club of those explorers who had overlooked the mouth of the Columbia. He returned to Nootka and was on hand for the launching of his ship, the *Northwest America*. (Someone forgot to tie the stern line, and, on hitting the water, she almost left on the outgoing tide, but was retrieved.) Then Meares loaded the *Felice* with otter furs and sailed off for China, leaving his associate, Douglas, to manage the little colony. (In Hawaii the natives stole the anchors from the *Felice,* but gave them back.) Meares sold the otter furs at a good profit. Then he approached some legitimate British traders and talked them into backing him. The following year he dispatched two new boats to Nootka. He didn't go himself; he was writing the narrative of his voyages, real and fancied.

As Meares' two boats, flying the British flag this time, were moving eastward around the world toward Nootka, Spanish war vessels were coming up from San Blas. The Spanish claimed the entire Northwest coast, and they disapproved of visits by ships of rival claimants. The viceroy ordered Don Estevan José Martínez and Lopez de Haro to go north and scare the British traders away.

Martínez found the *Iphigenia* still at Nootka. Since she had Portuguese papers, he gave permission for her to sail, but he warned Captain Douglas not to return. Then Meares' new vessels, the *Argonaut* and the *Princess Royal,* arrived, flying the British flag. The Spaniards seized them. Captain James Colnett of the *Argonaut* expressed himself so vigorously that

Martínez shipped him off to San Blas, and in that mosquito-plagued port he went mad.

The *Iphigenia* brought news of these events to Meares in India. He caught a packet to London, where he hired a press agent and stirred up Parliament. The government went on record as being ready to wage war to sustain the right of British merchants to buy cheap in the eastern Pacific what they could sell dear in the western part of the ocean. Spain backed down, agreeing that both nations should have the right to establish posts on the Northwest coast, promising to return the buildings which Meares said had been taken from him at Nootka, and undertaking to pay indemnity.

Meares turned the full force of his considerable talents to the task of preparing a suitable expense account, and in the fullness of time produced one that ranks as a triumph of imaginative literature. He claimed that his ships were hull-down with otter skins when seized; he inflated the going price for skins; and he reached his climax with a demand for $210,000, which he got. Meares thereupon retired from the fur trade and devoted himself to publishing his memoirs, whose accuracy was quickly challenged by other explorers.

Meanwhile the ripples caused by Meares' activities continued to widen. Spain moved to consolidate her claim to the coast. Martínez erected some buildings at Nootka. In 1790 a small expedition under Don Manuel Quimper explored the length of the Strait of Juan de Fuca, naming—among other places—Port Angeles (Porto de Nuestra Señora de Los Angeles) and the Canal de Haro, now part of the boundary between the United States and Canada.

The next year the Spanish sent north an expedition to found a military colony on the southern shore of the Strait of Juan de Fuca by establishing "a small battery on the mainland, respectable fortifications, provisional barracks for the sick, a bakery and oven, and a blacksmith shop, and to cut down all trees within musket shot." They chose Neah Bay, a poor spot, for the Makahs were unenthusiastic hosts, killing one Spaniard (Makah tradition describes him as a rapist) and threatening the others. The bay was so exposed and the bottom so rocky that the supporting frigate had to anchor far from shore, where her guns could offer no support to the men on the beach in case of trouble. (The captain of an American merchantman, the *Hope,* later wrote in his journal: "I cannot imagine what the Spaniards promised themselves by forming a settlement on a spot where it is five points of the compass open to the sea. I should suppose a good Harbour was the first and most material thing to be sought for.") That mistake killed the colony. After five months at Neah Bay, during which they provoked the Makahs to the point of war, the Spaniards gave up and abandoned the settlement before the winter storms forced the withdrawal of the frigate to safer waters.

That same year British warships were en route to the coast. The British expedition was commanded by Captain George Vancouver, who had visited the coast before with Captain Cook and had been chosen to negotiate with the Spanish representative, Juan Francisco de la Bodega y Quadra, over possession of Nootka.

The negotiations produced new controversy. Vancouver's instructions were to receive from the Spaniards the buildings and lands which Meares said had been seized from the British. Neither Vancouver nor Quadra could find any trace of buildings, but Vancouver interpreted the instructions as meaning he should take possession of the entire port of Nootka. The Spaniard wouldn't give it to him. The two diplomats referred matters to their home governments, which in 1794 solved the problem neatly by giving Nootka back to the Indians.

While on the coast, Vancouver carried out his instructions to explore. In April 1792 he was cruising the western shore of the peninsula and had reached a point about opposite the mouth of the Quillayute River when, according to his journal:

> At four o'clock a sail was discovered to the westward stand-ing in shore. This was a great novelty, not having seen any vessel but our consort during the last eight months. She soon hoisted the American colours, and fired a gun to leeward. At six we spoke her. She proved to be the ship *Columbia*, commanded by Mr. Robert Gray, belonging to Boston, whence she had been absent nine months. . . .

Like Vancouver, Gray was no stranger to the Northwest. Sponsored by a company of Boston men whom John Ledyard had interested in the fur trade, Gray had visited the otter-hunting tribes in 1788, commanding the *Lady Washington,* a ninety-ton sloop, which was consort to the *Columbia Rediviva*, 220 tons, Captain John Kendrick. They had met Meares at Nootka, and in one of his flights of fancy Meares later attributed to Gray a cruise around Vancouver Island.

While at Nootka, Kendrick took advantage of the powers vested in himself as master and sold himself the sloop. For the next six years he cruised the Pacific, never remembering to send payment for the *Lady Washington* to her former owners. His career ended with a bang: a British captain, saluting the entrance of Kendrick's vessel into a Hawaiian harbor, forgot to remove the grapeshot from his twelve-pounder, and the salutation killed Kendrick.

Gray, who had succeeded to the command of the *Columbia Rediviva* when Kendrick took the sloop, carried a cargo of otter skins to China, bought tea with the proceeds of his sale, and returned to Boston, the first captain to carry the American flag around the world.

In 1792 he was back, looking for new tribes with otter skins to trade. Gray cruised with Vancouver as far as the entrance to the Strait of Juan de Fuca. En route he told Vancouver that to the south he had seen signs of a great river. Vancouver was unconvinced; he had just been through the same waters and felt, as he wrote in his journal, "that we could not possibly have passed any safe navigable opening, harbour or place of security for shipping on this coast." The ships parted; Vancouver went into the strait and discovered the inland sea he named for his subaltern, Peter Puget, while Gray sailed south to discover the great river, which he named for his ship, the *Columbia*.

While en route to the Columbia River and immortality, Gray made other discoveries, the most important of which, Grays Harbor, bears his name. His log describes the event:

May 7, 1792, A.M.—Being within six miles of the land, saw an entrance in the same, which had a very good appearance of a harbor; lowered away the jolly boat, and went in search of an anchoring place, the ship standing to and fro, with a very strong weather current. At 1 P.M. the boat returned having found no place where the ship could anchor with safety; made sail on the ship—stood in for the shore. We soon saw, from our mast head, a passage in between the sand bars. At half past three, bore away, and run in northeast by east, having from four to eight fathoms, sandy bottom; and as we drew in nearer between the bars, from ten to thirteen fathoms, having a very strong tide of ebb to stem. Many canoes came alongside. At 5 P.M. came to, in five fathoms water, sandy bottom, in a safe harbor, well sheltered from the sea by long sand bars and spits. Our latitude observed this day was 46 degrees 58 minutes.

With Gray was the brother-in-law of one of the *Columbia*'s owners, eighteen-year-old John Boit of Boston. He kept a journal:

May 7—Vast many canoes came off, full of Indians. They appeared to be a savage set, and was well arm'd, every man having his Quiver and Bow slung over his shoulder. Without doubt we are the first civilized people that ever entered this port, and these poor fellows view'd us and the Ship with the greatest astonishment. Their language was different from any we have yet heard. The men were entirely naked, and the women, except a small apron made of rushes, was also in a state of nature. They was stout made, and very ugly. Their canoes was from the Logs, rudely cut out, with upright ends. We purchas'd many furs and fish.   .

May 8—Vast many canoes along side, full of Indians. They brought a great many furs which we purchas'd cheap, for Blankets and Iron. We was fearfull to send a Boat on discovery, but I've no doubt we was at the Entrance of some great river, as the water brackish, and the tide set out half the time. This evening heard the hooting of Indians, all hands was immediately under arms. Several canoes was seen passing near the Ship, but was dispers'd by firing a few Muskets over their heads. At midnight we heard them again, and soon after, as't was bright moonlight, we see the canoes approaching the Ship. We fired several cannon over them, but still persisted to advance, with the war Hoop. At length a large canoe with at least 20 Men in her got with ½ pistol shot of the quarter, and with a Nine pounder, loaded with langerege [langrage] and about 10 Muskets, loaded with Buck shot, we dash'd her all to pieces, and no doubt kill'd every soul in her. The rest soon made a retreat. I do not think that they had any conception of the power of Artillery. But they was too near us for to admit any hesitation how to proceed.

May 9—Very pleasant weather. Many canoes along side from down River and brought plenty of Skins; likewise some canoes from the tribes that first visited us, and their countenances plainly show'd that those unlucky savages who last Night fell by the Ball, was a part of the same tribe, for we could plainly understand by their signs and gestures that they were telling the very circumstances, to their acquaintances from down River, and by Pointing to the Cannon, and endeavoring to explain the noise they made, made us still more certain that they had no Knowledge of fire arms previous to our coming amongst them. I am sorry we was obliged to kill the poor Devils, but it could not with safety be avoided. The Natives brought us some fine Salmon and plenty of Beaver Skins, with some Otters, and I believe had we staid we shou'd have done well.

Gray and Vancouver met again at Nootka before returning to their homelands. They exchanged notes on their experiences. After getting home to Boston, Gray made no effort to publicize his discoveries. His mission, after all, had been to get otter skins, and where he found them was nobody's business (does Macy's tell Gimbel's?).[3] Vancouver, who had been assigned to explore and add to the world's knowledge, reported Gray's findings as well as his own.

The controversy over the Northwest coast simmered down. In 1793 the Spanish viceroy, Revilla Gigedo, wrote a secret report, advising his government that the otter trade offered a shaky economic basis for colonization; that the Northwest coast had little else to offer, being too heavily forested for farming; and that if no major river route to inland trade was to be found in the vicinity it would be uneconomic to subsidize colonies in the Northwest simply as a means of keeping

---

[3] In 1816 President Madison asked for information about Gray's voyage. Charles Bulfinch, one of the owners of the *Columbia*, copied passages from the original log, including the entries describing the discovery of Gray's Harbor and the Columbia River. In 1838 William Slocum, an army officer assigned to study the problem of possession of the Northwest coast, traced the original log to Gray's niece, to whom his effects had passed; she was using it for waste paper and had already destroyed the account of her uncle's greatest discoveries.

other countries away. So Spain withdrew her claims to sole possession.

When the dispute boiled up again it was in the form of controversy between the United States and Britain over possession of the Oregon country. The Olympic Peninsula played little part in the arguments, except as the western shore of Puget Sound, which both parties coveted. (William Slocum, who reconnoitered the Northwest for the government in 1835, reported: "In a military point of view [Puget Sound] is of the highest importance to the United States. We should never give it up." And Lieutenant Charles Wilkes, after his visit in 1841, also stressed the value of the Sound to a maritime nation. "Not a shoal exists within the Straits of Juan de Fuca, Admiralty Inlet, Puget Sound or Hood's Canal, that can in any way interrupt their navigation by a seventy-four-gun ship.") But as for the Olympics themselves, shouldering up between the sound and the sea, they were too heavily forested to be worth anything. The otter herds had long since been decimated; trade with the Indians was confined to barter for whale oil and beaver and seal skins. Once during the negotiations the British suggested that the Americans take the peninsula as a sort of three-sided island and, in return, concede the rest of the land north of the Columbia. The Americans said, very flatly, "No."

When the settlement was finally reached in 1845, the border ran down the Strait of Juan de Fuca. The United States got not only the sound but the peninsula. In all its six thousand square miles there was not a white settler.

2

Port Townsend:
A Matter of Customs

i

In an era such as ours, which is marked by the attitude that the government owes the citizen a living, it is instructive to look back a century to the time of the pioneers. Then the rain-forest country was full of robust individuals straining every effort to find places for themselves on the public pay-roll, or at least to secure for their scrawny villages some life-blood from the federal exchequer.

Most of the settlers who came to the Northwest in the early fifties were farmers. Those who settled on the Olympic Peninsula found themselves surrounded by giant trees. Unable to expand their farms, without equipment to log the forest, with furs becoming scarce and the Indians more conscious of their value, the pioneers were often desperate for money. The story of the 1850s is the story of their search for a cash crop. Until they discovered the commercial value of the forests, the federal government provided the largest pay-rolls.

ii

On April 22, 1850, the schooner *Albion*, Captain Richard O. Hinderwell, lay in Discovery Bay near the northeast tip of the Olympic Peninsula. A rakish vessel, 126 feet long with a twenty-five-foot beam, she flew the British flag. On her deck were lashed seventeen spars ranging in length from seventy to ninety feet, and averaging about two feet at the butt, eighteen inches at the tip. These spars were the product of four months' intensive labor in the cold forest bordering the bay. They were the cause of an international incident.

Ships' captains had long been impressed by the marine potential of the rain forest. This set them apart from all other visitors and the resident tradesmen and farmers, who considered the forest as little more than an encumbrance that would have to be cleared before cities could be built and farms planted. But nautical men, looking at the straight-boled firs that rose branchless for more than a hundred feet, thought at once of spars. Captain John Meares replaced a broken spar with one cut from a peninsula fir in 1788, and four years later Captain Vancouver did likewise.

During the 1840s the Hudson's Bay Company put the *Beaver*, the Northwest's first steamer, into service hauling supplies and farm products to and from the post at Nisqually, near the southeastern extremity of Puget Sound. As the side-wheeler thrashed the green waters of the sound her captain, William Brotchie, stared at the still untouched forest reaching down to the shore—mile after mile after mile of fir, hemlock, cedar, spruce, growing right down to the slate-gray beaches. He thought of the shipbuilders of his native England.

After the boundary settlement of 1845 had disrupted Hudson's Bay Company business in the Puget Sound area, Captain Brotchie went home to England. There he approached various shipping interests with the proposal that they contract to supply Her Majesty's Navy with spars from the rain forest. In 1848 he was outward bound as supercargo on the *Albion,* with orders for spars from Vancouver Island or the north shore of the peninsula. If Brotchie's intention ever was to cut spars north of the strait, he soon changed his mind in favor of pirating logs from Discovery Bay on the American side, where the trees were straighter, the banks lower, and the Indians more cooperative.

The Clallam Indians were downright helpful. After receiving some of the "clothing, tobacco, female ornaments, clasp-knives, files, fishhooks and needles" listed in the *Albion's* trading stock, the Clallam chief, known as King George, gave permission for the Englishmen to work in the forest, and assigned numerous Clallams to help.

Even so, it was no picnic, this pioneer logging venture on the peninsula. The ship's carpenter, William Bolton, was in charge; he said later he had never known anything like it—the resilient toughness of the timber, the spurts of sap that all but drowned the choppers when they got through the bark, the groan of the fir as it started to fall, the sheer bulk of the logs. Bolton did not take the biggest trees—no shipping needing spars of two hundred feet or more—but even the smaller ones were almost impossible to move, once down. When the branches had been lopped off and the boles squared, teams of Indians, a hundred strong, were called on to drag the spars to the water. Often the four-inch hawsers snapped as the log edged forward. It might take a week to move a spar a hundred yards. Still the men from the *Albion* and their Indian helpers worked on, beaver-slow, gnawing into the fringe of the endless forest. In four months they dropped and trimmed and squared eighteen trees and loaded all but one.

Then, on the morning of April 22, while the sun was still behind the fringe of firs on the eastern shore of Discovery Bay, a small boat appeared and moved alongside the *Albion*. She was flying the American flag. She carried a half-dozen soldiers from Fort Steilacoom up the sound, and a man who identified himself as Eben May Dorr, the customs inspector for Oregon Territory, whose headquarters were at Astoria on the Columbia River.

After a brief look at the schooner, the customs inspector informed the captain that he had violated a number of revenue laws, ranging from failure to register entry to illegal trade. As a consequence, said Eben Dorr, the customs had no alternative but to seize the vessel.

Captain Hinderwell and Mr. Brotchie replied that they had not known there was a customs office anywhere on the Northwest coast—not improbable, since the office had only been created by Congress in January, and Dorr had assumed his title only a month before. As for illegal trading with the Indians, the Englishmen could ask quite seriously where they were expected to obtain permission—Washington? And taking trees illegally? If there was anything no one would miss, it was a tree.

The *Albion* was taken under armed guard to Steilacoom, way up the sound, where she was held pending action in the federal district court in Clarke County, Oregon Territory. The court libeled ship and cargo. Anglo-American relations in the Northwest were strained at the time, and the local officials do not seem to have been inclined to lean over backward, or even remain neutrally upright, on behalf of the British owners—an attitude which may have stemmed from the fact that several influential pioneers were anxious to buy the *Albion* at government auction.

She was sold at Steilacoom. The British captain estimated his ship's worth at $50,000; she was knocked down to the winning bidder for $1450. The buyers celebrated their windfall by breaking open the ship's stores and treating the little town to a brandy and champagne drunk. The Hudson's Bay factor at Nisqually, on hand to observe the proceedings, remarked in his journal that it seemed to him the sale had been conducted in a manner "both riotous and hurried."

The new owners loaded the schooner with potatoes, beef, and hand-dressed pilings, and sent her south to San Francisco under Captain Robert Fry, a discreet man who had instructions to sell not only cargo but vessel.

Fry got a good price for his truck and lumber, San Francisco being ill housed and ill fed, but the gold rush had made the port the end of the line for many a vessel, and the price of schooners was depressed. He finally sold the ship to a landlubber for use as a floating rooming house.

In time there came to the United States customs office at Astoria an offer from the British owners of the *Albion* to pay a considerable fine to redeem her. But she had been sold again, this time as junk, and her ultimate owner loaded her with ballast and sank her as fill along the San Francisco waterfront.

The case of the *Albion* called attention to the fact that Oregon Territory was too large to be policed by one collector. In February 1851 a separate Puget Sound customs district was created. Simpson P. Moses, a handsome young Whig from San Francisco, was named inspector, with headquarters at Smithfield. This was hardly a plum, as appointments went. Moses may well have hoped for some less barbaric land to be promised him. In September, some weeks after his appointment, he wanly wrote his superiors in Washington asking "for such information as the Treasury Department may possess as to the precise location of the port of entry."

Moses finally found his way to Smithfield. He campaigned briskly against Canadian smugglers, whom he suspected of carrying on much trade with the Salish Indians of Puget Sound; but he found that having headquarters at the southern end of the sound was a handicap. Not many smugglers bothered to come down that far. When not lurking in a rainy cove in hopes of catching some Canadian with rum or black-market beads, he was dashing off long reports to his superiors, recommending that the station be moved farther north, where it would be easier to keep an eye on the Canadians.

In 1852 Isaac Ebey succeeded Moses as collector. He too was an apostle of change. First he talked the residents of Smithfield into changing the name of their town to Olympia in honor of the nearby mountains. Then he talked the Treasury Department into permitting him to move the port of entry to Port Townsend, on the northeast tip of the peninsula.

iii

Port Townsend, a community of about forty persons, was two years old when the federal bounty began to flow from Washington.

The first settler had come in April 1851, a swarthy, full-bearded young bachelor of twenty-nine. His name was Alfred A. Plummer. He had been born in Boston, where he had learned the trade of harness-maker, an easy trade not to grow rich in. The news of gold in California fired his imagination, but he lacked passage money; he got around that by joining the Army, signing on as a saddler, and asking for western duty.

The Army shipped Private Plummer to El Paso, where he resigned, collected his pay, and started to walk across Mexico. He crossed the desert of Chihuahua, the mountains of Durango, and trudged at last into the lovely, malarial port of Mazatlán. There he caught passage to San Francisco, and arrived in May 1850.

Plummer used his remaining funds to lease a plank building, which he christened the Plummer Hotel. Among the clientele at the Plummer was Captain Lafayette Balch, master of the brig *George Emery*. Balch was a combination chamber of commerce and travelers' aid for Puget Sound. After listening to the captain declaim on the wonders of Steilacoom, where, as Balch put it, "there is still opportunity," Plummer locked his hotel and booked passage on the *George Emery*. With him went a friend, Charles Bachelder. They worked for a time in Steilacoom, and, in the spring of 1851, they set out to found a town of their own.

Plummer and Bachelder paddled north through the narrows and along the eastern shore of the peninsula. The site they chose was on the inner curve of a blunt question mark of land, Quimper Peninsula, which thrusts up between Discovery Bay and Puget Sound. Captain Vancouver, who named it, described the anchorage in front of their homestead as "a very safe and more capacious harbor than Port Discovery; and rendered more pleasant by the high land being at a greater distance from the water-side. . . . To this port I gave the name of Port Townshend, in honor of the noble Marquis of that name." The Americans dropped the "h."

Plummer and Bachelder immediately filed their claims (Bachelder's was never perfected), gave the customary presents to the Clallams, built a two-room log cabin, and planted a garden. Six months later they had visitors, Loren Hastings and Francis Pettygrove, who said they wanted to start a town.

The founding fathers were delighted. Hastings had some money, and Pettygrove, a merchant from Maine, was an old town-founder, having been one of the creators of Portland, Oregon—in fact, he had given the town its name. The new-comers paddled away and returned in February 1852 with their families. A town site was plotted: 144 blocks, each 220 feet square, with streets 63 feet wide. It was the first town on the peninsula. The men adults formed a company to exploit the fishery—the nearby streams were almost choked with salmon during the spawning season, and the Clallams were adept at catching them—but the problems of preserving the catch until it reached a market proved too great. The enterprise did not prosper.

The men who had come to farm and to fish stayed to cut lumber. Captain Balch, stopping by on his trips from California, reported that the people to the south needed wood even more than they needed food. San Francisco burned down every few months. Timbers were needed in the mines and for the docks that were being pushed out into San Francisco Bay. There was always a market for lumber. There was a new steam mill down at Portland, but reaching Portland meant risking a ship on the Columbia bar. If you need cash, Balch advised, cut me some lumber.

Pioneers always need cash. The town's manpower was soon largely devoted to cutting down trees, squaring logs, and hauling them to the water. But that is slow work at best, and these men were amateurs. Lumber prices were high, but it takes time to saw boards by hand. "If blisters sold by the board foot," the saying went, "I'd buy gold mines." Sometime in 1853 a rude mill was built. Theodore Winthrop, who visited Port Townsend that year, described it as a "town of one house on a grand bluff, and one saw-mill in a black ravine." The mill was water-driven, and, like the other water-driven mills, on Puget Sound it was not spectacularly efficient. A pioneer sawmill worker recalled in his memoirs the operation of one of these handmade, water-driven rigs:

It was driven by an overshot wheel twenty-four feet in diameter and thirty inches in width, which required three minutes to make one revolution and the machinery was so geared up that every time the wheel revolved once the sash-saw would be raised and lowered at least ten times. The cog gearing was made of fir blocks and would wear out after one week's service, necessitating the replacing of one every hour or so, while the only belt was the one reaching to the drum to which the sash was attached. This belt, made of cow skins with the hair still on one side, would stretch to such an extent that when we were not making a new block for a cog we were taking up the slack. We made a new one one day which measured forty feet. The first afternoon we used it we cut out a surplus foot four times, and by the time it was worn out —it lasted a week—we had fifty feet of surplus hide and still forty feet of belt. There was no waste material about the mill anywhere!

My special task in this work was to "off-bear" the mill's output, to do which, however, was not difficult. The logs were delivered on a hillside just above the mill by a team of oxen and we could easily saw one every half-day. When we wanted a new log we cleared the mill of all obstructions and removed the "chunk" which retailed the "boom" on the hillside. This done, the log would surrender to the law of gravitation and with great velocity roll into the mill, usually taking its place on the carriage without assistance. In fact the speed made by the logs in this operation was the only rapid motion ever seen about the mill, and was an event to which we looked forward twice a day with great interest.

But the one feature about the mill which I enjoyed to the full was the progress of the carriage, as it pushed the log into the saw. It was a constant struggle as to which would surrender. Sometimes the saw would give up, and as the carriage endeavored to proceed against the dead saw, the mill would shake and tremble for a moment and all motion would cease, while the water would pour over the stationary wheel until the extra force would cause the belt to slip, when the wheel would turn half over, empty out its buckets and again come to a standstill. Sometimes a cog in the carriage gearing would break while the saw was savagely eating its way through a knot and, having no resistance, the remaining machinery would virtually run away with itself until the excited foreman succeeded in shutting off the water. . . .

But when everything was running smoothly it was great fun. Having set the log and started the works going, there was a good long rest in store until the saw reached the further end. There was nothing unseemly about the gait of the carriage. It was deliberate part of the time. With the screws turned, the dogs firmly driven in and the water turned on, as soon as the big wheel became filled, the picnic began. . . .

Of course in a mill of this character, it was utterly impossible to saw the lumber accurately. Nearly all the planks which were intended to be an inch thick were two inches at one end and a half-inch at the other—ofter a mere feather in the middle. For this reason a house we built was a foot wider at one end than at the other and was narrower in the middle than at either end and for the same reason we had great difficulty in making a roof that would force the water to run from its comb to its eaves.

A haywire rig such as this might supply a community with lumber but could not turn out the quantity or quality necessary for the export market. So Port Townsend was fortunate in its new position as a port of entry. Now incoming ships would have to stop; no longer would they sail past en route to the bigger towns farther up the sound. Port Townsend would get the first chance at the sailor's dollar.

The town began to grow.

iv

One difficulty with a federal payroll is that it means federal inspectors. For Port Townsend, one trouble with being port of entry for Puget Sound was J. Ross Browne.

After the presidential election of 1856, the faithful followers of James A. Buchanan lined up hopefully. Among the job-hunters was a heavy-shouldered young Democrat from New York, J. Ross Browne. He listed his qualifications for government service as including employment as blubber-stripper on an Antarctic whaler, squirrel-hunter in the Kentucky backwoods, ferry-keeper, flatboat hand, short-story writer, and —all-important—campaigner for Buchanan. He was offered an appointment as special agent for the United States Treasury Department on the Pacific Coast. Browne said later, "At great pecuniary sacrifice (in a prospective sense, for I hadn't a dime in the world), I announced myself as ready to proceed to duty."

Browne's reports may well be unique in the history of the Treasury Department. What experience he lacked as an accountant he attempted to compensate for by his talent for burlesque. His reports on the revenue-service operation on Puget Sound were models of unrestrained unenthusiasm. Of the revenue cutter based on Port Townsend he wrote:

> She finds occasional occupation in chasing porpoises and wild Indians. It is to be regretted that but little revenue has yet been derived from either of these sources; but should she persist in her efforts there is hope that at no distant day she may overhaul a canoe containing a keg of British brandy— that is to say, in case the paddles are lost, and the Indians have no means of propelling it out of the way. . . .
>
> Now and then they run on the rocks in trying to find their

way from one anchorage to another, in which event they require extra repairs. As this is for the benefit of navigation,
it should not be included in the account. They generally
avoid running on the same rock, and endeavor to find out
a new one not laid down upon the charts—unless perhaps,
by some reckless fly—in order that their vessels may enjoy
the advantage of additional experience.

Nor was Browne swept off his feet by the charms of Port
Townsend, which now termed itself Hub City of Puget
Sound:

Port Townsend is indeed a remarkable place. The houses,
of which there must be at least twenty in the city and sub-
urbs, are built chiefly of pine boards, thatched with shingles,
canvas and wood slabs. The streets of Port Townsend are
paved with sand, and the public squares are curiously orna-
mented with dead horses and the bones of many dead cows.
This of course gives a very original appearance to the public
pleasure grounds and enables strangers to know when they
arrive in the city, by reason of the peculiar odor, so that,
even admitting the absence of lamps, no person can fail to
recognize Port Townsend in the darkest night.

The prevailing languages spoken are the Clallam, Chinook
and Skookum-Chuck, or Strong Water, with a mixture of
broken English; and all the public notices are written on
shingles with burnt sticks, and nailed up over the door of
the town-hall. A newspaper, issued here once every six
months, is printed by means of wooden types whittled out of
pine knots by the Indians, and rubbed against the bottom of
the editor's potato pot. The cast-off shirts of the inhabitants
answer for paper.

Public affairs, Browne indicated, were oddly managed. He
said the jail, a log edifice, had been built on beach sand and
that some Indian prisoners, "rooting for clams, happened to
come up at the outside." He went on to discuss the manner
in which the pioneers determined those best suited for civic
leadership:

On the day of election, notice having been previously given on the town shingles, all the candidates for corporate honors go up on the top of the hill back of the waterfront and play at pitchpenny and quoits till a certain number are declared eligible; after which all the eligible candidates are required to climb a greased pole in the center of the main public square. The two best then become eligible for the mayoralty, and the twelve next best for the common council. These fourteen candidates then get on the roof of the townhall and begin to yell like Indians. Whoever can yell the loudest is declared mayor, and the six next loudest become members of the common council for the ensuing year.

One purpose of Browne's visit to Port Townsend was to have an audience with the Duke of York, a chief of the Clallams. Opinions differ about the duke, whose Indian name was Chetzemoka. Local residents considered him strong and intelligent, a friend of the white man, and a pillar of strength for his people. William Welsh, an authority on Port Townsend, says, "His part in the development of the Northwest, and more especially, Port Townsend, has reserved a place for him on the historical honor roll of the region. . . . Beautiful little Chetzemoka Park is named for the gallant Indian who many times saved the settlement from extermination." But Theodore Winthrop, who rented a canoe from him in 1853, begins his description of the incident with the remark, "The Duke of York was ducally drunk." And Browne, who called on him four years later, said that not only the Duke but his two wives, known to the whites as Queen Victoria and Jenny Lind, had had a snootful:

> I complimented him upon his general reputation as a good man and proceeded to make the usual speech, derived from the official formula, about the Great Chief in Washington, whose children were as numerous as the leaves on the trees and the grass on the plains.

"Oh dam," said the duke, impatiently. "Him send any whisky?"

No, on the contrary, the Great Chief had heard with profound regret that the Indians of Puget's Sound were addicted to the evil practice of drinking whisky, and it made his heart bleed to learn that it was killing them off rapidly, and was the principal cause of all their misery. It was very cruel and very wicked for white men to sell whisky to the Indians and it was his earnest wish that the law against this illicit traffic might be enforced and the offenders punished.

"Oh, dam," said the duke, turning over on his bed and contemptuously waving his hand in termination of the interview. "This Tyee no 'count!"

Browne's accounts of life in the Pacific Northwest came to the attention of a congressman who, during a debate on the budget, inserted some quotations in the Congressional Record. And Browne sent articles to magazines and newspapers for publication. In time some of the documents were reprinted in the Olympia *Pioneer and Democrat* and reached Port Townsend.

Pioneers may have callused hands, but their skins are thin. The dullest barb pricks them painfully. Browne's broadax cut deep into Port Townsend's pride. Civic leaders, including Plummer, Pettygrove, and Hastings, composed a long and humorless letter of protest. Browne replied with an open letter in the San Francisco *Bulletin*, in which he apologized, after a fashion:

You do not think it can possibly have escaped my memory that I found you engaged in your peaceful avocations as useful and respectable members of society. Now upon my honor I can not remember who it was particularly that I saw engaged in peaceful avocations, but I certainly saw a good many white men lying about in sunny places fast asleep and a good many more sitting on logs of wood whittling small sticks, and apparently waiting for somebody to invite them into the nearest saloon; others I saw playing billiards and some few standing about the corners of the streets, waiting for the houses to grow.

This apology was not accepted. There followed a vigorous public correspondence, the result of which, Browne was to argue later, made Port Townsend the Northwest city best known to Californians.

During this period a bearded young Scot passed through Port Townsend en route to Olympia. His tattered appearance attracted little attention, but when he bought a new wardrobe and paid for it with gold dust poured from a poke made of the scrotum of a bull elk, he no longer went unnoticed. All at once he had a hundred friends and a thousand questioners. He was a reticent man, but he could not keep his secret. His name was McDonald, and he had found the gold himself— up in Canada, on the Fraser River. He and a partner named Adams had spent the preceding year on the Fraser and Thompson Rivers, and they had, in what was then a fresh and lovely phrase, "struck it rich." Long afterward some people paused to wonder what had become of Adams, and the legend grew that McDonald had arrived with gold enough for two. But at first no one had time for such speculation. Everyone along the coast was outfitting—or helping others to outfit— for the rush to the Fraser.

Marine traffic picked up . Port Townsend had more than its share of visitors. For this Browne publicly took credit:

> The people of California were well acquainted, through the Newspapers, with at least one town on Puget's Sound. If they knew nothing of Whatcomb, Squill-chuck and other rival places that aspired to popular favor, they were no strangers to the reputation of Port Townsend. Thousands, who had no particular business there, went to look at this wonderful town, which had given rise to so much contro-

versy. The citizens were soon forced to build a fine hotel. Traders came and set up stores; new whisky saloons were built; customers crowded in from all parts; in short it became a gay and dashing sort of place and very soon had quite the appearance of a city.

So it was that when official duty brought Browne back to Port Townsend he was met not by a tar-and-feather brigade but by a delegation from the common council, who made speeches of welcome. Then they escorted him to a saloon, where, Browne recalled in an article in *Harper's Monthly*, "we buried the hatchet in an ocean of the best Port Townsend whisky." He was mellow enough to add a careful postscript. "It is due the citizens to say that not one of them went beyond reasonable bounds on this joyous occasion, by which I do not mean to intimate that they were accustomed to the beverage referred to."

This time few took offense. Browne kept up a correspondence with several of his former antagonists, sending them presents from out-of-the-way places. In 1867 he came back again, this time in a private capacity. Waiting for him on the dock, a bottle of whisky under his arm, was the Duke of York. And in the Port Townsend *Weekly Message* there appeared a poem of greeting:

> Welcome stranger, to our clam beach,
> To our clams and tangling whisky.
> The Duke and wives all wait to greet you:
> Toothless, blear-eyed, dusky matrons—
> Matrons soaked in strychnine whisky,
> On the clam beach at Port Townsend.
> All were drunk, though patient waiting,
> For the *hyas Boston tyee* [1]
> Who remembered them in Lapland
> And their dear Port Townsend whisky.

[1] Chinook jargon meaning "big American chief."

Several generations of Port Townsend residents cherished the reputation that their waterfront first achieved during the Fraser gold rush. Even the reformers took pride in the gaudiness of night life down on the beach; one Christian lady boasted, "Sodom and Gomorrah wasn't in it." A pamphlet issued by the Chamber of Commerce a few years ago wistfully quoted a retired admiral on the good old days:

> There was a man's town! Port Townsend was wild and prosperous then. A little too wild for a young ensign from the East. The first night I spent in a hotel there a man came down with smallpox in one room next to mine, and in the other a man was murdered.

There were giants in those days.

You could smell the whisky in the dirt along Water Street to a depth of ten feet, they said. There was one saloon for every seventy inhabitants—man, woman, and child. Local bad men formed a union known as the Forty Thieves. So many men, after visiting Victoria, returned to Port Townsend with bottles concealed in their high rubber boots that peninsula philologists claim the town gave to the language the word "bootlegger."

v

The Presidential election of 1856 had brought J. Ross Browne to Port Townsend. The canvass of 1860 brought Victor Smith, another Treasury special agent.

President Lincoln appointed, as Secretary of the Treasury, Salmon Portland Chase, a man described by his biographer as looking "as you would wish a statesman to look . . . a picture of intelligence, strength, courage and dignity." Around this paragon crowded the usual throng of office-seekers; these were described by a contemporary observer as "unpractical authors, sore-throated, pulpitless clergymen, briefless lawyers, broken down merchants, poor widows, orphaned daughters, all claiming to have helped elect Lincoln." Among them was Victor Smith, a debt-ridden newspaperman from Cincinnati.

Smith had special claims on Secretary Chase. He had not merely supported Lincoln for the presidency; before the Chicago convention he had backed Chase, his fellow townsman, for the nomination—backed him not from propinquity but from principle, believing that Chase was a stronger anti-slavery man than Lincoln. Smith was an abolitionist red-hot, a quick man with the epithet, a doubter of others' motives, a crusader, earnest and impatient and humorless. Chase's secretary said of him, "He believed in spirit rappings; he whined a great deal about progress; was somewhat arrogant in manner and intolerant in speech; and speedily made himself unpopular. . . ." He was not an easy man to have around. Chase may well have been thinking of the merits of absence when he proposed that Lincoln send the gaunt, sandy-haired reformer to the most distant customs house in the United States territories.

Smith was not enchanted with Port Townsend. He quickly decided the community was "a collection of huts," its water supply inadequate, its harbor a mere roadstead, its citizens certainly oafs and probably copperheads. After a few days in town he wrote to the Treasury Department, outlining the need for reform and saying:

> I recommend that the Port of Entry be transferred from Port Townsend to Port Angeles, which may be done by the Secretary of the Treasury, as Congress has never legislated on the subject. (See Act of July 21, 1852, Chapt. LXVIII.)

While waiting for word from the east authorizing this economic castration of Port Townsend, Smith went about town building up goodwill. He hired the editor of a local weekly as assistant collector, then fired him for incompetence. He deplored the local practice of importing Hudson's Bay whisky without bothering to pay duty. He even criticized the view. Sometimes he tried to be nice: at a party honoring his arrival he expressed his pleasure at finding his hosts as intelligent as the country folk back where he came from.

Port Townsend did not cotton to Victor Smith.

In time word leaked out that Smith had recommended removal of the port of entry. He denied it, explaining with something less than candor that he had done nothing more than outline the situation to higher authorities.

Then someone learned that Smith and four other men had acquired title to a town site at Port Angeles. Smith could explain that: the Port Angeles Townsite Company had been organized as a patriotic endeavor to promote the national welfare by developing land across the Strait from the British naval station at Esquimalt. Didn't the people of Port Townsend realize that Britain was likely at any moment to come into the war on the side of the Confederacy? It was imperative that the harbor of Port Angeles be developed in the interests of national safety. Port Townsend remained unconvinced as to the purity of his motives.

When his letters recommending the creation of a military district at Port Angeles failed to get results, Smith decided to go east and by personal interview convince the nation's leaders of the British menace and the steps needed to combat it. He was fresh out of assistant collectors, and he felt it unwise to deputize any of the Port Townsend citizens, whom he suspected of having subversive tendencies. He asked the captain of the local revenue cutter *Joe Lane* to lend him an officer for six weeks. Second Lieutenant J. H. Merryman got the job.

Smith left quietly for Washington—so quietly, in fact, that Port Townsend got the impression he had fled the field. The *Weekly Republican* saluted his departure: "Poor Victor has gone, unwept, unhonored, and unhung."

Lieutenant Merryman brevetted Founding Father Hastings as deputy collector, and together they went over the records of the custom house. First—oh, shades of Judas Iscariot! oh, whelp of Benedict Arnold!—they found a copy of Smith's recommendation to shift the port of entry. (The absent collector was hanged in effigy when that word got out.) Then they began to go over the accounts. To their delight, Smith came out fifteen thousand dollars short.

Merryman wrote a report to Secretary Chase, picturing Smith as an embezzler—and an inept one at that. Port Townsend settled back happily to await the arrival of Smith's replacement. Two months passed, two sweet months of clear skies, fresh breezes, good deer-hunting, happy clamdigging. The chinooks were biting off the point. Never had Port Townsend whisky given off a better glow. The Bank Exchange, the Whalesmen's Arms, the Banner Saloon, and lesser dives, all radiated relaxation and joy. Victor Smith was gone.

Then in July the mail from San Francisco brought a copy of the *Bulletin* with a story that Victor Smith, Customs Collector for the Puget Sound District, was in town, arranging the transfer of the revenue cutter *Shubrick* to Port Angeles, the new port of entry.

But you couldn't believe everything you read in the papers.

On a warm, overcast evening early in August a small paddlewheel steamer rounded Point Wilson and approached the town. Her running lights glinted off the bronze of her swivel guns as she jockeyed up to Fowler's Wharf. Word spread that she was the *Shubrick*. A crowd gathered as she tied up. Down the gangplank came Victor Smith.

No one stepped forward to welcome him. In silence the people of Port Townsend let him pass. In silence he walked toward the custom house.

Lieutenant Merryman was told that Smith was coming. He put the records in the safe, locked the safe, and pocketed the key. Then he locked the custom house door and waited.

The collector approached the deputy collector and announced himself ready to resume his duties.

Merryman said he could not permit Smith to do so.

Smith asked why.

Merryman said Smith was a felon and an embezzler, that it had been his painful duty to write the report revealing that sad fact to their superiors.

Oh, that! Smith said he had explained everything to Chase. Just a matter of bookkeeping. Merryman hadn't understood his accounting system, that was all. Now the keys, please.

Merryman said he would await official confirmation of Smith's clearance before letting him back into the office.

Smith turned and walked back to the *Shubrick*. From the saloons came the echo of laughter.

An hour later Lieutenant Wilson, the skipper of the *Shubrick*, came to the custom house. He was a pleasant young man with a soft voice and a courteous manner. He said it was his unpleasant duty to tell Merryman that on instructions from Collector Smith he had ordered his men to load the cutter's twelve-pounders with double shot. They were at this moment trained on the custom house. If the records were not surrendered within fifteen minutes, the bombardment would begin. It would be prudent of persons residing nearby to leave their houses.

Merryman, after a quick consultation with the city council, gave up the keys. A party from the *Shubrick* loaded up the records and carried them to the cutter, which at once cast off and moved out into the bay.

The next morning a delegation of citizens rushed off to Olympia to see the territorial governor. He rounded up a delegation of officials to find out what the hell was going on at Port Townsend—or, as Governor Pickering phrased it, to study "the complicated and delicate questions of law and conventional usage, or professional etiquette, always to be rightfully observed between officers representing coordinate branches of the same government."

After talking to the outraged citizens, United States Commissioner Henry McGill issued warrants charging Smith and Wilson with "assault with intent to kill." The United States marshal deputized a posse to row him out to the *Shubrick*, which had reappeared off the harbor. The marshal boarded the cutter, but he couldn't find Smith. He did locate Lieutenant Wilson and read the warrant to him. Wilson refused to accept it, arguing that he couldn't be served with a warrant on the deck of a government vessel. The marshal rowed ashore to ask what to do next.

The commissioner told the marshal he could too serve the warrant. The commissioner said he had better get right back out there and do it. Back they rowed. But as the rowboat approached the cutter Wilson ordered that the paddlewheels be started. They kicked up enough waves so that the rowboat could not approach.

Two days later the *Shubrick* dashed into Port Townsend at dawn, threw a line aboard the old cutter *Joe Lane*, and towed her off in triumph to Port Angeles. Then the *Shubrick* disappeared. She was thought to have gone to San Francisco. When, in September, she was sighted approaching Port

Townsend a rumor swept the city that Smith had turned privateer and had come to sack the town. But the cutter churned past, going up the sound to Olympia, where Smith looked up the United States marshal and declared himself ready to explain everything.

A grand jury was assembled. Most of Port Townsend wanted to testify. Civic leaders chartered the schooner *Potter* to carry a delegation of forty men to bear witness against Smith.

The cruise to Olympia took on some aspects of a community picnic. The passengers hung up a sign rechristening the sloop "Revenue Ship Number Two." When they passed the *Shubrick*, anchored off Nisqually flats, they fired a derisive salute.

Smith was indicted on thirteen counts involving charges of resisting a duly authorized officer, embezzlement of public funds, procuring false vouchers, and assault on the people of Port Townsend. But the record was sent to Washington for review. Another special Treasury agent was dispatched to investigate; according to Smith's enemies, he came "armed with lime and brush." Smith was cleared of everything. The indictments were quashed.

Smith immediately filed a complaint against the master of the *Potter*, accusing him of firing a broadside on the high seas, and against the Port Townsend delegation for "illegally impersonating a government vessel." These too came to nothing.

During the next few months Smith busied himself with construction of a residence at Port Angeles, and a large building which he rented to the government as a custom house. Port Townsend leaders were even more active; they built up a dossier against Smith and deluged the President and Secretary of the Treasury with manifestos, pamphlets, letters, accounts, editorials, and printed copies of sermons, all denouncing the transfer of the port of entry and the continued existence of Smith.

Lincoln at last decided enough was enough. He fired Smith. He wrote a note to Secretary Chase, explaining that while the charges against Smith had not been proved, "the degree of dissatisfaction with him there is too great for him to be retained."

Chase wrote a letter offering to resign. President Lincoln later told a friend how he had handled the situation.

"I walked to Chase's house," said Lincoln. "I went directly up to him with the resignation in my hand and, putting my arm around his neck, said to him, 'Chase, here is a paper with which I wish to have nothing to do; take it back and be reasonable.' I told him that I couldn't replace the person whom I had removed—that was impossible—but that I would appoint anyone else whom he should elect for the place. It was difficult to bring him to terms; I had to plead with him a long time, but I finally succeeded, and heard nothing more of that resignation."

Lincoln also told Chase that the Secretary could appoint Smith to some other post. Chase then appointed Victor Smith special agent of the Treasury Department, assigned to Puget Sound. Smith didn't even have to move.

Later that summer the stream that ran past the custom house and Smith's residence in Port Angeles went dry. No one knew why, or bothered to investigate. A landslide deep in the unexplored mountains behind the town had dammed the stream, forming a lake. With the winter rains the lake grew. On December 16 the dam washed out. A flood roared down on the town.

Collector Gunn was standing near the door of the custom house, listening to his two deputies, who were singing hymns. Over the song he heard a strange sound up the valley. Gunn looked out, saw a wall of water rushing toward him, and bolted for safety. He made it, but the collectors didn't. The custom house was swept away downstream.

Just above the Smith residence a log jam formed, momentarily diverting the waters. Victor Smith was en route to Washington, D. C., for more consultations, but Mrs. Smith was at home. She managed not only to save her four children but to pull a drowning woman from under a log jam.

The bodies of the two deputy collectors were recovered the next day. Some Makah fishermen found the custom house floating in the strait and towed it ashore. But a strongbox from Smith's house was missing.

In February, Smith's brother, Henry, who had been appointed lighthouse-keeper on Tatoosh, appeared in justice court in Port Angeles. He said he had information that his brother's strongbox was concealed in an Indian village nearby. It contained, among other things, $1500 in legal tender notes and $7500 in twenty-dollar gold pieces. Eight Clallams were arrested, and one was convicted. But no trace of the gold was discovered. The Indians said they had used the notes to start a fire with which they burned the strongbox.

In March 1864 Smith left Washington, en route for Port Angeles. He and another Treasury agent were given a large amount of currency to deliver to the subtreasury in San Francisco. Their ship, the *Golden Rule*, struck a reef and went down in shallow water. Most passengers abandoned her. Smith stayed aboard until a rescue party arrived. But when the safe was pulled up from the submerged hold it was open. The missing currency was never traced.

Smith went on to San Francisco, where he caught the *Brother Jonathan*. In her safe was a large sum of money to pay United States troops in the Northwest. Off Crescent City the *Brother Jonathan* hit an uncharted rock. She rolled off the rock and went down, taking 170 passengers with her, among them, Victor Smith.

The following March, President Lincoln appointed Fred A. Wilson as collector at Port Angeles. Wilson was a native of Port Townsend. He immediately proposed that the station be returned to his home town. Territorial Representative Alfred Denny introduced a bill to that effect. It passed Congress on July 25, 1865.

The cannon on Union Dock boomed as the *Shubrick* came in, bearing the records. They were carried in triumph to the old custom house. Port Townsend whisky flowed like Port Townsend whisky that night.

Afterward things settled down for a while and got dull.

3

The Lumber Ports

i

The young man stood on the dock at New York, studying the vessel on which he had just booked passage to Australia. She was a schooner, old, with rusted iron and corroded brass, and sheet he could see light through. Nothing about her looked good. Australia was a long way off and, it being July, there would be winter storms in the southern seas. On the other hand, gold had just been discovered near Canberra—a strike bigger than the one in California three years before, they said —and the adventurers of four continents wanted passage Down Under.

His ticket still in his pocket, young Cyrus Walker thought it over and came to a characteristic decision: he sold the ticket to another would-be prospector for somewhat more than he had paid for it and went back to his hotel. After all, he was only twenty-five, and there would be another chance to get rich quick.

Still, it could hardly have been anything but depressing, this giving up a planned trip to a far-off land where perhaps fortune waited, smiling; so it is not surprising that when young Walker got back to his hotel he fell into conversation with a middle-aged stranger in the lobby. The man identified himself as E. S. Brown, millwright. On learning that Walker was from Maine, Brown mentioned that he was to sail the next day for the Isthmus and California to join another State of Maine man, Captain William Talbot, who, with his partner, Andrew Pope, was in the process of expanding his company's operations to include the Pacific Coast.

The Popes and the Talbots had been cutting Maine trees and shipping Maine lumber from around East Machias as far back as 1767. It was just natural, come '49, for Captain Talbot to load his brig, the *Oriental*, with timbers for the mines and sail around the Horn. It was natural, too, that when he arrived he found two other members of the home team, Frederick Talbot and Andrew Pope, already on hand, picking up dollars inside the Golden Gate by lightering men and supplies ashore and hauling them to hotels and warehouses.

After studying the California scene, Captain Talbot decided that what the prospectors most needed—among the commodities a God-fearing man might be expected to supply —was lumber. Maine being too far away to serve as woodbox, he would have to let some light into the Western forests. The improvised waterpower mills then in operation were for amateurs. So he had sent for his millwright to come out and build something that would really make lumber.

Brown's story fascinated Cyrus Walker. He had tried school-teaching and surveying, but was convinced that in neither profession was he likely to earn fifty thousand dollars quickly. Since Walker had his ambition focused squarely on the speedy accumulation of this sum, he decided to go to California with the millwright. There seemed to be money in lumber.

As a young surveyor from Maine, Walker probably was familiar with logging operations. The long voyage to California with Brown gave him an opportunity to learn something about sawmill operation. He was a quick student. By the time Walker reached San Francisco he talked like an operator. Captain William Talbot listened briefly and hired the young man to work with the Puget Mill Company, which Talbot had just organized to cut Douglas fir up on Puget Sound. Walker would sign on for only a year—he wasn't sure there was fifty thousand dollars in the Northwest—but during the next half-century his name came to mean Pope and Talbot, and Boss Lumberman, to the people of the peninsula.

ii

In June 1853 the schooner *Junius Pringle* rounded Cape Flattery in fair weather and stood down the mountain-bordered strait. The dark mountains of Vancouver stretched off to her port, while to starboard the Olympics rose steeply from the narrow beach to a jumble of peaks, still carrying the winter's snow.

Captain Talbot and Cyrus Walker paid less attention to the snowy heights than to the lower terraces, solid with such a forest as the Down Easters had never seen. The trees averaged more than two hundred feet—Sitka spruce, grand fir, red cedar, western hemlock, Douglas fir.

Douglas fir, the dominant tree on the peninsula, has also been called Oregon pine, red pine, Puget Sound pine, Oregon spruce, red spruce, Douglas spruce, red fir, yellow fir, Oregon fir, and spruce fir. Its scientific name, *Pseudotsuga taxifolia,* is a compound of Greek, Japanese, and Latin, and means "false hemlock with foliage like yew." David Douglas, the Scottish botanist and explorer who is honored by its popular name, described the tree in his field books as "one of the most striking and truly graceful objects in nature." Then he added prophetically, "The wood may be found very useful for a variety of domestic purposes."

From the decks of the *Pringle* the foliage of the Douglas fir appeared yellow-green in the sunlight but dark, almost black, when shaded. The broad lower branches drooped gently, the upper branches curved up at the tips, and the crowns formed perfect pyramids. The boles were seen to be very straight and of great size. Even from a distance the men were struck by the symmetry of the massive cinnamon-brown columns. When the ship anchored at Discovery Bay and the party went ashore and into the forest, they were awed by the trees' height and by the thickness of the furrowed bark, sometimes a foot through to sapwood. They measured fallen trees and found them 250 to 280 feet long and twelve to fourteen feet through at the butt.

Captain Talbot took the *Pringle*'s longboat, and Cyrus Walker an Indian dugout, and they set off to explore the upper sound. Talbot wanted a mill site near the strait—no use making ships sail any farther than necessary—but one with a deep harbor and a low bank or sandspit for the mill.

They paddled off in picnic weather. The sockeye were running, and they passed scores of small canoes, paddled by naked Clallams, who maneuvered the boats in pairs as they stretched nets of kelp strands horizontally under the green water, then, as schools of migrating salmon swept past, raised the nets full of fish. The fishermen shouted, "*Suk-kegh, suk-kegh,*" as they emptied the nets into the dugouts, and ashore old Indian women, wrapped in tattered blankets held loosely in place by ropes of frayed bark, called back, "*Suk-kegh, suk-kegh.*"

They paddled by a stand of tall cedars with long-beaked black canoes suspended between the boles, and the Indian paddlers said these were the graves of chiefs. Closer to the beach was another graveyard, bright with blankets raised like flags over the graves. The sun glinted off tin pans and mirrors hung from trophy poles.

Around Point Wilson they came on the cabins of Port Townsend spread along the waterfront, and on the high bluff a house of planks, not yet painted but still a pleasant reminder of home.

They rode the tide south down Admiralty Inlet. Past Klas Rock, a black knob spangled with purple starfish and wearing a waving skirt of iodine-colored kelp, they turned into Mats Mats, a promising cove. A raft of coots skittered over the water, honking protests at the intrusion. Inside the narrow entrance was a small, circular harbor, lined with cedar; the wind that moaned in the branches of the trees barely riffled the surface of the water—a perfect harbor. But when they took soundings it was barely a fathom deep.

They paddled on, and the sound of hammers rang across the water as they approached Port Ludlow. They landed and talked to Captain William Sayward, a gaunt, red-bearded Maine lumberman who had come West a few months earlier, seeking taller trees to harvest. He already had his saw in place on a spit overlooking a lagoon. Talbot told Walker it was a wonderful site.

They rowed close to the cliff at Tala Point, so close they could see the big salmon lying head to current in the shadow of the bluff. They entered Hood Canal, a narrow inlet more than fifty miles long, and scouted its western shore as far as Dabob Bay, where they landed and ate with the Indians—oysters and the huge clams called goeducks and a thirty-pound salmon grilled over a smoldering log.

They crossed the canal and started back east. About five miles from Foulweather Bluff, where the canal meets the sound, they poked into a small bay, which the Indians called

Teekalet—"Brightness of the Noonday Sun"—and the Wilkes Expedition had named Port Gamble in honor of Robert Gamble, a naval officer wounded in the War of 1812.

An oval harbor two miles long, half a mile wide, spread inside the narrow entrance. The banks were heavily timbered. To the west was a level spit. The harbor was deep, the channel good. Captain Talbot sent the canoe back to fetch the *Pringle*. The search for a mill site was ended.

They hastily built a bunkhouse, a cookhouse, and a store out of lumber the *Pringle* had brought with her from California. Walker surveyed the ground for the mill while work crews felled some large cedars and began squaring off foundation timbers. When, in September, Pope and Talbot's spanking new schooner, *L. P. Foster*, her sails not yet bleached white by the sun, arrived, 155 days out of Boston, with the machinery, the frame of the mill was ready to receive it.

The building was small, only forty-five feet by seventy feet. It was set only a few feet above the high-tide level; a plank tail reached down to the water. There were a drum and cable for pulling the floating logs up to the mill, from which they were to be jockeyed onto the carriage by men armed with handspikes. The boilers, engine, and saw were rafted ashore and raised into position. Sometime around mid-September the fires were started in the boilers and steam was raised. The first log moved down the carriage and nosed against the little up-and-down saw. Port Gamble was in business. The first planks were used to close the walls of the mill.

That first "muley" saw at Port Gamble could turn out about two thousand feet of lumber [1] each working day of eleven and

---

[1] A foot, or broad-foot, of lumber represents an area one foot square and one inch thick. (A five-room house of lumber requires about twenty thousand feet.) The term is used for measuring both cut lumber and logs, or standing timber. When applied to stumpage—standing timber—the qualifying phrase "log scale" is often added to signify that the estimate allows for loss through trimming.

a half hours—six A.M. to six P.M., with time out for lunch.

Four months later two new saws arrived from Maine. One was a sash saw, which is like a glorified bucksaw and cuts the logs a slice at a time; the other was a live gang, a series of vertical blades set side by side in a frame and capable of cutting an entire log at one run of the carriage. Mill capacity shot up to fifteen thousand feet a day. That year—1854—the little lumber schooners picked up 3,673,797 board-feet in the cove at Teekalet, plus 42,103 feet of piles, 64,000 shingles, 223 masts and spars, and 71 barrels of salted salmon and 2000 gallons of dogfish oil—the latter received from the Indians and white settlers in trade at the company store. The books showed a gross business of $70,999.60. Puget Mill Company was capitalized for $30,000.[2]

Though his year was now up and his salary as timekeeper was less than a hundred dollars a month, Cyrus Walker decided to stay on to learn more about the lumber business. He still thought his future lay elsewhere. He did not even bother to stake out a homestead, so sure was he that he wouldn't stay on Puget Sound long enough to prove it up.

Down on the spit the little mill sawed away at the great forest, swallowing the logs pulled from the millpond, disgorging them as planks and laths. It worked every day but Sundays and Christmas and the Fourth of July. There was, however, a two-day time out for the Indian War on November 19 and 20, 1856.

A raiding party of Haidas from Queen Charlotte Sound entered Teekalet in seven black, high-prowed war canoes. They made camp on the far side of the cove. The sawmill workers holed up in an eight-sided plank fort and waited

---

[2] Production figures are from *Time, Tide and Timber, A Century of Pope & Talbot*, by Edwin T. Coman, Jr., and Helen M. Gibbs (Stanford: Stanford University Press, 1949).

for the attack, but it never came. On the second day of the siege the U. S. S. *Massachusetts* steamed into the harbor and began to lob cannon balls toward the canoes, which were valuable. The raiders quickly agreed to go home.

In 1858 a second mill was built farther out on the spit, where there would be less danger if the forest caught fire. There had been many fires that year. One captain noted in his log that the smoke was so thick off the Skagit River that he had to anchor; hundreds of suffocated birds fell about the vessel.[3]

The new mill was the biggest in the West, fifty-five feet wide and two hundred and fifty feet long. The carriage that pushed the logs through the blades was 124 feet. But the real wonder was the headrig: it was equipped with two parallel circular saws, fifty-six inches across, with twenty-four teeth —the latest thing from Maine, where they had been introduced only two years earlier.

The Circular Mill, as it was called, could handle logs up to nine feet thick and could turn out ships' planks fifty and sixty feet in length. Together the two mills could cut seventy thousand feet a day. Puget Mill was now the biggest enterprise in the Pacific Northwest.

To man the mill more workers were needed. Chimacum Indians did much of the common labor and were good workers, but their tribal customs made them likely to quit

[3] Logging operations caused a great increase in forest fires, though they had not been infrequent in earlier days. The dry summer months left the woods vulnerable. The Hudson's Bay factor at Nisqually noted in his journal on August 14, 1835: "The country around us is all on fire, and the smoke is so great that we are in a measure protected from the excessive heat." On October 1, the following year, the journal entry reads: "The weather is gloomy from the smoke around us." On October 18: "The country around us is all on fire." Pioneers for some time looked on forest fires as beneficial, since they cleared the land of what one called "those damned, outrageous conifer weeds."

whenever the salmon were running, or when the deer came into the lowlands, or an invitation arrived from a neighboring tribe to attend a celebration, or the hops were ripe in the Puyallup Valley, or simply when they felt like it. They had, after all, the ultimate independence of men who can live off the land.

Skilled white workers were imported from Maine, mostly from the Pope and Talbot hometown of East Machias. Other workers drifted in from the goldfields, driven to day labor by failure there. Pay was thirty dollars a month for a six-day week, eleven and a half hours a day. The men were paid weekly, or on demand, usually getting their wage in silver half-dollars.

The mill could no longer rely on nearby settlers who were clearing their lands, to supply the logs. Teams of loggers were dispatched to cut trees along the water's edge, trim them, and roll them into the water. At first the logs were floated to the mill on the tide, poled along by men who rode them, or, less often, guided by men in rowboats. That was too slow. A steam tug, the *Resolute,* was brought up from San Francisco.

And suddenly there had evolved a new pattern of logging, different from that practiced anywhere else, a pattern forced on the operators by the size of the trees, the absence of roads for bringing in logs and hauling away lumber, the presence of the broad highway of the sound—a pattern that was to change little for the next thirty years.

iii

A typical Puget Sound mill squatted at tidewater with the town spread out behind it. Beside the mill was the wharf, usually built so that it sheltered the millpond. If times were good the schooners lay alongside the wharf three or four deep, waiting for loads.

The timber in that era came from the lands near the water. If the land was claimed, the settler might receive a price for his stumpage; if the land was unclaimed, or claimed but not occupied at the moment, the loggers simply took the trees.

Swampers went in first and cut away the brush, the interlocked tangle of salal and Oregon grape, vine maple, salmonberry, huckleberry, blackberry, and brier, which made the forest almost impenetrable. Next came the fallers. They learned not to try to cut through the swollen boles of the giant trees, for the bark was from eight to twelve inches thick and the wood hard with gum. Instead they cut notches in a tree, six to ten feet from the ground, drove in a four-foot springboard, and, standing on that narrow perch, began to chop. (In the 1870s the cross-cut saw was introduced for falling.) The fallers worked in pairs. James Stevens, in his autobiographical novel, *Big Jim Turner*,[4] tells how the work went:

> This is how we worked, Rud and me. It might be a Douglas fir or a Sitka spruce six foot through, more or less. I chopped from the left, Rud from the right. The first thing on a big stick was to notch for the springboards, our working footrests. Sometimes we were up ten feet before setting in above the pitch pockets and the spread of the trunk to the roots. Then each planted his calk-booted feet far apart, sprung his knees, bowed his back, and swung from the hips with the ax. Shunk-shink! Shunk-shink! Rud led, I followed. On then, swing and swing, the thudding clang of the axes a powerful beat, boot-size bark chips flying; then a richer ring in the ax beats with soft, white sapwood chips first-big a-sailing; and then the cut into the true tree, the gold and red heartwood—if it was a king fir. At summer's end on the

[4] New York: Doubleday, 1948.

island of spruce I could have notched a big tree blindfolded. Any tree it was a deep notch to guide the fall. Then we set the springboards to the other side of the tree and began to saw timber. The prime thing was timing for the sawing team. Rud Neal and I were one man in the pull and ride of hands on the saw handles, in the turns of teeth and rakers from one position to another in the kerf, in the feel of just when to stop and slush coal oil in at binding pitch, in the time to wedge against the bind, in the sense of the tree's death shudder before crackling groan and fall notchward— the signal to yell "Timber-r-r!" and jump from the springboards for shelter from limbs broken and flying.

After the trees were down their branches were lopped and they were sawed into lengths the mill could handle. Getting the logs to salt water was the key technical operation. They were too heavy for wagons; they could be dragged only by ox teams. Logging was limited to areas that could be reached by skid roads along which the teams could pull the logs.

These skid roads seldom reached more than two miles back into the woods. They were made by placing logs of from twelve to eighteen inches in diameter across the trails, ten feet apart. In the center of each crosspiece was a rounded notch that served as guide for the log. The bark was peeled from the bottom of the log so it would offer less resistance. Before each haul-out a boy ran ahead of the oxen, daubing the notches with grease boiled out of dogfish livers by the Indians.

Brandon Satterlee, a newspaperman who spent his boyhood at Quilcene, recalls in his autobiography, *The Dub of South Burlap*,[5] a young Indian nicknamed Glease, who sang a four-word chantey—"Chickamin, luckutchee, klootchman, lum!" as he took the four steps between the skids.

[5] New York: Exposition, 1952.

In his left hand he carried a bucket of skid grease, in his right a swab made of a piece of sacking on a broomstick. With the word "chickamin," he plunged the swab into the bucket and took the first hop; the second hop at the word "luckutchee"; the third at the word "klootchman" and at the fourth he was at the next skid, and as he said "lum" he brought the swab down on the skid and started the chant again.

"Chickamin, luckutchee, klootchman, lum."

In the Chinook jargon these words mean money, clams, women, whisky.

Behind the grease monkey would come the team, dragging a turn of logs—one, two, or three logs, depending on their size, the grade, the strength of the team, and the skill of the driver. Billy Forbes, a former bullwhacker, fell into a conversation with Stewart Holbrook, the logging historian, one day in 1944, and from it came this account, first published in *Green Commonwealth:* [6]

Driving bulls was the top job. A good teamster got $100 a month and his board. He earned it, too, for a 16-hour day was the regular thing for bull teamsters. The bulls weighed up to 1800 pounds. Dehorning wasn't the usual thing, but we used to put brass caps on the ends of the horns. Except for the wheelers, as the butt or last team was called, the animals were mostly oxen. But the wheelers were always bulls. I mean bulls. In Mason county logging we used from four to seven yoke to a team.

The skid road held skids eight feet apart. Logs were twenty-four feet or longer. I have hauled 120-foot logs that were to be made into ships' spars. On a good level road, a six-yoke team of bulls could do four turns daily on a one-mile haul. One mile from water, or other landing, was the longest haul you could handle with bulls and still make money. A turn of logs would run from 10,000 to 12,000 board-feet.

[6] Seattle: Dogwood Press, 1945.

Accidents to bulls were not so common as many people seem to think. In a dozen years of bullteaming I never injured but one bull seriously. This happened when a turn made a quick run on a steep grade and broke the animal's leg. Bulls were worried by almost nothing except yellow jackets. Hornets sure would raise hell with a bull's life. Little else troubled them, but it didn't do to work them in heavy rain because this caused the yokes to chafe the animals' necks.

I have heard a lot about hell-raising bullwhackers who jumped on the backs of the wheelers and walked right on up to the lead team on the top decks of the beasts. Those kind of drivers didn't last. A brutal bullwhacker couldn't get the best work out of the animals. And if not handled just right, they would injure themselves and be unfit for logging. A good ox-driver always kept his animals in fear of him, the fear of respect, but he never beat them needlessly. I used a regular goad stick five feet long, made of hickory or oak. It had a one-inch steel brad in the end, but I kept several washers around the brad and never took them off unless a team became unruly.

My first bullwhacking was done in 1883 along Mill Creek on Big Skookum. Before that I had greased skids on the same skid road. In my early days old B. S. Chase was reputedly the greatest bull-teamster in the region. He wore a long beard and made considerable noise, but not so much noise as Tom Swan made. Tom was the noisiest driver I ever listened to anywhere. You could hear him a good mile through the timber. Make out the words, too.

Very important to a bull driver was a good hooktender. He was the man who made up the turn, who supervised hitching the logs together with chains and dogs, and followed along to take care of any hangups. At the landing the chains and dogs were thrown over the yokes to be carried back to the woods. A good hooktender got $75 a month and board.

The hand-skidder was the hooktender's helper. He carried a maul with a steel handle. He used it to drive the dogs into the logs. To remove them, he used the handle as a pry. A good hand-skidder always took the best care possible of his maul, taking it to the bunkhouse with him in wet weather.

After the logs had been spilled into salt water they were herded between long boomsticks, which were then chained together, and left floating inside some quiet cove. Eventually a tug would show up, hitch a cable to the boom, and tow the raft to the mill.

iv

Tugboats and their captains came to rival bullwhackers and their teams in logging legend. The *Resolute*, Puget Mill's first towboat, was hardly on the sound in 1859 before she collided with a full-sized steamer, the *Northerner*. The tug escaped with little harm, but the steamer's paddlewheel was badly damaged. Her owners filed suit. Puget Mill Company had not retained a lawyer, but it did have one in its employ, Christopher Hewitt, an ex-barrister from Illinois who was earning a living carving yokes for the skid-road bull teams. He asked to be allowed to handle the case. He carried it through three years of appeals and wound up arguing successfully before the United States Supreme Court. One of the justices was so impressed by Hewitt's brief that he called it to the attention of the President. Lincoln, who had known Hewitt in Illinois, promptly appointed him Chief Justice of Washington Territory.

Meanwhile the *Resolute* went on pulling logs. Her master was Johnny Guindon, a bugle-voiced man of few words. One midsummer day in 1868 Guindon was guiding the old sternwheeler up the narrow passage between Squaxin and Hope Islands. It was a hot day, he had a long boom, and the current was against him. The *Resolute* was straining for every inch, when, with a roar heard ten miles across the water, her boilers went up. Four crewmen sank with the shattered hull. Guindon and the mate were blown clear. Guindon was badly scalded in the blast, and after he was in the water a chunk of boilerplate smashed his leg; but he clung to wreckage until an Indian came out from Squaxin, picked him and the mate up, and took them to Olympia. From there Captain Johnny wired the owners: RESOLUTE BLOWN UP BOOM GONE TO HELL AND I'M AT THE PACIFIC HOTEL.

After he got back on his feet Guindon was given command of the *Politkofsky*, an improbable sidewheeler the Russians had built at Sitka. She was thrown in with the Alaska purchase. The government sold her to the Alaska Commercial Company, which sent her to San Francisco for refitting. En route she stopped at Victoria, where the *Colonist* found her worthy of editorial mention, saying, "She looks as if she had been thrown together after dark by an Indian ship-carpenter with stone tools. We hear she is to be rebuilt. She needs it."

Odd though she looked, the *Polly* was sturdy. The best of cedar had gone into her at Sitka. One of her engineers described her as "not much for handsome but hell for stout." She lasted until the Klondike gold rush, when her engines and bridgework were removed and she was towed back to Alaska as a barge.

Puget Mills had shared their first towboat with another lumber company; their second they kept all to themselves. She was the *Cyrus Walker*, built in San Francisco in 1864 of selected Douglas fir from Port-Gamble. Her 128-foot hull crouched between two huge paddlewheels. When new she packed more power than any other towboat on the coast.

Once the *Cyrus Walker* served as a warship. That was in 1867. Up in the strait a Makah and a Clallam had fallen into argument over fishing priorities; the discussion ended as such pleasantries often did, with the Makah on top and the Clallam dead. The Indian agent at Neah Bay arrested the murderer. The tribesmen asked what the fuss was all about. The agent explained that the killer would have to stand trial and that he might be hanged. This seemed unreasonable to the Makahs, so they took the prisoner away from the agent and wouldn't give him back. The agent sent word to Washington; the Indian Agency consulted with the War Department, which telegraphed Fort Steilacoom to send troops to the rescue. A lieutenant, thirty-two privates, and a surgeon, plus two howitzers, were loaded aboard the steamer *Eliza Anderson*, but she developed engine trouble and gave up at Port Gamble. Pope and Talbot loaned the United States Army the *Cyrus Walker*.

The next morning, with the engineer pouring slabwood into her furnace, she moved, full steam ahead, into Neah Bay. The soldiers landed with the howitzers. The Makahs disappeared into the underbrush. The soldiers shot the howitzers a few times, beat the bushes, and finally rounded up a respectable show of prisoners, whom they loaded on the tug. The *Cyrus Walker* paddled out to Tatoosh.

In time Makahs began to come out in canoes to negotiate for the prisoners. Every time one stepped aboard the tug he was disarmed and shoved down in the hold. Eventually there were sixty angry Indians down there, including the chief.

The lieutenant felt he was in position to negotiate from strength. The chief was brought on deck, and the lieutenant explained matters to him. White man's justice called for the murderer to be tried. The chief said he understood, that he did not like the bilge on the tug and would be glad to turn the murderer over. The trouble was, the man was gone. The chief didn't know where to find him.

There was an interval of gloom while everyone thought. Then the chief had an idea. The murderer's brother was available—why not arrest him instead?

The lieutenant and the Indian agent retired to consider the idea. There were more negotiations, and the *Cyrus Walker* at length sailed off, taking the brother and two friends to Steilacoom, where they were jailed for two months. The Makahs went back to their reservation, and the *Cyrus Walker* went back to towing logs.

The third of the Pope and Talbot tugs was the *Goliah*.[7] She was the second vessel (the *Ajax* was first) built for the specific job of towing ships. Commodore Cornelius Vanderbilt had bought her in 1848 to move ships in and out of New York Harbor but, after a brief experiment, sold her.

The *Goliah*'s new owners were in financial trouble, and she was libeled. A United States marshal came aboard. From there on, accounts differ. One story is that the marshal went ashore for a short beer and came back to an empty dock; the other is that he took a nap and woke up off Staten Island, bound for the Golden Gate. With or without the marshal, the *Goliah* made it, though on the last leg of the trip fuel ran low, and she steamed into San Francisco with her boilers fired by the wooden partitions between her cabins.

After serving in Northern California as tug, freighter, and riverboat, and once being abandoned as junk, she was bought by Pope and Talbot and sent north. Her first captain on the sound was Old Man Libby—Captain S. D. Libby—the prototype of a towboat man. A friend described him as having "a voice like a trumpet, eyes that could pierce a Flattery fogbank, a face tanned and seamed by salt air, and a battery of

[7] Goliah is the name of an obscure Skagit chief. The tug was christened in New York. Historians are not sure whether she was named after the Indian or was a typographical error.

expletives that was the despair and envy of the opposition."
But, of course, he had a heart as big as Mount Rainier.

The *Goliah* did some work with log rafts, but her primary
function was to bring in sailing vessels from Cape Flattery,
where they often encountered adverse winds. Pope and Talbot vessels got first call, but when others showed up the *Goliah*
would haul them to port for a price. If no other tugs were in
sight the price was high; if a rival tug also spoke the wind-
jammer a price war started. Throat-cutting became bloodiest
when the *Goliah* and her most powerful rival, the Tacoma
Mill Company's *Tacoma*, went after the same vessel. One
day both spoke a British brig off Tatoosh.

"I'll tow you in for three hundred dollars," shouted Captain
Libby.

"I'll make it two hundred," boomed Captain Chris Williams
of the *Tacoma*.

"Great balls of seagull sweat! I'll do it for one hundred."

"Fifty."

"By God, I'll tow you in for nothing and buy you a new hat
to boot!" cried Libby.

And he did.

v

Lumber, not being perishable, was moved by sail long
after the introduction of steam. The forest of spars of ships
waiting dockside for loads was a sign of a lumber town by
day, as was the glowing wire cone of its waste burner by
night.

Lumber schooners remained a common medium of transportation along the coast until the turn of the century.
Caroline Leighton, the wife of a customs official stationed
at Port Townsend, made several voyages in them, and her

journal contains the following description of a winter passage
in 1867:

> We left Puget Sound at short notice, taking passage on the
> first lumber-vessel that was available, with many misgivings,
> as she was a dilapidated-looking craft. . . .
> The sky looked threatening when we started; and the
> captain said if he thought there was a storm beginning he
> would not try to go on. . . . If he could find Port Angeles,
> he would put in there. A gleam of sunshine shot through
> the fog, and showed up the entrance; and we steered tri-
> umphantly for that refuge. . . . But just as we were about
> rounding the point to enter, and were congratulating our-
> selves on the quiet night we hoped to spend under the shel-
> ter of the mountain, the captain spied a sail going on towards
> the ocean. He put his vessel right around, determined to face
> whatever risks any other man would. . . .
> Passing Cape Flattery is the great event of the voyage. It
> is always rough there, from the peculiar conformation of the
> land. . . . Our captain had been sailing on this route for
> fifteen years, but said he had never seen a worse sea than
> we encountered. We asked him if he did not consider the
> Pacific a more uncertain ocean than the Atlantic. At first he
> said "Yes"; then, "No, it is pretty certain to be bad here at
> all times."
> We expected to sail on the water; but our vessel drove
> through it, just as I have seen the snow plough drive through
> the great drifts after a storm. Going to sea on a steamer gives
> no idea of the wind and waves—the real life of the ocean—
> compared to what we get on a sailing vessel. Every time
> we tried to round the point great walls of waves advanced
> against us, so powerful and defiant-looking, that I could only
> shut my eyes when they drew near. . . .
> Finally . . . the captain announced that we had made the
> point, but we could get no farther until the wind changed;
> and while we still felt the fury of the contrary sea, it was
> hard to recognize that we had much to be grateful for. We
> saw one beautiful sight, though, a vessel going home, helped

by the wind that hindered us. It was at night, and the light struck up on her dark sails, and made them look like wings as she flew over the water. What bliss it seemed to be nearing home, and all things in her favor.

I could hear all about us a heavy sound like surf on the shore, which was quite incomprehensible, as we were so far from land. But the water drove us from the deck. The vessel plunged head foremost and reeled from side to side with terrible groaning and straining. If we attempted to move we were violently thrown in one direction or another, and finally found that all we could do was lie still on the cabin floor, holding fast to anything stationary that we could reach. We could hear the water sweeping over the deck above us, and several times it poured down in great sheets upon us. We ventured to ask the captain what he was attempting to do. "Get out to sea," he said, "out of the reach of storms." . . .

One of the sailors was a Russian serf, running away, as he said, from the Czar of Russia, not wholly believing in the safety of the serfs. He had shipped as a competent seaman but when he was sent up to the top of the mizzen-mast to fix the halliards for a signal, he stopped in the more perilous place and announced that he could not go any farther. It seems that every man on board was a stranger to the captain. It filled us with anxiety to think how much depended on that one man. One night there was an alarm of "Man overboard!" If it had been the captain, how aimlessly we should have drifted on! I liked to listen when we were below to hear the men hoisting the sails and shouting together. It sounded as if they were managing horses, now restraining them, now cheering them on. When the captain put his hand on the helm, we could always tell below. There was as much difference as in driving. In the midst of the wildest plunging, he would suddenly quiet it by putting the vessel in some other position, just as he would have held in a rearing horse. . . .

At length, one night, as I lay looking up through our little skylight at the flapping of the great white spanker-sheet, my special enemy and dread, because the captain would keep it up when I thought it unsafe, it seemed such a lawless thing and so ready to overturn us everytime it shifted—a great cheerful star looked in. It meant that all our trouble was over. One after another followed it. I could not speak I was so glad. I could only look at them and feel that our safety was assured. The wind had changed.

Not all the lumber ships made it. Some were broken on the beaches, some foundered within sight of the ports where they sought safety, others simply disappeared. Here is an account written by Captain Frederick Masher of the bark *Atalanta*, which went down fifty miles off Cape Flattery on December 16, 1890:

We left the mill at Port Gamble in tow of the tug *Tyee*. All went well until I put sail on off Flattery; the vessel then began taking water, but, being lumber-laden, I did not think it worth while to go back. We got down as far as the mouth of the Columbia, and the wind shifted from northwest to southwest, with snow squalls, and it was then that the forty years that the *Atalanta* had been afloat told on her. The sails all blew away on the night of the thirteenth, and soon after the heavy deck load of eighty-foot timbers broke adrift, and on the morning of the fourteenth the fore and main mast went by the board, the foremast smashing the longboat, destroying our means of leaving the vessel. The seas were washing over us fore and aft at the time, and, as we had been many hours without food, I went to what was left of our cabin and found a can of tomatoes and one of peaches. From these each man was given a mouthful to relieve his thirst. About noon of the fourteenth the vessel commenced to break up, and about 3 p.m. she parted just abaft the main hatch, leaving fourteen of us on the after-house, with nothing to eat or drink, the two cans having been lost in the excitement. Night began to set in, and a night in the month of December off Vancouver Island is a long one, even when one is comfortably situated. The mizzenmast went shortly after daylight and took nearly one-half of our limited raft. Through all that day and the next night the sea was making a clean breach over us, but on the morning of the sixteenth we sighted land, which was a relief even though it was far away. The steward, John W. Wilburn, became temporarily insane at noon on the sixteenth, the first officer's leg was broken, and all hands were inclined to feel despondent. We had full made up our minds that we would either be dead or ashore before morning, as we were all very badly chilled. The sailors exchanged addresses in case any should get ashore, and in this way we passed the longest night I have ever experienced. When morning came we we were still afloat, but few of the men could speak on account of thirst and cold. The rudder had become jammed with a lot of the deck load, forming quite a raft, and, as our house was breaking off piece by piece, John Anderson, the second mate, and four men went to it so as to make room for us on the house. They had hardly crawled on the timber before it parted from the rest of the wreckage, and we drifted away from each other at 8 a.m., and by a singular coincidence we both came together again at 5 p.m. in an eddy that sent us directly on shore, and we landed within 200 yards of each other in Clayoquot Sound, having drifted 170 miles on the raft in four days and four nights, in the month of December, without losing a life. The Indians were very kind to us, and we were taken to Victoria by the sealing schooner *Katherine*.

vi

In 1862 Captain J. P. Keller, who had managed the mill at Port Gamble for Pope and Talbot since bringing the equipment around the Horn in the *Foster*, died unexpectedly. The partners offered the manager's position to Cyrus Walker. He refused it, explaining that he was really just passing through, didn't intend to stay, was just there to learn the business. They then offered him a chance to buy a one-tenth interest in Puget Mills. Walker, who had watched the valuation of the enterprise rise from thirty thousand dollars to three hundred thousand dollars in eight years, realized that here at last was his coveted fifty thousand. He accepted. For the next half-century his was a decisive voice in the Northwest lumber business.

It was a time of corporate expansion, of the swallowing of the weak by the strong, and Puget Mills, with the backing of Pope and Talbot's Eastern and California capital, was the biggest fish in the Puget Sound pond. In 1870 Walker built a new mill, known as Number Two, to replace the little one he had helped raise in 1853. That boosted plant capacity at Port Gamble to 160,000 feet daily.

In 1877 Puget Mills acquired a bankrupt mill at Utsaladdy on the tip of Camano Island, north of Port Gamble. The mill had specialized in spars and continued to shape them for the navies of France, Spain, and Great Britain, but Walker also installed a headrig capable of cutting seventy-five thousand feet. Daily potential now totaled 235,000 feet.

The following year Puget Mills bought out the mill at Port Ludlow, just across the canal on the peninsula proper—the mill site Walker and Talbot had so admired in the summer of 1853. They tore down the old mill and put up a huge new one, 65 by 394 feet, capable of turning out a hundred thousand feet daily. And that meant a potential of 335,000 feet, plus lath and spars.

Walker's unique contribution to logging policy during this period was his decision to acquire but not cut stumpage. Other operators of the day harvested land as soon as they bought it. Not Walker. He bought sawlogs from gyppos,[8] as the independent contractors are called, but when he bought land it went "into the icechest" to await a day of higher

[8] The term "gyppo" in logging is believed to have been derived from "gypsy," applied to the independents because they moved from place to place. It has no opprobrious connotation.

prices for lumber. Some old-timers say that Walker simply could not bring himself to harvest his own lands in the wasteful manner of the day—cutting only the best trees, cutting high stumps, smashing up the seedlings, and leaving the area a firetrap of slash.

With the Pope and Talbot bankrolls behind him, Walker was able to buy stumpage in large chunks and, except for one big block along the Chehalis River in southwest Washington, always on tidewater. The first big purchase was made in 1861, before Walker took over. The commissioner administering the lands received by the University of Washington, a land-grant college, from the federal government, put some stumpage on sale. Puget Mills took 15,260 acres at $1.50 an acre.

Until 1863 the government would accept military scrip, which had been used in payments to army veterans and was heavily discounted, at its face value when applied to the purchase of land in the public domain. Walker bought scrip and used it to acquire another seventeen thousand acres.

Captains of the company's cruisers, whose business carried them to all points on the sound, were instructed to keep their eyes open for available tracts. And they certainly did. By the time the company tapered off in its buying, around 1892, Puget Mills owned 186,000 acres of timberland, with more than 1,500,000,000 feet of timber.

Part, but by no means most, of this land was acquired under the Timber and Stone Act of 1878, which permitted "any citizen or person who has made a declaration of his intention of becoming a citizen" to buy 160 acres of timberland at $2.50 an acre. On Puget Sound the practice was for millowners to march platoons of sailors from the lumber vessels into the woods to claim 160 acres, which the sailors immediately sold to the company. An anecdote of the era tells of rival millowners studying a map of Puget Sound, lined for miles with the shallow waterfront holdings of Puget Mills.

"Why don't they *ever* buy land back from the water?" someone asked.

And a rival agent said, "Because Cy Walker's afraid them sailors would get lost."

vii

The late 1870s and early 1880s were a time of low prices and overproduction in lumber. For several years Walker accepted for Puget Mills a subsidy of nine hundred dollars a month offered by an association of rival millowners to keep the Port Ludlow mill idle. During this period the town was desolate. Henry Hall, a shipwright who had lived there in the seventies, returned for a visit in November 1881, and penciled in his notebook: "This town consists of a store; a sawmill which has been 4 years in building and has not been started yet; a hotel, the Phoenix, of which I am the only guest, and which only lodges its guests; a cook house, run by China-men, at which meals are obtained; a few cabins for the work-men in the shipyard; two or three houses; and the shipyard. A lonely place." But within a decade the town became the lumber capital of the world.

In 1885, after a long courtship, Cyrus Walker married Emily Foster Talbot, one of the daughters of one of his bosses, and brought her, amid much welcoming commotion, to reign in the manager's house at Port Gamble. The house burned down soon after, and Walker ordered built in Port Ludlow a new establishment, fit for a king—or anyway for a lumber baron— a house he called the Admiralty and which local residents saluted as "the biggest damn cabin on the sound."

The Admiralty was built of the best Douglas fir and western

red cedar, and lots of it. It was about a block long, three stories high, and on top was a cupola and on top of that a flagpole of Sitka spruce from which flew the biggest American flag you ever did see. A neat lawn slanted down the hill toward the town and mill, and on the lawn, under the shade of maples and elms and cedars of Lebanon brought sixteen thousand miles around the Horn in sailing ships, stood a bronze cannon, a relic of the War of 1812. On the Fourth of July the cannon was fired, and it saluted the arrival of visiting celebrities who came to Port Ludlow, as they often did, to talk business with Cyrus Walker.

They might, if times were slack, find Walker working down at the mill. It was his custom to prowl the area looking for dropped spikes and even nails, and, on finding them, to turn the trophy over to a foreman with a stern lecture on economy. Archie Binns, the novelist, who was born at Port Ludlow, where his father supervised the loading of the lumber fleet, recalls in a book of memoirs, *Roaring Land*,[9] that during one dull period his father was called from the docks to help build a wooden sewer from the cookhouse:

> Father could not complain because his helper on the job was Cyrus Walker. The lean and bearded Yankee millionaire held the spikes which father whaled with a sledge hammer, swung from over his head. Father had had little experience in that kind of work and he was afraid of missing the spike and crushing his helper's hands, but Cyrus Walker seemed to have no misgivings.

But usually when visitors arrived Walker was on the dock in his best dark broadcloth, his beard combed and the pitch scrubbed off his hands, and he would walk with them up to the Admiralty. The doors of the house did not open like ordinary doors; they slid, like the doors on a boat; and the big

[9] New York: McBride, 1942.

front doors slid back to a central hall resembling a ship's saloon, with antique spindle-legged chairs on the rich red carpet. "Upstairs," says an early guidebook, "the high boards of the bedsteads reach almost to the ceiling. In each room is a marble-topped dresser. The bathrooms are as big as kitchens."

A dynasty of Chinese cooks—grandfather, father, and son —presided over the huge kitchen range at the Admiralty. Their table was said to equal that of the best San Francisco hotels; it is not recorded how they prepared Walker's favorite dishes—codfish and johnny cake, Skowhegan style. The cellar was ample, though Walker, a teetotaler and absent-minded in matters he felt unimportant, sometimes had to be prompted before he sent down for the choice libations his guests thirsted after.

When dinner was over there would be brandy and cigars and a ritual stroll in the garden, which was filled with flowers and trees brought to Port Ludlow from the seaports of the world. Then they would spend a moment on the veranda, looking down on the long mill with its white stack; the big New England houses along the waterfront; the wharf and warehouse; and out in the harbor the lumber vessels, waiting their chance at the dock, many with the Pope and Talbot pennant, others with flags representing half a dozen nations —ships, barks, barkentines, and the new workhorses of the lumber trade, the schooners, which could operate with smaller crews than the square-sailed craft, and sometimes a relic of the past, a clipper ship, ill-suited to the lumber trade but still beautiful.

They came from every seaport, and they carried the Douglas fir to exotic places. They took timbers fifty feet long, six inches square, each wrapped individually in burlap, to South Africa so Cecil Rhodes could build a grape arbor. They carried millions of feet of coarse fir to Argentina to be used as flooring on cattleships, other millions of feet of cheap core-wood to Australia for use in the mines. The brigs and brigantines loaded for the South Sea Islands, for with their square sails they could take advantage of the trade winds, make good passages, and yet be able to anchor at the small island ports, where, after discharging lumber, they picked up copra for San Francisco. The big schooners ran down to California, while the little ones carried beams for haciendas at Guaymas and Mazatlán and Topolobampo, and sometimes worked beyond the Mexican ports, running as far south as Callao, Peru, though they carried too small a cargo to show profit on such a run.

This, then, was Port Ludlow's flowering. It did not last, for the great circular saws in the headrig were chewing up the trees faster than they grew. In time the company had to dip into its vast holdings and use its own trees; then they too were gone. And after that there was nothing to do but ship away the machinery and burn the hulk of the mill so it would not be a fire hazard. The smaller houses were carted away for sale; the others were razed. The Admiralty was spared that fate; it served for a time as a hotel, then burned. The lumber ships stopped coming. Even the ferry stopped coming. About ten persons live in Ludlow now.[10] It is again, as Shipwright Hall described it in 1881, "a lonely place." But in its day Ludlow was queen of the lumber ports.

---

[10] Port Gamble, across the canal, is still in the lumber business, though the cut is greatly diminished.

4

The God Terminus

"It would seem that every community on the Sound called Puget's, on the Strait called de Fuca's, on the Harbor known as Gray's offers sacrifices of land and labor and good hard cash at the altar of the Roman god Terminus," declared the editor of the improbable Quilcene *Megaphone* in 1892. "The fervor with which men supplicate the favors of the gods of rail is most wondrous to behold and hard to comprehend."

The editor of the *Megaphone* had brought his own family of four west from Wisconsin, and then off into the Olympic wilderness, to live on the earnings of a weekly paper published in a community of fewer than a hundred people, on a creaky press driven by a waterwheel of his own designing, in a shack at the edge of the forest. But that was different. Who could question that Quilcene would have a railroad? Was it not on the right of way of the Port Townsend & Southern railway? And with thousands of tourists and businessmen passing through daily, were not many of them sure to recognize the opportunities looming everywhere on Quilcene Bay—recognize too the quiet charm of the sea in the forest, the healthful climate, the cultural opportunities, to say nothing of the restorative powers of the fecund Dabob oysters?

There was faith in the world in those days, and tidewater was alive with true believers, their hopes high and the ink not yet dry on their railroad stock. Tacoma might already be the railhead for the Northern Pacific, but that development was just the aberration of a bunch of Easterners who hadn't visited the scene. The Union Pacific would surely recognize that, where Puget Sound was concerned, "The West Side Is the Best Side." It was not even too late for the Northern Pacific, if it had learned its lesson. Tacoma, indeed!

From the seventies through the nineties you could find reason for believing anything you wanted to believe about the inevitability of a given railroad's reaching a given location. It was like betting on the races if nine out of every ten horses didn't exist. Men casually staked their small fortunes and years of their lives on hunches, on the 144-point dreams of brochure-writers, on the say-so of friends or acquaintances, or on a scrap of conversation overheard in a bar.

There was Union City, the Venice of the Pacific, on the narrow stretch of land connecting the Olympic and Kitsap peninsulas—a lovely spot, and destined, said its promoters, to be the meeting place of the Grays Harbor & Puget Sound, the Union City and Naval Station, and the Port Townsend & Southern lines, none of which ever was finished, though the Port Townsend & Southern did get some steel laid. In 1892 the Union City boom sounded loudest, for the word was out that there, definitely, the rails of the Union Pacific would meet the sea. Land sold for a thousand dollars an acre. The town's lone mill couldn't saw lumber fast enough to meet the demand for new houses. The tents of the settlers lined the shore at night, and, remarked a visitor, when they cooked their meals over fires on the beach "it seemed an army was bivouacked there, awaiting the call."

The call never came. On the very day that construction equipment arrived at Union City the Bering Brothers Bank of London, which was deeply involved in international finance, suspended payments on its obligations of twenty-one million pounds, touching off the panic of 1893. The Union Pacific failed, and railroad building shuddered to a stop. The settlers took down their tents and went away.

Union City's unrealized glories were of dimmest luster compared to those of Boston Harbor at the entrance to Budd Inlet, a radiant metropolis with a mile-long wharf, a towering smelter, a drydock, an array of sawmills, a half-dozen warehouses, and a depot big enough to accommodate the rush —all imaginary. The proprietors got as far as removing some of the forest from their dream city, and putting out pamphlets and running free excursions up from Tacoma and Seattle, and selling lots to the credulous as far removed as Tallahassee and Copenhagen—a practice from which federal authorities finally made them desist—but they never built a city or laid a rail.

Down on a Grays Harbor mudflat during this period shimmered Ocosta-by-the-Sea, another predicted site of the Northern Pacific's meeting with salt water. Ocosta was conjured up after representatives of the Tacoma & Grays Harbor line, an N. P. offshoot, had been unable to come to terms with the principal proprietor of Hoquiam concerning the land they wished to acquire for depot and dock. The railroad was more than willing to let the citizenry in on a good thing, and for that purpose organized expeditions to the promised land. A couple of big sheds had been put up and brevetted depot and warehouse. Ocosta came complete with boardwalks too, which was fortunate; otherwise some of the customers might have disappeared in the bog. And the boardwalks were shaded by cedars of considerable size, which had been sawed off and stuck in the mud. Small wonder that on the day Ocosta was offered up to colonists and speculators three hundred lots found takers.

It was a custom of the period for citizens of a community, denied the terminus they hankered after, to announce that, sure as pitch is sticky, they'd build the thing themselves. Protocol called for a gathering in the town hall, marked by energetic speeches by the town founder, by a man of the cloth who had himself acquired a few lots, and by other interested parties ad infinitum, to be followed at suitable length and on a sunny day by a combined picnic and rail-laying party, which would get approximately nowhere. After this everyone would go home and brood.

The citizens of Aberdeen, on hearing of Ocosta's good fortune, announced the customary meeting, but departed from script by actually completing a railroad. They ran a line from Aberdeen over to the track of the Tacoma & Grays Harbor railway. Their rail had been retrieved from the hold of a ship that had been lost in the harbor some years previously, and it showed the effects of long submersion in water, but so did almost everything else in Grays Harbor. So Aberdeen became the terminus, and Ocosta sagged back into the mud.[1]

While one group of pioneers clung to the fancy that the Northern Pacific was impatient to push lines along the eastern shore of the peninsula, another envisioned the Union Pacific as awaiting only the proper moment to begin the even more difficult task of stretching steel across the western shoulder of the mountains to Sequim or Sekiu or Pysht or Whiskey Flat or that hardy perennial, Port Angeles.

[1] Once, as a cub reporter, I referred to Ocosta as a ghost town. There were at the time 157 persons living in the vicinity of that chimerical metropolis, most of whom were given to writing long letters of extreme directness, dealing with the questions of my ancestry, my judgment, and my concern for fact.

There is a bouquet to Port Angeles' promoters sometimes lacking in those of other peninsula communities, who all too often appear to have been motivated by something akin to self-interest and common sense. After the death of Victor Smith and the subsequent departure of the Treasury men, nothing much happened in the town until 1887, when it was selected as the headquarters for utopia. The Puget Sound Cooperative Colony, which was capitalized for one million mostly theoretical dollars, was thought up by a New York State judge, Peter Peyto Good, who wanted it to be the forerunner of a society untainted by capitalism. Good died before the colony got out of the dream stage, but his work was carried on by a friend, George Venable Smith, another lawyer deeply troubled by social injustice. Smith and Good had met in Seattle and discovered their common interest in bettering the lot of the working man, while they were organizing the anti-Chinese riots on Puget Sound, an endeavor that had a wide appeal for idealists of the day.

Smith and his associates raised enough money to buy fifty acres at the mouth of Ennis Creek, where, in the summer of 1887, they erected a small steam mill. With the mill they sawed lumber for the cabins of the colonists, and had enough left over to build a store, a sixty-ton sloop, and a meeting hall called Potlatch House, where they gathered to absorb culture and argue policy.

Economics interested them most deeply. They had foresworn the dollar, but they were desperate for a medium of exchange. Finally they printed scrip, which was distributed among the colonists once every three months, not strictly on the basis of need, nor on terms of absolute equality, but according to work performed. The foreman on each job had the right to reward special effort and ability with bonus hours.

The colony had a weekly paper, *Model Commonwealth,* better edited than many others in the state, and it expounded the true doctrine, scourged capitalists of varied stripe, and outraged the orthodox by reversing its column-rules in the traditional mark of editorial mourning when reporting the execution of four of the Haymarket rioters.

At its peak the colony had more than a thousand members. But in 1888 George Venable Smith, to the horror of a considerable portion of the populace, who thought they detected in the distance the rumble of the tumbrils, was elected judge of the Superior Court and retired from his position of manager. The change in leadership coincided with the pinch of hard times. The free spirits began to question one another's judgment. Although in 1889 assets were listed as $79,569 more than debits, the colony was continually strapped for cash. The cows were sold at public auction. After that there was a downhill slide to bankruptcy in 1894.

Hundreds of the colonists had come to love Port Angeles and stayed on, their hopes rising and falling with the rumors of the coming of the railroad. Most of these rumors centered around the activities of a handsome, pink-bearded surveyor, Norman R. Smith, son of Victor, heir to a tradition.

After his father's death Norman had been taken East. He went to school in Ohio. He served for a time as a page boy in Congress. He went to California and learned surveying under the redoubtable George Davidson—the same Davidson who, as a youth, had surveyed Juan de Fuca Strait. Then young Smith returned to Port Angeles.

He showed his father's energy, his father's impatience, his father's judgment, and great personal charm. He was elected mayor and, while mayor, wooed and won away Judge George Venable Smith's young wife—a marriage that rocked the community. He was sent east to try to retrieve for Port Angeles the position of port of entry, which Port Townsend had stolen back, and he returned with a government promise to rate Port Angeles as a sub-port, which was something. It was after this trip that Smith, who liked to think in terms of millions and was forgetful of his small creditors, encountered his tailor on Front Street. As the tailor approached, obviously intending to raise the subject of his bill, Smith pivoted gracefully and began an earnest conversation with a storekeeper. Timing his movements by the tailor's reflection in the store window, he managed to keep his back firmly to his creditor, who, in extremity, drew from a sheath his tailor's scissors and with a flourish trimmed off Smith's coattails.

Norman Smith was convinced that the Union Pacific would approach Port Angeles from the west, coming in between the mountain and Lake Crescent. So to gain control of the right of way he bought one iron rail, sawed it in two, and had it packed up to the pass, where he personally spiked it to the ties, becoming the proprietor of the Shortest Railroad in the World. No one ever tried to buy it from him, though.

In 1893 a railroad to connect Port Angeles with Everett was proposed. The sponsors brushed aside the objection that lying between the two ports was a lot of salt water. That, they said, could be solved by a rail ferry. But, they admitted, there was one little difficulty—money. It would help considerably if, as a token of good faith and sincere interest in the Port Angeles & Everett railroad, the people of Port Angeles, who would benefit immensely, would raise, say, $350,000. A mass meeting was held and the money pledged, with Smith making spectacular offers which some say totaled more than fifty thousand dollars. He didn't have fifty thousand dollars, nor did many of the others have the amounts they subscribed, except in land, the value of which the owners were inclined to overestimate. But it didn't matter. The railroad was never started, and no one lost the money he didn't have.

So it went, with the Oregon Railroad & Navigation not building a railroad in 1895; the East Clallam & Forks not building in 1896; and a putative syndicate of Chicago millionaires taking out a franchise and hiring a local man as engineer in 1898, but neglecting to supply him with locomotive or track.

In 1903 it was Smith's turn again. He interested Eastern capital in the Port Angeles Pacific, which was to run to Grays Harbor—incorporating the Shortest Railroad in the World as part of its track, Smith said. The company got a franchise. It got a right of way through town. It cut ties and it laid track as far as the city limits. It sent an engine—the Norman Number One, it was called—and it sent a flat-car, on which Norman Smith placed bleachers and took some fifty friends for a triumphant ride. Then it went broke. Smith hurried East, came back with a promise from an insurance company for two million dollars, and was hailed yet again as invincible. But the two million dollars never materialized, the receivers did, and Smith gave up. He moved to California, where he died in 1954, at Crescent City, not far from the reef where his father had gone down on the *Brother Jonathan*.

Smith's only peer on the peninsula, as a promoter of unbuilt railroads, was James G. Swan of Port Townsend, a vastly different type. Swan was a sort of Renaissance figure in the rain forest—scientist, author, judge, ethnologist, collector of art, collector of customs, teacher, oyster-grower, promoter, linguist, fish commissioner, diplomat, historian, deputy sheriff, admiralty lawyer, journalist, trader, artist, and representative for the Northern Pacific.

In 1848 it would have seemed easy to predict the course of Swan's life: hard work, shrewd trading, gradually accumulating wealth and respect in his native Boston, where his family had lived since before the Revolution and owned, in fact, some land the Battle of Bunker Hill had been fought on—a good life, but unexceptional. It was not at all the one he lived. Swan had been born in 1818, married in 1841, and was the father of a girl and a boy. He had read for the law and was doing well as a ship chandler. He was a grave little man with a rather thin voice, something of a scholar, it seemed; at least he always had a book thrust in the pocket of his coat. Then gold was discovered in California, and the respectable, conventional Mr. Swan sold out his shipping business, left his family, and took passage on the *Rob Roy* for San Francisco.

In 1851 Swan was working as purser on a Sacramento River steamer, the *Tehama*. One of the passengers, Captain Charles J. W. Russell, a big oyster- and clam-huckster from Willapa Harbor, just north of the Columbia, invited Swan to come north for a visit, which he did.

After spending a year with Russell, Swan went into the oyster business himself. It was mainly a matter of persuading the Indians to bring to him huge Willapa oysters, big as plates, which were put in barrels and sent to San Francisco. Success in the oyster business depended for the most part on maintaining good relations with the Indians, who pried the crop from the harbor rocks at low tide. Swan was as good a friend as the peninsula Indians ever had. He learned their language—not just the Chinook trading jargon, but the individual tongues of the varied tribes; he studied their art and their culture, viewing both with far less condescension than that shown by other observers of the period. As a Boston man with an interest in ships, he was particularly impressed with their great canoes, and though normally the writing in his journals is cool and objective, well adapted to scientific description, excitement shows through whenever he writes of the great black dugouts:

> The canoe which I had purchased was a beauty. She was *forty-six feet long* and *six feet wide*, and had thirty Indians in her when she crossed the bar at the mouth of the Bay. She was the largest canoe that had been brought from up the coast, although the Indians round Vancouver's and Queen Charlotte's islands have canoes capable of carrying one hundred warriors. These canoes are beautiful specimens of naval architecture. Formed of a single log of cedar, they present a model of which a white mechanic might well be proud.

In the summer of 1854 Swan was appointed customs collector for the coast between Willapa Harbor and Cape Flattery, a district that assured him of some exciting canoe rides. At the time there were only two white men known to be living in the entire stretch, and one of them was William O'Leary, a singularly taciturn Irishman who had holed up in a cabin beside a small stream emptying into Grays Harbor and went twenty years without speaking to anyone. Swan's district was not overburdened with customs receipts. His main function was to keep an eye on British and Russian traders, who sometimes visited the coast to trade with the Indians for sealskins, whale oil, dogfish oil, and an occasional sea-otter pelt.[2]

When Territorial Governor Isaac Stevens undertook to

---

[2] The otter herds, all but extinguished in 1840, began to reappear in the 1850s. Then professional hunters built wooden towers overlooking the kelp beds where the otters lived, and from these towers shot the otters at leisure, though recovering the bodies presented some difficulties. The herds disappeared completely, though there are recurrent rumors in the Indian villages that a pair have returned to the Hoh River area and are breeding. The otters have been protected by international treaty since 1911.

negotiate a treaty with the coastal Indians he chose Swan as an aide. On a cold, foggy February morning, Swan rode with the governor and twelve other white men to the meeting ground in a grove of trees on a bluff above the beach—site of the present town of Cosmopolis—where there had already gathered representatives of the various tribes.[3]

The negotiations broke down over the question of a reservation. Governor Stevens insisted that the Indians all retire to one reservation around Lake Quinault. Nakarty, a leader of the Chinooks, stated the case of those who refused.

"We are willing to sell our land," said Nakarty, "but we do not want to go away from our homes. Our fathers and mothers and ancestors are buried there, and by them we wish to bury our dead and be buried ourselves. We wish, therefore, each to have a place on his own land where we can live, and you may have the rest; but we can't go north among the other tribes. We are not friends and if we went together we should fight, and soon we all would be killed."

Swan felt this was a legitimate argument, and though at the time he was not able to convince the governor, a treaty providing separate reservation was negotiated the following year by Indian Agent Mike Simmons, a pioneer from Tumwater, who, though illiterate, was an authority on Indian languages and Indian customs.

In 1856 Governor Stevens became Congressman Stevens, and with him to Washington, D. C., went Swan as private secretary. While in the capital he became friends with the administrators of the Smithsonian Institution, which was then only ten years old; later he was to gather several of their most important collections. He also found time to write

[3] A census taken during the council lists the populations of the tribes of the central coast as: Lower Chehalis, 217; Upper Chehalis, 216; Quenaiults (Quinaults), 158; Chinooks, 112; and Cowlitz, 140; total, 843.

his first book, *The Northwest Coast, or Three Years' Residence in Washington Territory.*

Swan returned to the Territory in 1858 and settled in Port Townsend, thus raising its population to 531. He saw in the settlement "an inevitable New York," which was par for the course; most Puget Sound pioneers considered their communities certain to suffer in the near future the blessings of overcrowding. Seattle's pioneers referred to their first cabins as New York Alki, "Alki" being jargon for by-and-by. At Whiskey Flat, as Dungeness was then called, the saying was, "We're as big as New York, only the town ain't built yet."

In 1859 Swan became associated with a trading post at Neah Bay, where Samuel Hancock, a Virginia-born handyman, had tried unsuccessfully to establish a post in 1845. Hancock was one of the more colorful pioneers. He started west without even twenty-five cents to contribute toward the hire of a pilot for the covered-wagon train he joined, but with skill enough as wheel-maker, brick-baker, kiln-builder, and coal prospector to earn an interesting living in the Puget Sound country. He came to Neah Bay on an impulse and set himself up to trade in whale oil and otter skins, but the Makahs were not inclined to cooperate. They boycotted his store, broke his canoe, threatened his life. He spent one night crouched in his cabin with four Colt revolvers loaded and an Indian boy as hostage. The next day, according to his account in his autobiography (a book that reads in spots like fiction, and probably is), he bluffed the Makahs into tolerance by pretending to write a letter to President Millard Fillmore, tattling on them. He tore up the letter when they rebuilt his canoe. But he soon gave up on the trading post.

Swan did not fare much better. He soon abandoned trading for teaching, accepting appointment as a teacher for the Indian Service. It was a trying experience. The Makahs were suspicious of the school. They looked on it as an instrument for turning Indian children into imitation white men, which it was. The Makahs were not interested in Shakespeare or the Tudors or Latin, or even in methods of growing cotton. One of Swan's rare bursts of impatience with the Indians came when some of the Makahs asked him to pay them for sending their children to his classes.

One evening shortly after the end of the Civil War, while Swan was still on the reservation, the smoke of a steamer was observed on the horizon. Steamers were rare on the Pacific. Swan thought this might be the Confederate raider *Shenandoah*, then still at large, coming in to bombard the lighthouse on Tatoosh, or perhaps to ravage Port Townsend. He ordered the employees of the Indian Agency to run up the American flag and stand by to repel attack. The steamer entered the harbor after dark and anchored far out. The men ashore spent an anxious night until, with the dawn, they made her out to be Her Majesty's Ship *Devastation*, just in from the Queen Charlottes.[4]

In 1866 Swan returned to Port Townsend to practice law. He served seven years as probate judge, taking time out on one occasion to act as a deputy sheriff. That was when no one else wanted the assignment of arresting twenty-six Clallams who had surprised a party of Vancouver Island Indians on Dungeness spit and killed them all. Swan brought back the offenders for trial.

He also served as assistant United States Fisheries Commissioner and engaged in a loud scientific argument with

[4] Swan's worries were not unjustified. The *Shenandoah* at the time was en route from the Bering Sea, where she had destroyed a large part of the Yankee whaling fleet, to the California coast. Her captain, James Waddell, was contemplating the capture of the San Francisco–Panama mail steamer. He was also toying with the idea of capturing San Francisco and holding the town for ransom. Both projects were abandoned when he learned the war was over.

Henry Elliott over the swimming habits of seal pups. But the last thirty years of Swan's life centered on his efforts to get a railroad for Port Townsend. That endeavor proved more frustrating than teaching school at Neah Bay.

When the Northern Pacific was slowly pushing its line north from the Columbia River to Puget Sound in 1871, Swan called a meeting of Port Townsend business leaders and persuaded them to offer the railroad a large amount of local property if it would bend the line north and bring it to tidewater at Port Townsend. Any chance of that dream's coming true ended with the collapse of Jay Cooke, that flower of inflation. The N. P. terminus went to Tacoma, which was cheaper.

For nearly fifteen years Swan worked to raise the interest of editors and financiers in a railroad to Port Townsend. He sat at his desk "amidst Hydah gods and Cape Flattery devils, images in stone and wood, and implements of savage warfare," as one visitor put it, and wrote, with a stub pen dipped in purple ink, long, almost indecipherable letters on the merits of Port Townsend's harbor and the riches awaiting the sponsors of a railroad.

Local businessmen incorporated the Port Townsend Southern railroad in 1887. It was to run to Portland, and the only thing it needed to be a success was money. When no one offered to put up the money the populace, in approved fashion, started laying track themselves and laid the standard mile before giving up.

The Oregon Improvement Company, a subsidiary of the Union Pacific, agreed in 1890 to take over the franchise if Port Townsend would help out with a subsidy of a hundred thousand dollars. The gift was pungled up by popular subscription. Fifteen hundred laborers started laying track down to Hood Canal. This was the dream come true.

Port Townsend boomed. Population doubled to 3500 and doubled again. Waterfront lots sold for ten thousand dollars, and lots out of sight of water—in fact, out of reach of water—brought a thousand. Farmers who the year before had had trouble buying flour for the kitchen sold their homesteads for as much as a hundred thousand; Tom Bracken got a record $160,000 for his 160 acres. Real-estate transactions for 1890 totaled $4,594,695.93.

So was faith rewarded. And most of the old settlers promptly reinvested in Port Townsend. The ships that would come to meet the railroad would need a drydock; the inhabitants ponied up to subsidize construction of a floating drydock. A smelter had been started at nearby Irondale, and Port Townsend helped finance a rail factory that was to use its iron. The town was sure to grow to twenty thousand, and the old-timers raised sandstone warehouses and office buildings and hotels to meet the needs of the newcomers; for themselves they built on the bluff a handsome array of tall clapboard houses, capped with widows' walks.

The rails reached from Port Townsend to Quilcene before the bottom dropped out of everything. Brandon Satterlee has described how the news struck one community on the line:

It was one of those wonderful days when nature seems to cry out for all her creatures to luxuriate. Frank and I were setting type for the next issue; Father had been writing at his paper-strewn table and had arisen to fill his trusty corncob, when we heard the rumble of Telegrapher Lord's handcar. He entered the shop and handed Father a telegram with the remark, "Here's something for you, Sat, that I don't think you'll like," and immediately left. Father opened the envelope, read the message and dropped heavily in his chair. He stared at it a long time; then came over to my case. I thought I detected a note of worry in his voice as he said:

"Let me have your stick, Brandon. I'll finish this take and

you go up to Fil Hamilton's and tell him to come down here as soon as he can and bring the squire with him."

It was glad to get outside, and raced up the track like a pupil on the last day of school. I found Hamilton in his orchard and delivered my message.

He looked puzzled. "What's up, Dub?"

"I don't know," was all I could reply.

"Come out to the barn while I hitch up and you can ride back with me." On our way to the barn we stopped in the store and Fil told Squire McArdle. By the time we had the horse hitched to the buggy, he was at the barn. The men seemed to sense disaster and the trip to the office was made principally in silence.

Charley Hamilton, Lou Seitzinger and Jay Bristow were at the office when we entered. "What's up, Sat?" was Hamilton's quick greeting. He ignored the other men. Father walked over to the table and picked up the telegram. "I'm afraid this is it," he said with a sigh; then read:

"The jig is up. Reliable word reached me that Portland court today appointed receiver for O. I. Co. This kills all hope that road will be extended.—SWAN."

Frank had not stopped the rapid motions of typesetting, and the click of the type as he dropped them into the stick sounded like hammer blows in the long, deathlike silence that filled the room while the men absorbed the full import of this news. Hamilton opened his mouth in amazement, and the squire began to make the familiar nervous motion with his hands. From outside came the soothing plop, plop, plop, as each bucket of the water wheel passed under the spout of the flume and received its quota of water, and then the splash, splash, splash as it was discharged into the stream at the low point of revolution. In a madrona tree nearby a colony of crows set up a raucous scolding, while over the bay a flock of graceful, screaming gulls circled above the white sails of a yawl.

It was the comedian, Bristow, who broke the impressive silence with Len Flickinger's favorite expression, "There'll be hell poppin' an' no pitch hot." Bristow could afford to be facetious—he was the least affected.

Hamilton shot a meaningful glance at Father, and McArdle said in a low tone, "Let's go out on the beach." They went out together, and the other men, taking the hint, started up the track toward the townsite to spread the gruesome news. I picked up my composing stick where Father had laid it down when we came in. Through the window beside my case I saw three troubled men sit on a log at high-water mark. I would have given much to hear their conversation. Frequently Hamilton arose and took a few nervous steps back and forth.

When Frank filled his stick and dumped the type on the galley, he broke the silence:

"Did you hear that telegram Dad read?" he asked.

"Yes. Doesn't sound very good, does it?"

"Not a bit. Judge Swan would never send a message like that if it wasn't true. Nobody in the world wants to see the road extended more than he. . . . I wonder what will become of us."

That was in Quilcene. In Port Townsend it was even worse. The real-estate boom collapsed. Those who had become suddenly rich became suddenly bankrupt. The floating drydock was towed off to Dockton, down the sound. The machines in the nail factory were sold for junk. Cobwebs gathered in the sandstone warehouses. For a time even the brothels closed.

Judge Swan was one of those who stayed on. He still believed. He still wrote long letters in his tiny hand. In time even Port Townsend found his faith a bit funny. It was his habit to go each evening to a small restaurant near Union Dock to eat a quiet meal and read the paper. One evening a young man decided to have some fun at the Judge's expense. Taking a seat near Swan's, he launched a discussion on the economic future of Puget Sound. His central theme was that the future of Port Townsend was as nothing when compared to the possibilities of Seattle. Within a year, he predicted, no right-thinking man with a decent desire to better himself would remain in a tomb like Port Townsend unless Seattle saw fit to raise a twenty-foot fence to keep out those who would share in her inevitable wealth.

Judge Swan laid down his paper. He listened in silence to the young man's monologue. At last he rose and walked over to the table and leaned closer, as if to make certain he had heard correctly.

Then, certain no mistake had been made, he raised his heavy cane and brought it down with an echoing thump across the youth's shoulders. That attended to, he shot his cuffs, straightened his black frock coat, stroked his beard, and stalked from the restaurant with the air, said an enraptured observer, of one who has performed a meritorious deed and has done it most effectually.

Judge Swan died in 1900, still believing.

No railroad has yet been built to connect Port Angeles or Port Townsend with the transcontinental lines.

5

Home: No Place Like It

i

John Muir, who visited the Olympic Peninsula in 1889, reported with some amazement that "in these Washington wilds, living alone, all sorts of men may perchance be found—poets, philosophers, and even fullblown transcendentalists, though you may go far to find them."

He was quite right, except that the woods were so full of latter-day Thoreaus, Marxists in tin-pants, kelp-eaters, single-taxers, theoretical and practicing free lovers, and cooperators of assorted kidney that no far journey was needed to locate them. Nor were they all lonely spirits; they had a tendency to swarm. Besides the hive of free spirits in the Puget Sound Co-operative Colony at Port Angeles there were, around the turn of the century, an odd lot of egalitarians at Equality in the tall timber of Skagit County; some Edward Bellamy socialists attempting to live by the book at Glennis, near Tacoma; and a contingent of cooperators on Burley Lagoon, who supported themselves by cutting cordwood and rolling cigars. But it is generally agreed that in all the wilds, and perhaps in all the world, there was really no place like Home.

Home was different not because it was utopian—for a

time you could hardly fell a tree without waking some dreamer—but because it was not doctrinaire. Home was a backwoods Greenwich Village, where, intellectually at least, everything went. Outsiders came to refer to Home as a colony of anarchists, or—to catch the exact flavor of many editorial references to the community—"a festering nest of poisonous anarchists." The colonists themselves, while disagreeing with this judgment, never could get together on what they represented politically. This failure was not from want of effort; they gave the matter considerable thought.

Probably the best expression of the town's opinion of its purpose came in an editorial written by the last publisher of its weekly paper, a remarkable organ which in various incarnations went under the names *New Era, Discontent—Mother of Progress, The Demonstrator,* and *The Agitator.* This editorial brought its writer to the outraged attention of the prosecuting attorney of Pierce County and led in time to the collapse of the colony. It was a plea for tolerance and it began: "Home is a community of free spirits who came into the woods to escape the polluted atmosphere of priest-ridden conventional society. . . ."

The first of Home's free spirits were refugees not from conventional society but from an experiment in socialism. In 1895 there had been founded at Glennis a colony to put into practice the ideas advanced by Edward Bellamy in his best-selling *Looking Backward.* Either something was missing in Bellamy's how-to-do-it, or the people involved weren't up to being characters in a novel. After less than two years, Glennis went broke.

Die-hard Bellamists could point out that times were tough all over. More orthodox communities were also going bankrupt. But, looking back on their experiment, some of the colonists concluded the root of their troubles had been in the Glennis charter: it had been too rigid. Three men—George Allen, O. A. Verity, and F. F. O'dell—decided it would be pleasant to live in a community where the only requirement was that a man respect the right of others to do and think as they pleased. To live so, they reasoned, it would be necessary to get away from the big cities. They had seen the polluting influence of capitalistic—though broke—Tacoma on the good socialists of Glennis. Better to be by themselves.

So they built a rowboat and scouted the shores of the Olympic Peninsula, seeking a place remote enough to bring out the best in their people. They found a remote and uninhabited spot at Joe's Bay on Von Geldred Cove, twenty miles up sound from Tacoma. A depressed speculator, tired of waiting for the real-estate operators' millennium, was willing to unload twenty-six acres on the free spirits at $2.50 an acre. The only difficulty was that their economic education at Glennis had left the trio without even sixty-five dollars. They set out to earn it. Allen, an honors graduate of Toronto University, taught school, while his companions exploited the natural resources of the area, digging clams and cutting cordwood and peddling the products to the bourgeois enemy. By the spring of 1897 they were in a position to become landowners themselves, and they drew up the Compact of the Mutual Home Colony Association.

There was some question about how much land each colonist might use. They settled it scientifically—sort of. They wrote to the Department of Agriculture, asking the number of acres under cultivation in the United States and the number of families in the United States. Dividing acreage by families, they got the figure of one and three-fourths acres. The average American family, they felt, did not live very well off this amount of land, but that was probably the fault of the System. With a Rule of Liberty, two acres should be enough for anyone.

To become a member of the colony a settler had only to pay the treasurer a sum equal to the cost of the land he selected. Not less than one acre nor more than two acres went to a member. The land remained the property of the association, but the member could occupy it indefinitely by paying the taxes. All certificates of membership were to be held for life and, at death, were to be willed. Improvements were considered personal property and might be sold or mortgaged. No officer of the association could contract debts in the name of the association (oh, bitter, bitter Glennis!).

These were all the restrictions imposed on the colonists— except that each was to remember the rule of tolerance. The founding fathers considered even these few thou-shalt-nots to be necessary evils, a sort of decompression chamber between life under capitalist pressures and the expansive existence dreamed of, when all confining conventions would shrivel up and blow away.

ii

In June 1897 Founding Father Verity published the first issue of Home's first paper, *New Era*. The paper was printed on a portable press with a shirttailful of type that Verity had bought for five dollars in a Tacoma second-hand store. It was written not to tell the colonists about the world but to tell the world about the colony. Subscriptions were announced as costing a dollar a year, but there were few paid subscribers; copies went free to every free-thinker whose address the editor could discover. Just as the capitalist press in Tacoma and Seattle sounded the praises of the material advantages of life on Puget Sound, *New Era* thumped the tubs for Home's spiritual advantages:

> Liberty we have, so far as *we* are concerned, but the laws of the state—of course—the ever-present thorn in the flesh—are the great barriers to the realization of Liberty. Now, one may at Home keep within the pale of the law or totally ignore it, just as he pleases. Most of us prefer the latter course and teach others to do the same.

In a subsequent editorial Verity went into a bit more detail about one of the liberties he had in mind: "The love principle of our being is a natural one and to deny it expression is to deny Nature."

This attracted the attention not only of postal authorities, who for the moment did not act, but of a number of passionate lovers of liberty, who did. Population grew. Radical circles throughout the land began to talk of the new colony in the western wilderness, the self-styled "oasis of freedom in the desert of convention." The libertarian promises of *New Era* appealed to radicals and satyrs, intellectuals and incompetents, reformers and ruffians, and to some who were simply curious.

One of the first to be tolled by Verity's hand-set lure was a tramp printer named Charles Goven, a product of Atlanta. Goven came across a copy of *New Era* in a Barbary Coast saloon, and, he said, as he read it he felt life take a new shape. A hard-drinking type, he felt an inner assurance that Home would be just the place for him to abandon alcohol; one look at New Era's typography—four pages, three columns—convinced him that the town needed a professional printer. Goven showed the publication to a Barbary Coast crony, James F. Morton, Jr., a Phi Beta Kappa from Harvard, grandson of the man who wrote the song "My Country 'Tis of Thee," and a newspaperman himself. Morton, who wrote editorials for anarchist publications, was as unimpressed by Verity's prose as Goven was by his printing. *New Era* needed them, so, deserting the beauties of life in San Francisco, they started north.

By the time Goven and Morton came ashore at Joe's Bay, *New Era* was dead, the victim of a lack of funds. They revived it under a new name. On May 11, 1898, they drew from the old flatbed press the first issue of *Discontent—Mother of Progress.* Judging from the first issue, they were most discontented about the current state of sex. They took up such burning questions as "Is sin forgivable?" (yes); "Is it possible for two women to live happily with one man?" (yes); and "Do women have the same rights as men in sexual relations?" (yes).

The San Francisco editorial contingent was soon reinforced by a pair of free-lances from Portland, Henry Addis and Abner Pope, editor and contributor to the *Firebrand,* which had lost the privilege of going through the United States mail. Both men had been tried for defiling the mails with obscenity. Addis had been convicted, appealed the conviction, and won. Pope, who called himself a Quaker, spiritualist, and anarchist, and who at seventy-four was an enthusiastic though perhaps only theoretical supporter of free love, refused to have anything to do with such state-inspired devices as court appeals. He felt that an appeal recognized the right of the state to put him on trial. He just didn't believe in government, Pope told the judge sweetly—wouldn't have anything to do with it. He did four months.

Pope and Addis both became contributors to *Discontent.* Pope wrote for the most part about the enchantments of anarchy, and he was pretty dull; Addis remained preoccupied with birds and bees, boys and girls. In some of his milder periods he referred to monogamy as the worst of all forms of prostitution, to the church as the mother of whores, and to men of the cloth as the pimps of puritanism.

Discontent's passion for Topic A did not seem to diminish its appeal. By 1900, when Home's population was seventy-five, including thirty schoolchildren, the paper had a circulation of twelve hundred and claimed subscribers in every state. One of its more enthusiastic readers was Emma Goldman, the best-known anarchist of the day, a gentle advocate of violence as a means of achieving serenity. The blond and blue-eyed Miss Goldman gave the editors of *Discontent* permission to publish one of her essays on free love. In it she blamed organized religion for prostitution.

Later Emma came in person to lecture in Liberty Hall on what was announced as "subjects of general interest." The idea was getting around that Home was a hotbed of sin as well as anarchy. Though the colonists never gave their neighbors any trouble, the neighbors suspected it might be because, after putting first things first, they simply lacked the energy.

iii

On September 6, 1901, President William McKinley was shot in the abdomen by a young man named Leon Czolgosz, who was immediately captured. He was quoted as saying he had shot McKinley because he believed that people who wielded political power should be killed. This was a position attributed to anarchists. Home was considered to be anarchist. Home was in trouble.

For several days McKinley seemed to be recovering. On September 14 he abruptly died, and the shock was great. That night, as a sort of memorial for McKinley, an anti-anarchist mass meeting was held in Custer Post Hall in Tacoma.

Veterans of the Grand Army of the Republic formed a Loyalty League.

Two days later the Loyalty League gathered again. A Vigilance Committee was assigned to investigate Home, which was described as "the nest that housed the viper, Emma Goldman." The free spirits of the colony, who up to that time had never had one of their residents in jail, were accused of every crime from murder to arson, and of practices ranging from rampant vegetarianism to keeping community wives and denying Holy Writ.

The *Ledger* carried a story saying the Vigilance Committee might find it necessary to charter a steamboat, load it with men, and raid Home. There were those who felt that only by driving the colonists into the brush and burning the town could the citizens of Puget Sound be saved from the fate of the martyred McKinley.

Ed Lorenz, the skipper of a paddlewheeler that served Home and other hamlets along the upper sound, brought the warning to the colony that a raid was in prospect. The bell at Liberty Hall tolled, calling all individualists to a mass meeting to discuss the common danger. The anarchists decided on non-resistance. Lorenz, accompanied by a Civil War veteran then in residence at the colony, returned to Tacoma to try to talk the Vigilance Committee into observing the laws of the land.

The Reverend J. F. Doescher, pastor of the German Evangelical Trinity Church in Tacoma, decided to see for himself what was going on at the colony. He stayed two days and preached in Liberty Hall. When he got back to Tacoma he hurried to the offices of the *Ledger*, buttonholed the editor, and demanded to be interviewed.

"They have made clearings, planted orchards, and made gardens," the divine told the editor. "The people are sober, industrious, and friendly. Their neighbors give them good witness. They are better citizens by far than those who have been shouting 'Exterminate the vipers.' "

The raid was called off. But a few weeks later a United States marshal was sent to Home to arrest Goven and two of his assistants on charges of "depositing obscene matters in the United States mails."

Home heard he was coming and decided to give non-resistance another try. When the marshal strode down the gangplank he was met by a welcoming committee complete with flower girls. The embarrassed officer was escorted to the best house in town. Pretty girls served him a five-course dinner, with ice cream. He was led to Liberty Hall as the guest of honor at an all-colony dance. The next morning, though, he took his three prisoners back to Tacoma.

The trial was held on March 11, 1902, and it was brief. After listening to presentation of the government's case, Federal Judge Hanford ordered the jury to return a verdict of not guilty.

Though the federal government had lost its criminal case against Home and *Discontent*, the authorities still had power to punish the community and the editor. In April the Post-master General took away Home's post office. A month later he ordered cancellation of mailing privileges for *Discontent* —*Mother of Progress*.

There was nothing for Goven to do but suspend publication.

iv

Home was not long without an editorial champion. *Discontent* rose, phoenix-like, from the ashes of censorship. She looked much the same, which is not surprising, since she was printed on the same press by the same people. She read much the same too, which isn't surprising, for Goven and Morton were still at the editor's desk. But now Morton was listed as publisher, Goven as printer, and the paper was named *The Demonstrator*.

In spite of its troubles, and perhaps in spite of its press, Home continued to grow. There were 107 inhabitants now. Nine houses in town had organs. There was still no saloon or jail or church, but there was a Home Colony baseball team ("Root for the Home team," the slogan went), and there were a debating society and a band and classes in pencil drawing and water color and Esperanto and Haha-Yoga and German and flower culture and spiritualism.

Cash was flowing into the community, too. An orchard of seven hundred trees was planted on the tableland behind Joe's Bay. The men sawed wood and sold cords to the wood-burning steamers that plied the sound; Home was a port of call for a dozen boats. The women and children picked huckleberries in season and sold them in Tacoma.

Liberty Hall burned down, and a new and larger community center was built and named, without particular appropriateness, Harmony Hall. It was two stories high. The *Demonstrator* was given free space on the ground floor. Upstairs there were meetings almost nightly as the colonists discussed diet, literature, free love, free silver, anarchism, spiritualism, bimetalism, phrenology, communism, and just plain sex. This made for easy reporting. There are accounts that describe Goven standing by the type-case, cocking an ear, and composing his story on the type-stick as the debate roared on above.

Equally interested in the debates was the butcher, who had to be alert for trends among his customers. Effective

speakers started fads. Let someone come out eloquently
enough against meat, and the butcher found himself stuck
with half a hog and a side of beef. Or a plea for an all-carrot
and no-peanuts diet might convince the customer who had
been living on nothing but calves' brains. The poor butcher
would arrange to ship his surplus meat to Tacoma, and then
along would come an apostle of raw beef and he'd be caught
short. Other speakers advocated fasting. It was enough to
drive a man mad, and it did; the butcher ended his days in
the state mental hospital.

Anyone was allowed to hold forth in Harmony Hall. Big
Bill Haywood came to town after his acquittal on charges
of murder. Elbert Hubbard spoke there and approved Home
in an essay in *The Philistine*. Harry Kemp recited his poems
from the stage and made up an "Ode to Liberty," long since
lost to history. Present too were disciples of Dr. Cyrus Teed,
an astronomer of sorts, who preached that the earth is a
hollow ball, with us inside.

Another visitor was Moses Harmon, editor of *Lucifer,* a
publication devoted to a discussion of marriage in terms offen-
sive to the constituted authorities of several states. Harmon
spoke out against "so-called legal and holy marriages" and
urged understanding of "the imperative of marital unfaithful-
ness, if we are to be redeemed."

If the males who mounted the platform in Harmony Hall
seemed an odd lot, the women were their equals. There was
the Lady of Mystery, who gave no name but dropped hints
that Count Tolstoi had given her a chalet. She was a vege-
tarian. Her neckpiece was made of ostrich plumes dyed to
resemble fur. She wore rings with the royal crests of five
sovereigns, and she left town quietly, her bills unpaid. There
was Elizabeth Gurley Flynn, the handsome Lady Wobbly,

who later led the I. W. W. free-speech fight in Spokane, the one in which the Wobs perfected their technique of violating anti-free-speech laws so overwhelmingly that the jails could not hold all the prisoners.

Some of the ladies were right out of a textbook on psychology—for example, Lois Waisbrooker. In October 1903 the Burley *Co-Operator,* house organ of the nearest non-philistine settlement, reported a visit of a good-will delegation to Home, and remarked that "an address was given by Lois Waisbrooker, who dwelt upon the necessity for the absolute freedom of women, economically and personally, before the race can make any further progress."

There is no detailed account of Miss Waisbrooker's dwelling upon the necessity, which is a pity, for she developed a full head of steam where discussion of sex was concerned. She had published a pamphlet on the subject. It was called *How to Free the Earth of the Sex Disease.* She and an associate, Mattie Penhallow—herself a former postmistress at Home —had emitted a periodical called *Clothed with the Sun,* which the Postmaster General felt was too hot for his men to handle. After that Miss Waisbrooker offered her ideas on the subject to the *Demonstrator.* Morton ran a note in the paper, saying he had been forced to reject Lois's contribution as "not in good taste," which, everything considered, was quite a tribute.

Morton by this time was developing interest in topics other than mating patterns. He had, in fact, discovered a new cure-all, the single tax. He was so enthusiastic that he packed his Gladstone and left for New York to help Henry George, who was running for mayor. George didn't make it, and, without Morton's relatively steady hand, neither did the *Demonstrator.* It ceased publication in May 1906.

v

Henry Dadisman, an elderly Virginian, bought two hundred acres adjoining Home in 1908. As soon as he was sure he approved of his neighbors he opened his land to the settlers on the two-fifty-an-acre terms of the association. Among the newcomers were a number of Dukhobors, fresh from Russia. Not even Home had ever seen anything like them.

At this stage the Dukhobors had not perfected the strip tease as a method of political protest. They did take an old Georgian delight in nude bathing. And they were accustomed to disrobing at home before starting for the beach. You could never be sure when you'd meet a bare Dukh en route to or from a dip in the chill waters of the sound. Most of the residents of the colony quickly adjusted to this new factor in their environment, and some free spirits took up the custom themselves. But a few held out. On this rock the colony split.

Among the immigrants to Home during this period was Jay Fox, no Dukhobor but a professing anarchist. Fox was a tall, lean agitator from Chicago. He had been present at the Haymarket Riot, and he carried in his shoulder a bullet from the McCormick Harvesting Machine strike. He was a newspaperman by trade and he revived the paper, this time under the name of *The Agitator*.

In his maiden issue Jay Fox promised to advocate "the modern school, industrial unionism, and individual freedom." He was as good as his editorial word. *The Agitator* stirred things up on behalf of literature, the graphic arts, and education, free trade and bimetallism and faith healing. But an editorial on a local topic attracted most attention.

Home had expanded until it almost touched the neighboring community of Lake Bay. Residents of Lake Bay had long prided themselves on being unlike residents of Home. They were farmer folk, and they did not want to rub shoulders with anarchists, particularly if the anarchists' shoulders were bare. They took to complaining to the constable whenever they encountered one of the Dukhobors clad only in goosepimples.

This in turn outraged the free spirits, who did not agree that freedom to go without seeing other people naked was a right to be cherished. Relations between the two communities relaxed a little during the winter, when not even the Dukhs felt much like nude bathing. But about the time the first trilliums pushed up through the fallen alder leaves four residents of the colony, two women and two men, were brought before Justice of the Peace Tom Larkin in Lake Bay on charges of indecent exposure.

The trial was short, and it revealed the horrifying fact that the complaints had been filed not by the bourgeois oafs at Lake Bay, who might be excused on the grounds that they knew no better, but by residents of Home. This was treason. Those who had turned the watchdogs of the state upon their bath-loving neighbors were obviously against the Home way of life. Fox said as much in an editorial:

THE NUDE AND THE PRUDES

Home is a community of free spirits, who came out into the woods to escape the polluted atmosphere of priest-ridden conventional society. One of the liberties enjoyed by Home-ites was the privilege to bathe in evening dress, or with merely the clothes nature gave them, just as they chose.

No one went rubbernecking to see which suit a person wore, who sought the purifying waters of the bay. Surely it was nobody's business. All were sufficiently pure minded to see no vulgarity, no suggestion of anything vile or indecent in the thought of nature's masterpiece uncovered.

But eventually a few prudes got into the community and proceeded in the brutal, unneighborly way of the outside world to suppress the people's freedom. . . .

Fox went on to suggest that the only thing Home could not tolerate was intolerance. He called on the good, old-fashioned, liberty-loving colonists to boycott anyone who summoned the constable to arrest a nude neighbor.

Under ordinary circumstances Fox's essay would have caused little stir, but times were far from normal, even for Home. The outside world was intruding evermore on the gentle anarchists. The community could not agree on how to handle its foreign relations. Some felt that Home could best retain independence by ignoring the philistines; others thought it might be well to put on a show of conforming; and some felt Home should do everything possible to attract attention to itself as an island of liberty in a despotic sea. The discussions in Harmony Hall were bitter.

The winter of 1910–1911 was a winter of violence. The Los Angeles *Times* was strikebound. In September an explosion and fire wrecked the plant, killing four men. Anarchists were blamed for the dynamiting, and Home was suspected of harboring the men who had planted the bomb.

Among the visitors to the community during the winter were assorted agents of the William J. Burns Detective Agency, complete with false mustaches. Burns himself showed up, disguised as an atlas-peddler. Their visits to Home produced little more than routine reports, but the Burns organization did manage to break the case. They picked up Joe and Jim McNamara, officers of the Structural Iron Workers Union, who, to the consternation of their supporters, eventually confessed to the bombing.

The manhunt went on for two members of McNamara's band, David Caplan and Matthew Schmidt, who had helped the brothers pick up the dynamite. Here Home became directly involved. Caplan had lived for a time at the colony, and Schmidt was arrested in New York on a tip given the

Burns people by Donald Vose, the son of Gertrude Vose, a resident of Home.

All this did nothing to underwrite Home's reputation as a community of philosophic agriculturalists busily not minding one another's business. Nor did it lessen the intramural clamor. The bitterness of the period echoes in memoirs published by Detective Burns and Anarchist Goldman.

Burns's picture of Home Colony is contained in his book with the nonstop title *The Masked War: The Story of a Peril that Threatened the United States, by the Man Who Uncovered the Dynamite Conspirators and Sent Them to Jail.*[1] The detective was not a man to underestimate the danger from which he had saved the Republic:

> Home Colony is the nest of Anarchy in the United States. There are about 1200 of them living there without regard for a single decent thing in life. They exist in a state of free love, are notoriously unfaithful to the mates thus chosen, and are so crooked that even in this class of rogues there does not seem to be any hint of honor.
>
> The colony did have a post office, but when McKinley was assassinated the people of this community gave a celebration of the event ending in a debauch. The government took the post office away from them. They do share, however, in rural free delivery. . . .
>
> Jay and Esther Fox (are) publishers of the *Agitator.* Agent reported: "I ascertained from my landlady that . . . Fox is a free lover; the woman with him is a Jewess. They have two children—a girl about fourteen and a boy about twelve. The children I became acquainted with at my boarding house. They were soliciting subscriptions for the paper edited by their father. I purchased a copy . . ."

Emma Goldman, in *her* autobiography, *Living My Life,*[2] selected a far different cast of villains:

[1] New York: George H. Doran, 1913.
[2] New York: Knopf, 1931.

Matthew Schmidt had been sacrificed to the vengeance of the Merchants' and Manufacturers' Association, the Los Angeles *Times* and the State of California. One of the main witnesses against him was Donald Vose. In open court, face to face with his victim, he admitted being in the employ of Detective William J. Burns. . . .

There was no more reason for withholding the publication of what I considered Donald Vose's perfidy. The January 16 issue of *Mother Earth* contained the too-long-delayed article about him. Gertie Vose stood by her son. I understood the maternal feeling, but in my estimation it did not excuse a rebel of thirty years' standing. I never wanted to see her again.

It was against this background that Fox's editorial on "The Nude and the Prudes" appeared. His plea for tolerance was interpreted as an appeal to anarchy, a call for citizens to defy the laws of the land. So interpreted, it was called to the attention of the prosecuting attorney, who was also shown statistics indicating that there had been a two-hundred-percent increase in arrests for nude bathing in the months following publication of the editorial—the summer months.

Four months to the day after Fox had polished off the prudes editorially, Deputy Sheriff J. M. Tillman, a former resident of the colony, informed the editor that he was under arrest for "tending to encourage or advocate disrespect for law or for a court of justice."

vi

The trial of Jay Fox began on November 2, 1911, in the oak-paneled courtroom of Superior Judge William O. Chapman in the Pierce County Courthouse.

The prosecution's case was handled by two young deputy prosecutors, A. O. Burmeister and W. G. Nolte (both still practicing law in Tacoma in 1955). Their case was simple. They claimed that the editorial, on its face, tended to encourage disrespect for the law, and had actually resulted in more persons strolling starkly across the clam-beach, to the embarrassment of their moral betters and in defiance of state law.

Fox's defense was entrusted to Colonel J. J. Anderson, a Populist orator who had a way with the juries of his day. Anderson's first line of defense was that the state law against abuse of the rights of free speech and free press was unconstitutional. Judge Chapman overruled Anderson. The defense then entered a demurrer which argued that the editorial did not in fact tend to advocate disrespect of law. The judge recessed the case for several weeks and then ruled:

> There is a difference between moral laws and policy laws. Moral laws are the very fiber of the nation. . . . [They] are the fundamental laws based on man's belief in a Deity and are like the axioms of mathematics which must be accepted. . . . Such laws are not subject to attack. An article advocating the putting aside of all restraint would be seditious and the writer should be punished.

Judge Chapman said it was up to the jury to determine whether the editorial did indeed tend to encourage disrespect of moral law. If so, Fox was guilty of a crime.

The trial came to a close on January 11, 1912. The courtroom was packed with people from Home, and with Tacomans who had turned out to look at the Home folks. In the state's closing arguments young Burmeister told the jurors:

> You cannot uncover yourself, although beautiful in form and shape (a glance at the two women members), in the presence of the court. . . .
>
> Remember that Fox said, "The well-merited indignation of the people has been aroused." Of what people? The law-

and-order faction—this conventional society faction of yours and mine? No! These people who believe it is man's right to commit incest, robbery, rape and so forth, if he wants to in that community.

Anderson pointed out for the defense that there never had been an arrest for incest, robbery, or rape in Home. Then he called for Basic American Fair Play:

> Why doesn't the prosecutor proceed against every other paper in Tacoma, against every paper in the state? They criticize the laws and the courts freely.
>
> Oh, I can tell you why he does not. Because the other papers have power behind them, they have sympathy behind them, they have votes behind them.

The audience broke into applause. Women stood and threw kisses at Anderson. The judge beat his gavel until there was silence, then warned the spectators that he would clear the court if the demonstration were repeated. Anderson concluded his set-piece without further interruption:

> The young man for the state has made much of the fact that Fox's newspaper is named the *Agitator*. As if agitation were something bad. Why, if it wasn't for agitation of the waters of Puget Sound it would become a stagnant pool, breeding disease and pollution.
>
> Agitator? What was George Washington, Simon Bolivar, Louis Kossuth, Abraham Lincoln and Wendell Phillips, and scores of other patriots, if they were not agitators?

Deputy Prosecutor Nolte closed for the state:

> It is not time for them to come in here and cry that we have encroached upon their liberty. The State of Washington was organized long before Home Colony was. The laws were fixed here long before Home Colony was founded. They knew that this state was an organized society at the time and if they didn't like it, why did they come here? They didn't want that liberty which is the liberty that means

freedom under law and order. They just wanted the right to do as they damn please.

The jury was out twenty-seven hours. When they filed back in it was to announce that Fox was guilty as charged. The foreman handed the judge a note asking "liency." Fox was sentenced to two months in the county jail.

The State Supreme Court upheld Fox's conviction. The United States Supreme Court refused to consider an appeal. In February 1913 Fox surrendered himself to the sheriff in the basement of the Pierce County Courthouse, and the double iron doors clanged shut. He spent the next six weeks reading aloud to his fellow prisoners from the works of Ibsen and Tolstoi. Their reaction to this recital is unrecorded. The readings ended only when Ernest Lister, a Democrat with Populist leanings, took office as governor. He granted Fox an unconditional pardon.

The editor returned to Home, vindicated—but the colony was dying. Not even Home's tolerance could stand the strain put on it by the trials of Fox and Matthew Schmidt. This was not a new world free of petty bickering. They began to move away. Fox suspended publication of *The Agitator,* admitting sadly that "papers in the East can do the job better." The Mutual Home Colony Association was disbanded.

Some people loved the place too much to leave—Fox among them. He is still living on the shores of Joe's Bay in 1955. But the past was lost. They knew it for sure when Joe Kapolla came down out of his tree.

Kapolla had arrived in Home around 1908. He and a man named Franz Erkelens found a beautiful spot near a spring, but the ground was too soggy to hold up a house. Nearby was a giant tree trunk that had been broken off about twenty feet above ground; four new sprouts, each about sixteen inches in diameter, rose from the base of the tree.

Joe and Franz sawed off the new growth even with the broken trunk. They laid a floor eight feet square across it. They put up a roof, built walls, installed bunk beds covered with cedar-bough mattresses, and drove some nails for coat-hooks. The main trunk leaned a bit, so they nailed boards to the upper side and had a stairway.

Downstairs, the kitchen was in a tent. One edge bordered the spring, which they used as an icebox. A stump served as kitchen table. Blocks of wood, sawed to different heights to compensate for the slope of the ground, were their chairs. The man at the head of the table could lean slightly and dip cool clear water from the spring. The man to his left could, without getting up, reach everything on the stove. Everyone liked to eat with Joe and Franz, especially since there were no dishes to wash. The boys just put them in the creek until they were clean.

Franz moved out in 1910, but Joe stayed in the tree (except for a few days spent in jail after his conviction for nude bathing) until 1917. When the United States went to war Joe climbed down and took a job in the shipyards in Tacoma, of all places. He returned later, but he moved into a house on the ground. The dream was over.

Home was like any other place, except for its memories.

6

Grays Harbor:
The Era of Violence

i

Billy Gohl was a short, round-headed, heavy-shouldered man
in his forties. He had brown hair, which he wore parted in
the middle, bartender fashion; and, indeed, he sometimes
tended bar. His eyes were big and blue and wide-set—honest,
you might say. In an era of free-flowing mustaches he went
about bare-lipped. His chin was square, his neck short, his
chest heavy. He was tough and he looked tough, which was no
disadvantage in the Grays Harbor of the Big Cut.

Billy was a great talker. His conversation centered on his
business pursuits and his hobbies. If the reports of his lis-
teners to policemen, sheriffs, and grand juries are to be
credited, his conversations were unforgettable. You'd start
chatting with Billy about the weather, and the next thing you
knew he was launched into a recital about a house he had
burgled, a hotel he had burned, a ship he had pirated, a man
he had murdered, or a deer he had shot out of season.

"Nice weather for ducks," a bartender in a saloon on

Wishkah remarked one evening shortly before Christmas in 1909 when Billy rolled in out of the rain.

Billy slapped his sou'wester across his thick thigh, settled himself solidly against the bar, and said, "I've got to kill Charley. As long as that scissorbill is walking around, I'm looking right into the penitentiary." Charley was never seen again.

A cigar-store operator, whose competition had driven Gohl into temporary bankruptcy, told police that Billy approached him amiably on the street and remarked, "You ain't going to be in business so long yourself." That night the hotel housing the cigar store burned to the wet ground—two guests along with it, one of them being an elderly Swede who had annoyed Gohl some years before. Billy was in excellent spirits when he next saw the burned-out tobaccoman. "Ain't it funny how things work out?" he said. "I never dreamed there'd be a bonus in it."

One night in a bar he explained to a considerable group how he had rigged the bomb. "I used electricity to set it off," he said. "I had the damnedest time. I fastened the cord to his light circuit, but the son-of-a-bitch hadn't paid his light bill, and it was turned off. I had to run a wire in from clear across the street to make it go."

The burned-out tobaccoman felt the police should take the matter up with Billy. So did Sig Jacobson, a former associate, who complained to the authorities that Billy wouldn't pay him for the infernal machine he had used to start the fire. A detective was sent around to see Billy, but he came back with the word there was nothing to it. (It was not impossible to get arrested in Aberdeen at this time; Mac DeLane, the proprietor of the Pioneer Liquor Store, who happened to be an enemy of Gohl's, was jailed for smoking a cigarette on the street.)

Billy could be remarkably persuasive. A man who shot a friend at Gohl's suggestion told a jury, "Billy looked at me and said, 'You take him,' and I knew I had to. There wasn't anything else to do. He had a great deal of animal magnetism."

During one eight-month period while Gohl was active forty-three bodies were found floating in Grays Harbor. Some had been shot, some slugged, a few showed evidence of poison, and the majority appeared simply to have drowned after falling or being pushed into the water while drunk. These anonymous dead men, culled from the hordes of migrant laborers who had flocked to Grays Harbor to cut trees, came to be known as the Floater Fleet. Billy Gohl was credited with launching most of them. If he was responsible for even half of the floaters found in the harbor during his day, Gohl was America's most prolific murderer. Over a ten-year period the fleet numbered 124.

Gohl first appeared in Grays Harbor in 1900, one of many men who drifted in broke from the Yukon. He said he had been born in Austria, though one police report credited him to Madison, Wisconsin, and another to Bergen, Norway. He found a job in a waterfront saloon, where he attracted attention with a tale about eating a man during a cold snap near Whitehorse.

He is said to have picked up bonus money by recruiting seamen, usually unconscious, for misery ships that called at the Wishkah mills for lumber. A bartender could be most useful when shanghaiing was necessary to round out a crew. But this story may be libel, for that is one of the few crimes Billy never boasted of committing, perhaps because he soon graduated from barkeep to agent for the Sailors' Union.

Gohl was an effective agent. Aberdeen became one of the first ports on the Pacific Coast with a union hiring hall. People seldom talked back to Billy. Once during a strike, when there were rumors that a citizens' committee in neighboring Hoquiam was planning to intervene, Billy strapped on a pair of forty-fives, cradled a shotgun in his elbow, and boarded each streetcar as it came in from Hoquiam. As he searched the passengers he explained blandly, "to make sure there ain't nobody going around town illegally armed."

In 1905 the captain of the lumber schooner *Fearless,* which was tied up in port by a strike, sneaked a non-union crew aboard, cast off, and headed for the Pacific. A runner bounded up the steps to the union hall, over the Pioneer Saloon, and reported the getaway. Billy recruited a boarding party, commandeered a launch, and put out after her. The seagoing pickets were sighted as they approached the schooner in the dark. Somebody started shooting. The gunbattle lasted half an hour before the *Fearless* escaped over the bar, which was too rough for the launch.

Later Gohl was arrested. The papers said he was charged with piracy, but actually it was "aggravated assault." He was fined twelve hundred dollars. On leaving court he remarked, "It'll be worth every penny of it, for advertising."

Gohl seldom missed an opportunity to expand his reputation for violence. One of his stories was that after the *Fearless* returned he sent word to four of the scabs that another non-union boat was waiting to sail. "After I got them on my boat," said Billy, "I took them out to the bar at low tide. I made them get out on the spit. Then I held a gun on them until the tide came in."

A private detective was hired to check on Billy. "He's just trying to scare people," the operator reported. "He's all talk."

Gohl's headquarters were in the union hall, a gaunt, narrow room with flaking yellow wallpaper. A scattering of scarred tables stood stark under bare lightbulbs. There were some rung-sprung chairs and sturdy splintered benches. One day a friend told Billy that a rumor was going around town that Billy sometimes killed sailors who left money with him for safekeeping and then dropped the bodies through a trap door into the Wishkah.

"That's silly. There ain't no trapdoor here," said Billy. "And if there was it would just open into the saloon." Then he took the man by the arm and led him to the window. "Tell you what I did do, though. The other day some Swede came in and gave me some money to hold for him while he hit the cribhouses. I told him something was up. I thought a scab boat was coming in. I got him to put on a logger's outfit— there was some old stag pants around—and I told him to go out and sit on those pilings down there and keep a lookout for the boat. When he got out there I got my rifle and shot him from here, right through the head."

In 1909 there was a shift in political alignment at the city hall. Billy was arrested for stealing a car robe. He was indignant. "A auto robe, for Chrissakes!" he said. He was acquitted when a friend who rustled cattle on the Chehalis River said he had bought the robe at a pawnshop and given it to Gohl.

Gohl brooded about the fact of his arrest. Rumor reached him that the cattle rustler had been seen talking to a deputy sheriff. It was then that he told the barkeep at the Grand that he would have to kill the man. When the barkeep mentioned some weeks later that he hadn't seen Charley around, Gohl told him, "You won't. He's sleeping off Indian Creek with an anchor for a pillow."

A report of this statement reached Montesano, where the sheriff decided Gohl might not be joking. He waited for a day of low tides and went to Indian Creek. Not far off shore he found Charles Hatberg's body, weighed down by a twenty-five-pound anchor.

Gohl was arrested. He denied everything. "It's a frame-up," he said, and many believed him. Their confidence was shaken two months later when the schooner *A. J. West* returned from a run to Mexico. Aboard her was a very nervous seaman named John Klingenberg. He had been seen with Gohl the night Hatberg disappeared. He had tried to jump ship in Mexico, but the captain, who had received a telegram from the sheriff, kept him aboard. On its return run the schooner was held up two weeks at the Grays Harbor bar by adverse winds. The delay, said Klingenberg, "left me in a highly nervous state." When a sheriff arrested him at the dock he was anxious to talk.

Klingenberg said Gohl had asked him to go along to kill Hatberg so Hatberg couldn't tell anyone what he knew. They had gone to Indian Creek, where Gohl kept a small schooner. There they met a man named John Hoffman. Gohl asked Hoffman to go with them to Hatberg's cabin. After they were on the launch Gohl drew his gun and shot Hoffman in the back, wounding him. Hoffman begged for his life. Gohl sat on his chest and shot him through the forehead. They threw his body overboard and went on toward Hatberg's. "He'd have been in the way," said Gohl. Near the cabin they ran on a mudbank. Hatberg came out in a skiff and rowed them ashore. The three men spent the night in the cabin. Klingenberg said he didn't sleep much. The next morning Hatberg rowed them out to the launch. "You take him," said Gohl to Klingenberg. And Klingenberg did. "But," he told the deputy, "I didn't shoot him in the back." Gohl and Klingenberg went back to Aberdeen together. A few days later Gohl suggested to Klingenberg that they go for a walk alone on the beach.

Klingenberg declined; the next day he shipped out for Mexico.

When brought to trial for his life, Gohl maintained that Hatberg and Hoffman were somewhere in Alaska, tending lighthouse. He didn't know exactly where; didn't have any idea whose body the sheriff had found off Indian Creek. The State then brought Hatberg's arm, which had been pickled, into court so the jurors could examine some identifying tattoo marks.

Gohl was sentenced to life. He was later transferred from the state penitentiary to a hospital for the criminally insane, where he died in 1928. Klingenberg was sentenced to twenty years in prison.

ii

The time and the place that spawned Billy Gohl were the toughest in the history of logging.

Mainly because of transportation difficulties, logging did not begin on Grays Harbor for nearly thirty years after it got under way on Puget Sound. The first logs were cut commercially on the harbor when an early homesteader, Charles Stevens, converted a singularly unsuccessful grist mill into a water-driven sawmill and shipped some planks to Portland. That was in 1881. The following year Stevens' little rig sawed out timbers for a big new mill that was being whacked up on the Hoquiam River for A. M. Simpson, a veteran logger from California. Simpson's loaded its first lumber in 1882.

A. J. West, a logger from Michigan, where they were running thin on prime timber, came to Aberdeen in 1884 and planted saws near the mouth of the Wishkah. So by 1885 each of the sister communities of Grays Harbor—Hoquiam, Aberdeen, and Cosmopolis—were sawing lumber.

The arrival of the industry on the harbor coincided with two great changes in logging methods. Each involved steam. They were the donkey engine and the logging railroad.

Several mechanics were experimenting with methods of dragging logs through the woods by machinery. John Dolbeer, a California mechanic who was logging in the redwood country, got to the Patent Office first, in 1882, with plans for the Dolbeer donkey engine. The donkey was an upright steam engine with a single vertical cylinder that turned a winch and thereby wound a line around a drum, pulling in the log. It was low in power and subject to fits and vapors and all other ailments that plague steam engines, but it worked. Other ingenious men introduced modifications that increased the power, strengthened the cable, and turned the drum to a horizontal position, which eliminated tangles.

The first donkey engine roared and rattled on Grays Harbor sometime around 1885. You can still get an ear chewed off in almost any beer parlor in Hoquiam and Aberdeen by saying flatly which outfit you think pioneered steam in the woods. Name your candidate, and twenty big men will rise to challenge you with facts, figures, and the vehemence of outraged faith. Soon after the donkey (some will say before) came the logging trains, tiny little locomotives—"dinkys"— hauling short flatcars over tracks that had no business staying together and often didn't.

The iron horse and the mechanical donkey drove the bull teams from the woods, and they let the operators escape from tidewater. Now it was possible to follow the receding tree line back into the foothills.

The donkey engine crouched in the yarding area near the railroad track. At the throttle was the engineer, or donkey-puncher, waiting for the signal that a log was ready. Back in the woods, usually out of sight of the donkey, buckers with cross-cut saws were cutting the fallen tree into sections. A chokerman slipped a heavy wire noose around the log. The hook-tender wrestled the business end of the cable into position and attached it to the choker—an operation requiring skill and brute strength.

Just as the signalman, or whistle punk, who had the easiest and worst-paid job in the woods, had replaced the bull-team grease monkey at the bottom of the camp hierarchy, the hooker had taken over the pay and prestige of the bull-whacker. Ranking not far below the camp foreman in authority, and required by tradition and the force of circumstance to make more noise than anyone else in the woods, the hooker was the stuff of which legend is made. A good hook-tender was expected to lift a hung-up log off a low stump by the sheer force and ingenuity of his profanity, and he sometimes made it.

When the hooker dropped his hand and jumped clear the whistle punk pulled his chain; the engineer threw in the throttle; the engine, which had been emitting a low, tinny gargle, suddenly roared deep-throatedly; the drum spun; the great steel cable snapped taut with force enough to rip a man apart; and the log, perhaps forty feet long and six feet through, charged across the yarding area, smashing anything it hit.

It was rough on the forest and rough on the men, but there were saws to be fed at the far end of the track. For back East in Michigan and Wisconsin and Minnesota the woods were wearing out, and the boss lumbermen from the river country were building mills at tidewater. "So let's cut timber, you guys. You're not getting paid to stand still."

It was strangely like war. They attacked the forest as if it were an enemy to be pushed back from the beachheads, driven into the hills, broken into patches, and wiped out.

Many operators thought they were not only making lumber but liberating the land from the trees, making room for farmers. They advertised the cut-over areas for sale as farmland, and they found takers, for the price was low and the dream of a bit of land of one's own was almost universal. They were called stump ranchers, these hopeful people who came from everywhere to farm this new-won land. They grubbed at the great roots; they fought the encroaching salal and alder and huckleberry and the spikey, insinuating, indestructible blackberry vines. They raised a few crops and gave up, nearly all of them, though many wasted as much as a lifetime trying to grow truck and grain on land that, it finally became clear, was meant to grow only trees.

Meanwhile the war against the forest went on, farther back in the hills. Every year more mills were built and there were more saws to feed. In each mill were an agony of sound and a menacing flicker of steel as the teeth of the circulars and bands cut and ripped through boards and cants and slabs, and the carriages bearing the forty-ton sticks made the floor tremble.

This too was a battlefield, and the general was the head sawyer. He stood in a cage with the log deck on one side, the headrig on the other, and in front of him the carriage roughly cradling the big stick to be cut. On the sawyer's judgment depended the amount of lumber that could be taken from each log. He worked by feel, by the instinct of deep familiarity, making his estimates from color of wood, depth of bark, from the very sound and feel of the rumbling carriage. He signaled his crew to stand clear, and he pulled the lever that thrust the log against the spinning band. The steel whined, and the wood screamed, and *thump* went a thousand-pound slab on the live roll to be carried away, and down the length of the log a swath of sapwood showed clear. Then back with the carriage, and forward, and back, and forward and back, while the log is flipped on its side by the giant turner. Square it down. Cut it up. It was growing before Columbus, and you're its master.

The treeline was deep in the woods now. The land was getting rougher, harder to work. The logging lokeys had gears. The ground was so steep and broken that even the big new donkeys had trouble snaking logs across it. So "high-lead logging" was born. Instead of pulling in the logs with a straight, level pull along the ground, the donkey yanked them into the air and swung them to the yard. The high-lead doubled the output in the woods, made possible the logging of steep hills, and gave to Hollywood and folk-lore the "high climber."

For high-lead logging you had to have a "spar," a tall tree limbed and cut off at the top so a block could be hung 150 feet or more from the ground, and the cable from the donkey reeved through the block. Some logger—he came to be called the high climber—had to go up the tree, lopping off the branches and then topping it. He was a brave man and a romantic figure. No sight in the woods is more thrilling than that of the high climber working on a great spar—the tiny man against the giant, leaning back on his safety belt, cutting a notch with his ax, lowering the ax on the line fastened from his belt, and pulling up the saw, which he handles with delicate strength as he saws off the top of the fir (itself a respectable chunk of tree, tall as an eight-story building) and sends it plunging to the forest floor, while the spar jerks and vibrates and the high climber, often as not, waves his free hand like a bronc rider or climbs the last few feet of the still-quivering bole and stands on his head.

High-lead logging was dangerous logging, and not just for the high climbers. The great logs swinging through the air could knock down a two-foot-thick tree without losing momentum. They simply splattered any logger who wasn't in the clear when they started to move.

And this was the day of "highball," or hurry-up. The price of stumpage was rising. A thousand feet of standing timber cost now what an acre had cost in 1880. Profit depended on speed, and speed on expensive equipment. The big operator thought of his investment, of the taxes the state was starting to levy on the vast blocks of land he had acquired, and he thought of his competition. Sugar it off. Cut and get out. Highball.

And the little operator, who knew his men personally and might spend a lot of time with them back in the woods, for whom each injury to a crewman was something personal, had to go along with the speed-up if he was to stay in business. So it was highball. And if luck was with the little fellow, and his engineering good, and the price still right when the lumber lay on the dock, he made a lot of money quickly, and after that he was not so likely to go into the woods. And even if he did go it was different. He was rich now, and his men were poor. There was a growing estrangement between the men and the operators, and a new tension in camps.

The camps were far from town. The men worked an eleven-hour day, a six-day week, and they stomped in from the woods, hairy and tough and profane, only on Saturday nights. The Nice People stayed off the streets Saturday nights. Many loggers didn't come out of the woods except for the big blow-ins, Christmas and the Fourth of July, when, by tradition, everyone got so drunk that the camps were down a week or more.

The logger was now the timber beast, a man apart, strange even to the millworkers. He was a bachelor, a migrant. He had come from somewhere else, and he'd be going somewhere else if there were still trees growing anywhere else when the big cut was over.

All day he fought the trees to the limit of his strength, down there on the wet floor of the forest, where the rare sunlight reached only in shafts. Usually it rained. Day after day the wind blew in from the southwest, warm and wet, and it cooled as it rose over the forest. It blew without gusts—a steady wind, bringing a steady rain. The clouds lay over the tops of the trees like thin putty. The rain came cascading down the drooping, shiny-needled branches; the needle-carpeted earth soaked the water and held it. It was like walking on a sponge. The ax handles were slippery; the swinging metal was cold and doubly dangerous; and nothing ever dried out. Eleven hours of this, dawn to dark, and then the stinking bunkhouses, alive with vermin, and if you didn't like it you drew your pay and there was another camp just the same farther on. There was satisfaction, the satisfaction of the Marine—the pride of battle, the knowledge you could do what had to be done, but what many shirked. And if that wasn't enough, blow her in at the holidays. Get drunk, get happy, forget it until the pay is spent and the woods are the only place there is to go.

Jim Stevens, who knows the woods as well as any man, gave this description of bunkhouse life in his *Homer in the Sagebrush:* [1]

That night the wind roared into a storm that beat from the open sea over the Grays Harbor bar and up the Wishkah. It rattled the shakes that roofed the bunk shanty and it puffed and whistled through the cracks between the rough boards of the walls.

"Might as well be bunkin' inside a picket fence," grumbled an old faller, as he tramped in from supper and lit his pipe.

[1] New York: Knopf, 1928.

The shakes overhead rattled from the rain and the wind. The loggers crowded the benches around the stove. They were all in their sock feet. All of them were wearing overalls or ducking pants stagged just below the knee. Red strips of drawers legs were revealed between pants ends and sock tops. Heavy suspenders stretched over backs covered with wool shirts, red, green or blue. There were several bald heads, but every man had mustaches. There were no cigarettes. Pipe smoke of a stinging smell curled over the bowed heads of the loggers, who were tired out from their eleven hours in the wet cold. Fresh tobacco juice soon made small puddles in the ashes of the heater bed. From rafters, beams and lines hung wet mackinaws, stagged shirts, paraffin pants, and underclothes which had been boiled to kill the latest crop of lice. The windows were shut tight and the steam from the drying clothes mixed its powerful various smells with that of bitter root tobacco burning in caked pipes. The coal oil lamps with rusty tin reflectors behind them smoked from shelves in each end of the bunkhouse. The light was so dim around the heater that its red sides shone and sparkled. A mumble of talk arose. Somebody was grouching about the cook.

"That belly burglar's so greasy he has to use sandpaper to pick up the dishes."

An old faller complained of his rheumatism. "It was better for a while here on the Coast. Never bothered me at first like she used to in Michigan. But now it's misery all the time."

A swamper had a lame ankle. "Widder-maker dropped from a snag. Come nigh gettin' me. But I dodged. Turnt so quick, though, I spraint my lousy ankle. Warn't so close to Christmas, I'd mope."

Christmas. . . . The mumble of talk turned to the good time to come.

"Hope I meet up with that woman in the Eagle I had last Fourth."

"Not me. Three drinks a day this trip is my limit. Got to save up for my old age."

"Yeah, you'll save, lad. You'll get the other ear chewed off this blow-in, that's how you'll save."

"Hear they's a new place opened where they sell the real double-stamp."

"Yeah. Paul Bunyan's runnin' it, ain't he? Redeye, rotgut, bug juice and forty-rod—that's the licker for loggers all the time. Double-stamp stuff for loggers? Don't tell me!"

"I learnt last Fourth how they mix their bar licker. First they take hundred eight-eight proof alcohol, then English breakfast tea for color, then prune juice for flavor—"

"You mean finecut for both color and flavor. That was it back in the river towns."

"I'll bust the faro bank this trip, then I'll buy a bullteam of my own."

"You'll buy a trip to hell ridin' out on the ebb tide if you don't steer clear of the tinhorn joints, old settler! The bustin'll be done by somebody with a blackjack and you'll join the floater fleet."

"Hear they got a new bar in the Heron Cribs. Built like a horseshoe. Some nights they gets one of the sportin' women out, strip her off, grease her with vaseline, put her and some cockeyed bum inside the bar, and then have a chase for your whiskers."

"Yeah? That makes me think of the time I went from Saginaw to Chicago. . . ."

iii

They called the part of town where loggers came to blow in their cash on liquor and women the skid road. The term came from Seattle, where the first saloons and bawdyhouses had sprung up along the skid road Henry Yesler built to move logs to his mill, the first steam mill on the sound. Soon the name was used in all tidewater lumber towns. The skid road. It didn't mean "red-light district"—not exactly. Like Barbary Coast, it implied a way of life.

Skid-road life was raw and clamorous, often ugly, always boisterous, and nowhere more so than in Aberdeen. The town was built on the flats where the Chehalis and Wishkah rivers met. The houses rose on bog-land filled with sawdust [2] from the mills. The streets was sawdust, and boards were laid across the sawdust to form sidewalks. The boards were worn and splintered by corks—spikes—set in the shoes of the loggers. Sometimes when a southwest wind drove a high tide up the rivers you could feel the ocean heaving and pushing up under the street.

There wasn't a basement in town. Buildings were set on pilings. Along the skid road the saloons and houses nosed against the sawdust bank, but their rears hung over the river. Stories of men being dropped through trapdoors to the waiting boats of shanghaiers or to death by drowning were quite true. Here the floater fleet was launched.

Privies hung from the rears of the riverside buildings, none more conspicuously than that of the Sailors' Union Hall above the Palace Saloon. It was painted red. One memorable day the schooner *Sophie Christenson* was moving down the Wishkah under tow, headed for Australia with a load of lumber from the American Mill. Her skipper, Captain Michael McCarron, had a negative attitude where Billy Gohl was concerned. As the schooner approached the hall McCarron had an irresistible impulse. He took the wheel, spun it dexterously so the vessel's head swung to the west. Her long jibboom clipped the outhouse, shattering it. The *Sophie Christenson* moved serenely downstream with the seat of the old-fashioned two-holer swinging from the boomstick like a scalp. It started a riot on shore, of course, but anything started a riot on shore.

2 Circular saws cut a kerf as much as an inch wide. There was more sawdust than could be used to fire the boilers. Where it couldn't be dumped it was burned.

Out of one brawl in a sporting house came a famous phrase. An embattled logger had just lifted a rival over his head when someone shouted, "Don't waste him. Kill the fiddler with him."

In many of the dance halls the piano was surrounded by a heavy wire screen to protect the professor from his critics. You threw a dollar over the screen when you wanted music. The big sign proclaimed, "The man that pays the dollar is the one that calls the tune."

Some of the houses were named for institutions of higher learning—Yale and Harvard and Princeton, among others— and you can imagine the jokes *that* led to. Another house was called, for a short time, after a high-toned institution for girls in Tacoma. The name was changed after a policeman called to inform the madam that the prosecuting attorney's daughter went to the school in question.

Most of the cribhouses sported bars, but the saloons were the places for serious drinking. Many of them crawled with pimps and sharpies. A few were models of high-proof decorum. There was only one Humboldt.

Stewart Holbrook has lovingly recorded the glories of the Humboldt Saloon, where the corked boots of the loggers chewed up the hemlock floor so quickly that the one-and-one-half-inch hemlock boards had to be replaced every six months; where no woman, bad or good, was ever allowed to enter, nor any fancy man, cold-deck artist, or panhandler; where the double-stamp whisky was really whisky and ninety proof meant ninety proof; where each year more than a half-million dollars in loggers' paychecks were cashed, and a man could leave some cash in the safe and be sure it wouldn't be returned to him until he was sober.

The Humboldt was run by Big Fred Hewlett of the State of Maine. Big Fred was a black-mustached behemoth whose love for loggers was as deep as his scorn for all lesser breeds. It was Hewlett, says Holbrook, who, when asked by a visiting Easterner for a Manhattan, impassively poured into a beer mug, a slug of gin, a slug of rum, a dash of brandy, and another of bitters, then splashed in some aquavit, filled the rest of the mug with beer, stirred the mixture with a huge forefinger, and slid it down the shining bar with the command, "Drink 'er down."

Loggers drank whisky.

iv

There were men for whom a bout with a sporting woman and a drunk in a good saloon, even the Humboldt Saloon, were not enough. Some loggers wanted to do more than forget. Some wanted security.

Archie Binns in *Sea in the Forest* recalls a day at Port Ludlow in the late 1890s when a loading car slipped partly off an overhead track. Cyrus Walker dispatched a workman to chain the lumber on the car and save it from sliding off and getting bruised. The lumber slipped anyway, and the man was crushed. A foreman passed the hat among the employees and collected for the funeral expenses. Then he added something new. He held out the hat to Walker, who said, "I would like to help that poor woman and her children. But I can give nothing. If I did, it would set an unfortunate precedent and give the impression that an employer has responsibilities to his employees."

That was the standard-brand attitude. Walker was not a harsh man; by the standards of the day, Pope and Talbot was a good place to work. But the attitude remained: If you don't like it, draw your pay; nobody says you've got to stay; it's a free country.

Hence the unions. On the peninsula the first unions in the lumber industry were organized among the workers in the shingle mills, whose occupation was particularly hazardous. A reporter who visited a shingle mill in the first decade of the twentieth century has left this description:

> Shingle-weaving is not a trade, it is a battle. For ten hours a day the sawyer faces two teethed steel disks whirling around 200 times a minute. To the one on the left he feeds the heavy blocks of cedar, reaching over with his left hand to remove the heavy shingles it rips off.
>
> Hour after hour the shingle-weaver's hands and arms, plain, unarmored flesh and blood, are staked against the screeching steel that cares not what it severs. Hour after hour the steel sings its crescendo note as it bites into the wood, the sawdust thickens, the wet sponge under the sawyer's nose fills with fine particles. If "cedar asthma," the shingle-weaver's occupational disease, does not get him, the steel will. Sooner or later he reaches over a little too far, the whirling blade tosses drops of deep red into the air, a finger, a hand, or part of an arm comes sliding down the slick chute.

Shingle-weavers' locals flared up by spontaneous combustion in all the lumber towns around the peninsula and sound in 1900 and 1901. The necessary elements were all present: danger, poor pay, job insecurity, a feeling of craft solidarity among men who lived close together, and the need of the operators for workers with some skill. In 1903 delegates met in Everett to form the International Shingle Weavers Union of America. The same year sawmill workers started to organize. In 1905 the International Brotherhood of Woodsmen and Sawmill Workers was chartered by the American Federation of Labor.

The operators were outraged. They were individualistic

men, accustomed to making their own decisions. Their feeling of responsibility toward their men was at best paternalistic. Not infrequently an operator would drop around to give an old hand who had joined a union some sincere and fatherly advice: "Don't get mixed up with those wild men; we'd hate to have to let you go."

Many of the employers were sincerely convinced that most of the men in the mills and woods *liked* taking risks and working long hours. "Gives 'em a feeling of independence. Makes 'em know they're men. I know how they feel, dammit. I started there myself."

After 1900 all the employers were caught in the bind between rising prices for raw materials and declining prices for the finished product due to increased production. The operators formed associations of their own to limit output and regulate prices and achieve a standard grading system for lumber, but they were too individualistic for their own good. W. B. Mack, an Aberdeen operator, told a meeting of the Pacific Lumber Manufacturers Association in 1911, "I don't see a ray of hope. . . . Every time a price is given, some other fellow cuts it. Everybody seems to be fighting everybody else."

There was a welter of strikes. They boiled up in Hoquiam, were settled, then erupted in Raymond and Aberdeen, Cosmopolis and Port Ludlow; then back to Hoquiam, where at one stage union men were loaded into boxcars for deportation to nobody knew where, but the mayor declared himself out of sympathy with the project, and railroad men refused to move the train.

These first strikes, though violent and productive of deep bitterness on both sides, were strikes for such limited objectives as a larger share of the profits and a safer place to work.

They were intended not to change the world but only to change conditions in a given plant. Then along came the Industrial Workers of the World, born of a meeting of forty-three unions in Chicago in 1905.

The I. W. W., or Wobblies, as they soon came to be called, didn't ask for a larger slice of the economic melon; they wanted the whole thing, flesh, rind, and pits, and they wanted it right away. The Wobblies believed in world revolution, not in the distant future but today. The Red Dawn would not be tomorrow but had come yesterday, and the Wobblies were at war with society. They claimed no common ground with the employer except the industrial battlefield. They considered the craft unions, even the militant shingle-weavers, to be merely creatures of the employers, nursemaids of reaction, traitors to the working class. They quoted Mark Hanna on "the labor lieutenants of the captains of industry," but they didn't mean this as a compliment.

The Wobblies considered themselves soldiers in a battle already joined. They were brave, unreasonable, ingenious, cantankerous, violent. To the rootless men in the forest camps they offered an outlet for frustration more exciting than a brothel. The I. W. W. appealed to idealists who wanted a better world and to outsized juvenile delinquents in corked boots who wanted to smash back at a world they never made. The Wobs were every bit as rough as the conditions that spawned them.

There were Wobbly halls in all the lumber towns, usually somewhere along the skid road, preferably near the "slave markets," as the employment agencies were known. These headquarters were bare, beat-up buildings, furnished with battered chairs and decorated with pictures of Joe Hill, the romantic radical poet who was executed by a firing squad in Utah for a hold-up he perhaps did not commit and thereby became for the Wobblies that martyr without whom no cause can be complete.

These halls were raided diligently by town police, and also by such elements of the outraged citizenry as the employers—now suffering from the Wobbly Horrors—could organize and arm. But the hall was always just a rented hall; and if some of the men who packed the rigging—that is, gave signed-up members their red cards and passed out the gaudy propaganda broadsides and the Wobbly song books—were driven out of town in various conditions of disrepair, there were sure to be more fellow workers swinging down from the freight cars a few days later.

The Wobs brought to near perfection a technique later employed by Gandhi. When their right to harangue the stiffs on some lumbertown skid road was denied, they swarmed into the town and started talking at every streetcorner, inviting arrest. When the jail got too full (in one strike in Spokane the demonstrators filled the city jail, the county jail, a deserted schoolhouse, and an M. P. barracks) and the cost of feeding the prisoners began to damage the city budget, the authorities usually backed down. But not always.

Up in Everett in the spring of 1916 the Wobbly speakers moved in when the town was already made tense by strikes of longshoremen, tugboat crews, and shingle-weavers. The first Wobbly organizer to hit town, one James Rowan, almost immediately got into a streetcorner argument with a craft-union organizer and was vagged out of town by the police. Soon another Wobbly showed up, and the police chased him out of town along with thirty-five sympathizers. This kept up through the summer. In the fall, with the strike still dragging on, a party of forty Wobblies arrived on a passenger steamer from Seattle for a free-speech demonstration. They were captured by deputized vigilantes, taken to the edge of town, stripped, and made to run a gantlet of men armed with clubs and with branches of devil's club, a prickly brush. All survived, but some were hospitalized.

A few days later the Wobblies, at the suggestion of a Seattle clergyman, the Reverend Oscar McGill, announced that they would hold a mass meeting on Sunday afternoon, November 6, in Everett. The idea was that the vigilantes would not resort to violence in public.

That Sunday 250 Wobblies left Seattle for Everett on the regular passenger steamer *Verona*, and another fifty left on the *Calista*, which was chartered. The *Verona* got there first. As she tied up at the dock the Wobblies were singing:

> We meet today in Freedom's cause,
>   And raise our voices high;
> We'll join our hands in union strong,
>   To battle or to die. . . .

From the dock the sheriff shouted, "Who is your leader?"

"We're all leaders."

"Don't try to land here."

Some Wobblies rushed the gangplank. Vigilantes concealed in the warehouse started shooting. Eleven of the Wobblies died, along with two deputy sheriffs; thirty men on the boat and fifteen on the dock were wounded before a Wobbly with a revolver forced the *Verona*'s engineer to reverse the engines. The towline snapped, and the steamer wallowed away. No one took the wheel until she was almost out of range from shore.

The police were waiting when the *Verona* docked in Seattle. Seventy-four men were arrested and charged with first-degree murder. One of them, Thomas H. Tracy, was tried and found not guilty. The charges against the others were eventually dropped.

The Wobblies had won their greatest legal victory, but on

the morning that Tracy's attorney, George F. Vanderveer, rose in superior court in Seattle to open the case for the defense, President Woodrow Wilson stood before a joint session of Congress in Washington to ask that war be declared on Germany. The war made the Wobblies more unpopular than ever.

In the spring of 1917 both the craft unions and the I. W. W. asked lumber operators for an eight-hour day, at three dollars, in the mills and either an eight-hour day or a nine-hour day, at $3.50, in the camps. The operators refused the demands and turned down government requests that they arbitrate; instead they formed the Lumbermen's Protective Association, which was empowered to fine any member five hundred dollars a day for operating less than ten hours per shift. In July men walked out of nearly every mill and camp in the state. It was the biggest strike the Far West had known.

After six weeks the men went back to work, their demands unmet. The craft unions authorized their men to return to the job, although they were to remain technically on strike until the eight-hour day was granted. The Wobblies also went back, but not exactly to work; they appeared in mill and camp, but practiced what they called "conscientious withdrawal of efficiency"—the slowdown.

The ingenious Wobblies, long adept at sabotage, could think of a lot of ways to botch a job. For instance, they could work eight hours and then quit. If they were fired, the next crew was unlikely to be better. They were accused of driving spikes in logs to break saws in the mills—a really terrible thing to do, since a saw that hit metal filled the mill with flying steel. The Wobblies denied doing this, but they did not deny that they were striking on the job. Signs of the grinning cat perched on the wooden shoe—the symbol of sabotage— leered from the windows of Wobbly halls.

Lumber production got in such a snarl that the War Department dispatched Colonel Bryce P. Disque to see what could be done to get fir and hemlock and pine, and especially spruce, moving out of the woods. Spruce was the glamour wood; it went into airplanes. As a result of the colonel's visit two strange new organizations appeared in the woods: the Loyal Legion of Loggers and Lumbermen, and the Spruce Production Division.

The 4-L, as the Loyal Legion came to be called, was called a "fifty-fifty outfit: half employer, half employee, and half you-know-what." All real power centered in the Army in the person of Colonel Disque. Each 4-L member, boss or worker, had to sign a pledge to help the war effort, "to stamp out any sedition or acts of hostility against the United States which may come to my knowledge. . . ."

Though the craft unions and the Wobblies expressed loud doubts about the impartiality of the War Department in any labor-management dispute, the workers did not act the worst of the wartime decisions. Colonel Disque became convinced that most of the union demands would have to be met if lumber was to be cut. He finally ordered the operators to cut shifts to eight hours and pay time-and-a-half for overtime; shortly after, he ruled that employers must furnish bunkhouses with clean bedding and change the sheets and pillow slips weekly at a charge of a dollar a week.

Disque's other responsibility, the Spruce Production Division, was one of the oddest outfits the United States Army has ever activated—and, admittedly, competition is tough. The Spruce Production Division was a body of soldiers assigned to work in the woods. They received the going civilian wage for their work, minus their Army pay, and minus $7.50 a week as ration allowance.

The deep rain forest in winter is not everybody's delight,

but seven thousand men [3] signed up or were drafted into the Spruce Division. After all, as the saying went, "It don't rain lead." In theory, the division took only experienced loggers; in practice, quite a few men showed up who couldn't tell a Swedish fiddle from a deacon seat and had never raised a callus. But they worked very hard, and they were not without casualties. The woods are dangerous, especially for amateurs, and during the flu epidemic of 1918 the men in the rain forest were hard hit.

That first winter most of the spruce soldiers were assigned to camps near existing roads and put to cutting down spruce and splitting them on the spot. This is as inefficient a way of getting lumber as can be devised, short of sabotage. But the men were there, the trees were there, and no roads led into the main spruce belts, so the logs could not be hauled out to mills.

As soon as the woods dried out in the spring the Spruce Production Division started laying track for logging trains— five miles of track in the Quinault area to help the Polson Logging Company get out spruce; five miles along the Pysht to help Merrill and Ring; and thirty-six miles from the Disque Junction, west of Port Angeles, to the Hoko River area out toward the tip of the peninsula, where stood the greatest spruce forest in the world.

The Siems-Carey-H. S. Herbaught Corporation was given a cost-plus contract to build the spruce railroad, using spruce soldiers as part of the labor force. They also had a cost-plus contract to build a huge mill on a site donated by the people of Port Angeles at the mouth of Ennis Creek—the old site of the Port Angeles Co-operative Colony. Siems-Carey-H. S. Herbaught also got a contract to supply 300,000,000 board-

[3] On the peninsula they'll tell you the figure was nearer twenty-five or thirty thousand.

feet of spruce a year from the new mill at a cost of $105 per thousand.

The contract called for the spruce railroad to be finished in six months, and it was. As an example of hurry-up engineering this was remarkable, especially when you consider that most of the crews were amateurs, working in rough, wet country, and at the end of a supply line bottlenecked by Lake Crescent, along which all personnel and equipment had to be ferried. The only trouble with the performance was that when the last spike was driven the war had been over for nineteen days. Not a log was hauled down the spruce railroad, not a board cut in the big new mill.

It took some time to get things untangled in the tall timber after the outbreak of peace. The government sold the mill, railroad, and a vast spread of spruce stumpage to Lyon, Hill and Company of Portland in 1923 for a million dollars, of which fifty thousand was in cash. Lyon, Hill sold to Sol Duck Investment Company in 1929, and they in turn sold the mill to the Olympic Forest Products Company in 1930. Olympic Forest Products changed the mill into a pulp mill and changed its own name to Rayonier, under which it thrives.

The spruce railroad line died hard. While the government was still trying to sell the road in 1921, the biggest wind in the recorded history of the peninsula puffed in off the Pacific. There was a gust of 114-mile velocity, and a steady wind for half an hour of 110-mile force. It blew the lighthouse keeper's bull off the island of Tatoosh, and it bowled over millions of board-feet of old trees in the spruce belt. The giant jack-straw pile of two-hundred-foot-long trees made logging impossible in a wide area on the west end of the peninsula. Not even the logs that had been felled in 1918 by the Spruce Production Division could be pulled free from the tangle. Loss of this timber greatly reduced the potential earning capacity of the line.

After its purchase by Lyon, Hill and Company in 1925, the spruce line was incorporated as the Port Angeles Western, and was used as a common carrier. Work was started to push tracks down the coast into the rich timber country of the Hoh, but funds gave out after only five miles had been laid. Steel stopped at the Calawah River, just north of the little logging town of Forks.

In 1951 a fall drought dried out the forest. A small fire broke out along the railroad right of way, not far from Lake Crescent. It was brought under control and patrolled by the Forest Service. The wind shifted unexpectedly on the night of September 18, and rose to fifty miles an hour. Some ember —Forest Service men say it probably was a smoldering root surfacing after slowly burning for a hundred feet or so underground—came to life. Sparks reached the live dry forest, and the fire roared up, out of control, and swept along the Calawah on to Forks.

Oscar Peterson, a retired Forest Service man who lives on a ranch at the edge of town, recalls that his wife woke about four A.M. and remarked, "That's funny! It looks like dawn already in the east." Two hours later the Petersons' son came in from Port Angeles. "The whole damn peninsula's on fire," he said. "It's coming down the Calawah."

The fire swept to the edge of town. Many fled. Others stayed and helped the Forest Service fight it. They started backfires, ripped out fire lanes with bulldozers, climbed onto roofs and stomped out the cinders.

"The updraft sucked burning branches hundreds of yards or more into the air," Peterson recalls. "They fell all over the place. But the fire was so intense it burned up the oxygen, and the branches came down charred but cold. They were all over the roof here, but dead. Otherwise the town would have gone, sure."

The town was saved, but thirty thousand acres of forest were gone. That killed the railroad. Another huge swath of timber it had expected to haul to the mills was lost. Residents of Forks filed suits totaling nearly a million dollars against the line. The Port Angeles Western went into the hands of receivers in 1953. After several attempts to get federal or state aid had failed to raise half a million dollars for new equipment, the line was abandoned. In 1954 the tracks were taken up for scrap.

Colonel Disque's other creation, the Loyal Legion of Loggers and Lumbermen, also came unstuck when the glue of patriotism and wartime profits was removed. In 1919 more than half of the employers dropped out, and a mill or camp could not be organized under 4-L terms without the employer's participation. The 4-L lingered on into the 1930s, a shadow of the past, and then, after the institution of National Labor Relations Board elections, it disappeared completely.

The A. F. of L. mill and camp unions tried to fill the vacuum left by the Loyal Legion. They failed. Memories of the collapse of the big strike of 1917 were too fresh. Not until the 1930s were they to be important again.

That left the woods to the Wobblies. They carried on the fight as before, and again they were met with violence, the worst of it in Centralia, a lumber and farm town fifty miles up the Chehalis River from Aberdeen. There, on Armistice Day, 1919, an American Legion parade unit paused before the Wobbly hall in the Roderick Hotel building on Tower Avenue. For days there had been rumors that the hall was to be raided. The Wobblies had even appealed to their old enemies, the police and the governor, for protection. Their lawyer had advised them they had a right to protect themselves if attacked. Inside the hall were armed men; other Wobblies with rifles were stationed in a hotel across the street and on a nearby hill. So when the Legionnaires stopped in front of the hall on that chill, bitter day, the whole town seemed to hold its breath.

It has never been determined whether the shooting started before the Legionnaires charged the door. But when the ugly business was over three young Legionnaires were dead, and so was a fourth veteran, Wesley Everest, who had been inside the building, and who had killed at least two of the others. Everest had been chased through town by the mob. They caught him on the bank of the Chehalis. He was taken to the city jail, but that night he was lynched. The mob castrated him before they hanged him from the bridge, and while he was hanging they shot him.

The trial of the Wobblies for the murder of the Legionnaires was held in Montesano, the county seat of Grays Harbor. Ten men were charged with murder: four had been in the hall, five had been in the hotel across the street or on the hill, and the tenth was the lawyer who had told the Wobblies it was their right to defend themselves if attacked. Seven were found guilty of second-degree murder and sent to prison for terms of twenty-five to forty years; two, including the lawyer, were not guilty; the tenth was insane.

The Wobblies had a new set of martyrs to set up alongside Joe Hill. They used them with skill. But things were different, somehow. The stiffs in the woods were sorry about Wesley Everest and the other guys, but hell! that's how things are. What do you expect me to do about it?

"Revolt," said the Wobblies. "Throw off your chains."

But the loggers didn't want a revolution. Better pay, shorter hours, yes. Revolution, no.

The era of raw violence had ended. As we look back, it seems probable that it ended on the day when Colonel Disque ordered the eight-hour day and the sheets changed every week, for then the timber beast became an industrial worker.

7

Olympic National Park: The Fight the Iron Man Lost

i

Paul Bunyan is no hero to the loggers of the Olympic Peninsula. It is no longer true that they have not heard of him—the figure of the huge logger looms up in too many advertisements for that, and Bunyan is a feature of forest festivals and splashes, as some Fourth of July celebrations are still called in the long-log country—but as they sit around the bunkhouses or the stool-and-counter restaurants or the backwoods taverns, loggers certainly do not talk of Paul or Johnny Inkslinger or Babe the Blue Ox. They are quite likely, however, to yarn about John Huelsdonk, the Iron Man of the Hoh.

When, in October 1945, the newspapers of western Washington carried on their front pages the news that John Huelsdonk had died peacefully after a brief illness at the age of seventy-nine, many persons were surprised. There were those who thought that Huelsdonk had never existed, that he was all myth and folk tale; others thought that the Iron Man stories must be based on the exploits of some pioneer, already long dead; and those, like myself, who had known the muscular fact of Huelsdonk's existence had simply taken it for granted that he would live on just this side of forever, like a Douglas fir.

The man did die, but the legend lives.

ii

Back around 1905, they'll tell you on the peninsula, a party of Forest Service men was working through the deep woods in the Hoh Valley. The going was rough. This is the most rainsoaked part of the rain forest. The great moss-hung trees rose darkly from a tangle of vine-maple.

The rangers struggled into a clearing back from the river, and there they rested in woods so deep that not a bird sang. There was only the faint rustle of needled branches high above. Amid the cathedral calm the men discussed the probability that no white men had ever been in this exact spot before them. As they talked they heard a strange sound in the forest, a clanking, a hollow rattle, almost metallic. They eyed one another uneasily. The noise grew louder, and the rangers stood up, watchfully facing the unknown.

Out of the woods came a man, big and bearded and heavy-chested. He moved at a slow trot. Fastened to the packboard on his back was a kitchen range. Seeing the rangers, the big man paused to pass the time of day. He was, he allowed, John Huelsdonk, and he was carrying in some goods for a neighbor.

"But good heavens, man," somebody protested, "isn't that stove awfully heavy?"

"Oh, the weight isn't bad," said Huelsdonk, shrugging shoulders and stove. "But sometimes it's hard to keep my balance on a log when that sack of flour in the oven shifts."

So goes the legend. There are other versions. One of them has Huelsdonk carrying a stove under each arm—obviously impossible, say historians of the period: there weren't *two* settlers on the Hoh who could afford new ranges.

However exaggerated the story of the flour in the oven may be, there is no question that in Huelsdonk's own homestead on the Hoh, miles from the nearest road, there was a kitchen range. Nor can it be questioned that Huelsdonk was an extraordinarily powerful man. I remember seeing him once in a grocery store in Hoquiam, where he happened to be shopping. Someone was kidding him about buying more than he could carry. Huelsdonk, who was then in his late sixties, picked up a fifty-pound sack of meal and held it at arm's length for at least a minute without showing the slightest strain.

They'll tell you on the peninsula that Huelsdonk was the greatest hunter ever to go into the deep woods, though there are other contenders. Certainly Huelsdonk was one of the great cougar-killers of all time. The cougar, or mountain lion, is the largest North American cat; it is usually four and a half to five feet long, exclusive of tail, and weighs from 100 to 180 pounds. Cougars are seldom seen, and the State Game Commission says there is only one authenticated instance of a cougar's having killed a human being in Washington State; but hunters hate them because cougars live off deer and elk and usually eat only the choicest bits of venison, the liver and loin. The attitudes of wild-life administrators about cougars keep changing. Sometimes cougars are considered natural parts of the forest life-cycle, and the bounty is lowered; at other times they are considered an unnecessary danger to deer, and the bounty goes up to as much as seventy-five dollars. Whenever the bounty made it worth while, Huelsdonk hunted cougars. For some years he supported his family by killing the animals for bounty. Cougars were his cash crop. His total kill was around three hundred cats.

It is not true, as they'll sometimes tell you, that Huelsdonk once killed a ten-foot cougar with his bare hands. The man who killed a cougar bare-handed was James Andrew Smith, a logger from Virginia, who in the summer of 1899, on a trail near Matlock, suddenly came on a small cougar feeding on a doe and impulsively grabbed the cat by its hind paws and broke its skull against a tree, thereby earning the nickname "Cougar Smith," which stuck with him until his death, fifty-four years later, at the age of 108.

Huelsdonk, however, once found himself in barehanded combat with a big cat. That was when he and Pete Brandeburry tried hunting cougars by candlelight. Pete and John often hunted together. Just at dusk on a moonless evening their cougar dogs raised a cat and, after a considerable chase, ran it up a big tree. It was dark by then, and John and Pete had a rough choice: they could wait all night in the cold, or they could try a shot by artificial light. Pete lit and held a candle. Its wavering light reflected from the green eyes and white teeth of the big cat crouched on the limb. Carefully Huelsdonk took aim and fired.

The cougar leaped toward Pete, who jumped back, tripped over a root, and dropped the candle. Huelsdonk felt rather than saw the cougar spring toward him. He leaped aside—leaped and fell and dropped his gun as he rolled fifty feet down the steep slope and banged into the root clump of a fallen tree. The dogs jumped the cougar. All the animals came rolling down the slope. They landed in a clawing, snarling tangle on top of Huelsdonk. He lay as quietly as possible. After what seemed a considerable period Pete got the candle lighted, found the 30-30, and with a desperately dangerous shot killed the cougar. The Iron Man crawled out from under, only slightly damaged.

They'll tell you on the peninsula that it was only fitting that Huelsdonk should be the man to end the career of Big Foot, the mightiest cougar ever to crush the skull of a deer. Big Foot began raiding ranches along the Hoh in the early 1930s. He was never seen, though there were those who swore they could distinguish his wild scream from the cries of lesser carnivores. Huelsdonk was not among them. He insisted that cougars practically never scream except in literature. The Iron Man said he had never actually seen a cougar scream, and while he had heard sounds that might have been cougar screams they might have been something else too. Whether or not Big Foot screamed, he left tracks, the biggest in memory, and they haven't shrunk an inch in the telling.

One afternoon in the fall of 1936 Huelsdonk was walking along a trail on some routine domestic mission when he noticed a large number of ravens. He guessed they must be feeding on a cougar's partly eaten kill. He hurried back to get his gun and his cougar dogs. An hour later the dogs raised the biggest cougar Huelsdonk had ever seen—and the toughest. The cat went up a tree and clung to a branch, snarling, while the Iron Man pumped shot after shot into him. The animal finally fell at Huelsdonk's feet. Big Foot measured eleven feet from his scarred black nose to the tip of his muscular tail.

They like to point out, when spilling tales about the Iron Man, that, though he hunted cougars for half a century, it was a bear that caused him the most grief. In the fall of 1933 Huelsdonk was on fire patrol on the Snahappish Trail. He was resting near a lookout when a bear charged from the underbrush and grabbed him by the leg. Huelsdonk couldn't break clear. The bear held him with teeth and claws. Then Tom, Huelsdonk's cougar dog, who had heard the struggle, came to the rescue. He jumped the bear and worried it into letting go of Huelsdonk, who picked up his revolver and killed the bear. His leg was badly torn, but he managed to walk back to the ranch. It took Mrs. Huelsdonk two days to persuade her husband to go to Forks to see a doctor. He walked all the way. At the little hospital the doctors hemstitched Huelsdonk with thirty-two stitches and managed to keep him in bed for three weeks, his only confinement until his final illness.

There are lighter anecdotes in the legend of the Iron Man. Once he and Pete came on a bear among the blueberry bushes at timberline. As Pete tells it, John froze to let his companion have the shot; but the bear sensed something wrong, looked around, saw Pete with the gun, and lumbered off toward the nearest tree. Huelsdonk had frozen so well that the bear tried to climb him. The Iron Man held the bear off with his gunstock until Pete put in a finishing shot.

So the stories go—true or partly true or so good they ought to be true; beloved and perhaps believed by the people of the peninsula because each story is a reason why a settler can feel superior to an outsider, can breathe more easily in a difficult world. This was the function Paul Bunyan served for loggers of an earlier day. But Paul and Babe did not exist, whereas behind the folk-hero of the Hoh was a very real person.

iii

John Huelsdonk was born in Lippe, on the lower Rhine, in 1867. (Family tradition says the name was originally van Huelsdonk, which they translate as "from the deep, dark forest.") When John was twelve years old he was uprooted from the German forests and taken by his parents to the plains of Iowa, where they sought freedom from Bismarck's persecution of liberals. The flight from the Iron Chancellor marked the end of the future Iron Man's formal education—grade school and one year of *Gymnasium*. He spent his adolescence on a Midwestern farm. When he was twenty-one he started west to find land of his own and a place to put his life.

Seattle was still rebuilding after its great fire, and the young emigrant found work there, first as a hod-carrier, later as a member of a survey crew. The boy from the plains made a minor name for himself by getting lost within the Seattle city limits. But within two years he was an old hand in the woods, good enough to qualify as member of a group assigned to make explorations for the state government on the Olympic Peninsula, which, only two years earlier, the territorial governor had described as "our *terra incognita*."

There are those who hate the peninsula on sight and consider it a great wet thicket, and others who covet it as a secret garden. Huelsdonk loved the rain forest from the moment he saw it, loved it so much that when the summer's surveying was done he returned alone during the winter rains to seek a farm site among the three-hundred-foot trees of the Indian coast. The trip was no picnic. The young farmer tumbled into the flooding Soleduck, lost all his equipment and provisions except for one watersoaked sack of flour. Alone, without matches or blankets, he lived for a week on raw dough that he mixed in the top of the flour sack.

Huelsdonk found the land he wanted, a lovely valley on the Hoh. He went out for equipment and returned to spend a year alone, building a cabin and getting the first seeds into the ground. As soon as there was something to bring a bride to, John went back to Iowa and married his foster sister, Dora Wolf.

Their honeymoon trip was hardly languorous: by train to Seattle, by lumber schooner to the mouth of the Pysht, around the cape in a high-prowed dugout manned by Makahs, and up the Quillayute and the Calawah in a shallow canoe that Huelsdonk poled himself; then twenty miles overland and uphill along elk trails to the Hoh and the log cabin shaded by the great trees, and the trees small against the dark mountains.

Dora Huelsdonk spent sixteen years on the Hoh and bore four daughters before she saw a town again. She knew loneliness as great as any earlier pioneer woman ever knew. She spent weeks alone while John was off packing, or working in a logging camp as hooktender and rigging-slinger, or running the trap line—any of the things he did so there would be some cash. She knew the steady rain of the long winters, the booming-whinnying call of the bull elk in mating season, the beauty of the forest steaming under the morning sun, the worry of days without word of her husband in a land of no telephones and no mail. And she saw the cabin grow into a big, comfortable ranch house, and her daughters into fine woodsmen and college graduates—one of them Justice of the Peace for the district. Her husband became the most respected man in those parts, and when a neighbor on a nearby mountain described him as "a man having a natural genius for pioneering as another man might have for music," she could take satisfaction in the fact that none would disagree.

Dora Huelsdonk went "outside" with the girls in 1909 to see the Yukon-Pacific Exposition in Seattle. She looked at the big city, and when someone asked her how she liked it she said, "Fine. And if I get back home I'll never leave it again."

Lena Huelsdonk recalls her excitement when, as a little girl, she went with the family, by horse and then by buckboard, to Clallam Bay—rattling her teeth for thirty-six miles over a corduroy road, and thinking all the time of what it would be like to see a city, a real city. And then: "I think mostly I was astonished to find things were not more wonderful. After living within sight of Mount Olympus and seeing the big trees up the Hoh, the tall buildings I'd heard about seemed relatively small."

Those first years were not the loneliest. The new railroads were bringing in a steady stream of newcomers to the Northwest, and during the 1890s there were always a few odd enough to try living in the Olympics. The Huelsdonks themselves practically populated the valley; Dora's and John's letters to Iowa brought their grandfather, father, mother, and a dozen brothers, sisters, and cousins west to try farming in the deep forest. For a time there seemed to be growing along the Hoh that sort of community which Thomas Jefferson described as the American ideal: a sturdy yeomanry, possessed of land and firearms and respect for education, a populace independent of great cities, cooperative but self-reliant.

Huelsdonk, like most of those who followed him into the valley in the early years, regarded himself not as a hunter or a logger but as a farmer. He raised cattle and chickens, truck vegetables, and even some tobacco. There was no sure cash crop. Money was hard to come by; luxuries were few. Once Dora obtained some sage and used it to flavor a hen when the district schoolteacher came to dinner. John found the taste of seasoning so unfamiliar that he whispered, "Cook another hen quick, Ma. This one et skunk."

A girl who grew up in a neighboring valley has recalled that when she was sick she had to be hauled out over the mud trail on a sled, forty miles across the mountains to Clallam.

In spite of real hardships and minor deprivations, the white population on the coast increased steadily. Each year a few more settlers' cabins rose under the damp firs. The Hoh was hardly in danger of becoming overpopulated, for there were not more than twenty-five families in an area of four hundred square miles. But those who came intended to stay. Nine-foot cougars and twelve feet of rain a year could not scare them off.

The United States government could, though, and did.

iv

On Washington's Birthday, 1897, President Grover Cleveland, as one of his last official acts, proclaimed a number of forest reserves, of which the largest, the Olympic Forest Reserve, placed under government custody 2,188,800 acres, nearly two-thirds of the entire peninsula, a wilderness empire of rock and grassland, forest and glacier.

The editorial pages of Western newspapers broke out with feverish essays in which Cleveland was damned as a lame-duck saboteur out to wreck the system that had made this country great. The mildest adjective applied to the outgoing Democrat was "impetuous." Yet the forest-preserve idea had a long history and distinguished sponsorship. As Arthur Carhart recently pointed out in *Timber in Your Life*, the first reserves were established in 1800 by President John Adams to make sure there would be a perpetual supply of live oak for the Navy. (The reserves were logged anyway.)

The movement that led directly to Cleveland's proclamation probably started with the naturalist John Muir. For twenty years he had been calling attention to the fact that the nation's forests were not inexhaustible, that they were being cut faster than they grew. In 1876 he proposed the appointment of a national commission to inquire into the wastage of America's timber resources, to survey existing forest lands in public ownership, and to recommend measures for their conservation.

The economic-political climate of 1876 was hardly favorable to proposals for government regulation of natural resources. It was an era of unashamed exploitation. Muir's idea was damned by most lumbermen and ignored by Congress. Still, the seed had been planted, and the idea grew. Muir made himself something of a one-man commission, visiting the nation's forests and writing of them in a series of popular books. After a visit to the Olympic Peninsula in 1889 he wrote what many consider the best short description of the Douglas fir forests:

> It is not only a very large tree but a very beautiful one, with lovely bright-green drooping foliage, handsome pendant cones, and a haft exquisitely straight and regular. For so large a tree it is astonishing how many find nourishment and space to grow on any given area. The magnificent shafts push their spires into the sky close together with as regular a growth as that of a well-tilled field of grain. And no ground has been better tilled for the growth of trees than that on which these forests are growing. For it has been thoroughly ploughed and rolled by the mighty glaciers from the mountains and sifted and mellowed and outspread in beds hundreds of feet in depth by the broad streams that issued from their fronts at the time of their recession, after they had long covered all the land.

The most effective propaganda against continued unrestricted cutting in the deep woods, however, was the situation of the lumbermen themselves. The denuded counties of Maine and Michigan and Wisconsin, the ghost towns in a half-dozen states, cried out for some kind of regulation. When the West began to feel the pinch of depression there came to Congress men hostile to "the interests" and committed to the ideas of conservation and regulation. They were, however, a minority. So it was that the first long step toward conservation was taken almost literally in the dark.

In 1891 the Fifty-first Congress undertook to rewrite the land laws, which needed clarification. The House and Senate passed differing bills. A conference committee was appointed to adjust the differences. The joint committee happened to be drawn exclusively from the Midwest and South; a majority were conservationists. Late one night, after talking to the Secretary of the Interior, they slipped into the compromise bill an entirely new section, which said:

> . . . the President of the United States may, from time to time, set apart and reserve, in any State or Territory having public land bearing forests, in any part of the public lands wholly or in part covered with timber or undergrowth, whether of commercial value or not, as public reservations; and the President shall, by public proclamation, declare the establishment of such reservations and the limits thereof.

Now this was most irregular. The rules prohibited the inclusion of new material in a compromise bill. But the session was drawing to a close, and the conservationists took advantage of the last-minute rush to maneuver the bill through both houses. For the first time the federal government had the power to limit the destruction of some of the forests.

President Benjamin Harrison, Republican, at once set up the Yellowstone Timberland Reserve and, before leaving office a year later, put thirteen million acres under federal custody.

The government might control the forest reserves, but who controlled the government? Certainly not the conservationists. They had slipped the reserve bill through Congress, but they were unable to persuade their colleagues to appropriate sufficient money to police the National Forests. Government agents might tack up No Trespass signs, but that didn't mean lumbermen had to pay attention to them. All they needed to do was tear down the signs and keep on cutting. Many did.

The forest-reserve program threatened to become a fiasco and a scandal. President Cleveland asked his Secretary of the Interior to study the problem and report back; the Secretary asked the National Academy of Science; the National Academy appointed a committee. By the time the report was ready Cleveland was about to leave office. But the chairman of the Academy committee, in a preliminary report to the president in 1896, had recommended the reservation of twenty-one million acres or more. It was this advice Cleveland took when he established the Olympic Forest Reserve in 1897.

v

Having been given custody of most of the Olympic Peninsula, the Secretary of the Interior asked Henry Gannett, chief geographer of the United States Geological Survey, please to find out what was in it. Gannett in person took the Northern Pacific to Tacoma, which offers a good view of the Olympics whenever it isn't rainy or cloudy.

A senator from Washington noted Gannett's arrival in the Northwest by asking his fellow senators, "Why in God's name do these scientific gentlemen from Harvard have to come out here and butt into our affairs?"

Gannett didn't intend to make the survey himself. He was looking for a timber-cruiser with an engineering background who could take charge of a small party. A timber-cruiser is a man who can walk through a forest at a reasonably brisk pace and come out with an estimate of how many board-feet of lumber each species of tree will yield. It is a job in which accuracy is all important. There are timber-cruisers whose accuracy is amazing, and there are timber-cruisers whose inaccuracy has led companies to bankruptcy. Gannett was determined to find a good one. He did, too—or rather Theodore Rixon, a former railroad surveyor, found him as soon as word got out that Gannett was offering $150 a month for three years. The surveyor for the party was Arthur Dodwell. They had four assistants.

Once the party was organized, Gannett went with Rixon and Dodwell to Shelton. From there they made a preliminary climb of Mount Ellinor. Standing on the top, Gannett swept his arm north and west in a great arc that covered icy peaks, glacier ruts, rivers, and endless miles of forest. "There's your work, boys. Go to it."

Three years later Rixon, Dodsworth, and company came out of the woods with topographical maps of ninety-seven townships. Rixon had a cruise estimate by species for each township. There were 2883 square miles of merchantable timber in the reserve, totaling 61,000,000,000 board-feet. Another 20,000,000,000 feet lay in private lands outside the reserve.

The results were set forth in detail in 1902 in an exceptionally well-edited government pamphlet. *Forest Conditions in the Olympic Reserve, Washington,* told much about the timber, but it neglected some of the sidelights of the survey. Nothing was said, for instance, about the August afternoon in 1900 when the party stood on the rocks above the Humes Glacier and stared up at Mount Olympus. Somebody mentioned that it had never been climbed.

"Never climbed?" asked Jack McGlone, a packer for the survey. "I guess I'll go up and look around." He started up the rocks.

Rixon shouted after him to wait, that he'd go along in the morning. But McGlone didn't want to waste the space he'd already covered. He kept going. In the early dusk he stood on the eastern peak of the three-forked mountain and penciled on a bit of the *Mason County Journal,* which he carried for ballast, a few notes on the climb. He tucked the paper in a tin can and built a cairn to cover it. Then he climbed down, rejoined the rest of the party at about three in the morning, and turned over his topographic notes on the mountain to Dodwell. They'd climbed so many mountains they thought nothing more about it.

Rixon too made a discovery. He was walking along a trail in the Soleduck Valley when he came on a woman, a pretty young woman. She was homesteading a ranch on Lake Crescent, and her name was Carrie Jones, and she liked the wilderness. Rixon named Mount Carrie after her, and the next year he married her.

vi

While Dodwell and Rixon were studying the potential of the reserve that Cleveland had created, Congress and President McKinley were giving it away.

Congress suspended Cleveland's proclamation for nine months, thus permitting prospectors and speculators to take up claims. Then they adopted the Forest Lieu Act, which provided that any person who had a lawful claim to land within a reservation could select and acquire full ownership of a tract of the same size anywhere in open public lands. Big owners, particularly the railroads, traded the government their deserts and mountaintops for the richest timberland in the public domain.

President McKinley, on the advice of the Commissioner of the General Land Office, issued proclamations in 1900 and 1901, reducing the size of the reserve by 750,000 acres. Most of this land was in the western part of Clallam County. In his annual report for 1901 the commissioner said:

> . . . this timber was not worth preserving, as it would be destroyed by storms; and it was good for farming. Twenty miles of seacoast would be restored to use by the elimination.

The Rixon-Dodwell report for the same area, which was issued in 1902, but was available to the Land Office Commissioner when he wrote his, made a different estimate:

> Taken as a whole this is the most heavily forested region in Washington, and, with few exceptions, the most heavily forested region of the country. The densest forests are found in the townships near the Pacific Coast, in the northwestern part of the Reserve, and in the southern tier of townships.

The Big Blowdown of 1921 made the Land Office Commissioner a prophet in his warning that the timber might be destroyed by storms. In his other estimates he did not look so good. Almost none of the land turned back to bolster agricultural pursuits ever produced so much as a radish. Some of it was claimed under terms of the old Timber and Stone Act, in which the claimant swears the land has no agricultural value.

Much of the rejected reserve was taken under provisions of the Forest Lieu act. The land companies organized by the railroads to dispose of the empires the government had allotted them as subsidy were quite willing to swap acres of sagebrush and canyon and glacier, even up, for acres of Sitka spruce, Douglas fir, and western red cedar.

When a check was made a few years later, old settlers noted that most of the land released from the reserve, as well as that which never had been reserved, was in the hands of a few large owners, only one of whom lived in the state. The largest holdings were those of the Milwaukee Railroad and its subsidiaries, 105,000 acres; the Clallam Lumber Company of Grand Rapids, Michigan, had 40,000 acres; and there were lesser blocks, ranging from 10,000 to 30,000 acres, belonging to people, banks, and corporations in California, Michigan, Illinois, and Oregon.

This did not sit well with the old-timers, especially those pioneers who had given up their homesteads when the reserve was created. It could be pointed out that they had not been forced to leave. They could have remained, as had the Huelsdonks on the Hoh; but instead they had gone away because they thought the reserve would prevent the growth of the area. They had opposed the reserve, but when it was trimmed and they saw the land they had sweated over slip into the hands of absentee owners, they didn't like that either, not a bit.

Meanwhile the conservationists had found a champion in Gifford Pinchot, a young Connecticut millionaire who had dedicated himself to saving the nation's forests. Pinchot studied forest management in Europe, served on the National Academy of Science's forest committee, and applied his own theories of perpetual-yield logging to Commodore Vanderbilt's private forest in North Carolina. In 1898 McKinley named Pinchot chief of the Bureau of Forestry.

The administrative situation in which Pinchot operated was complicated. The Bureau of Forestry was in the Department of Agriculture, but the forest reserves were in the Department of the Interior and were managed by the General

Land Office, an agency not unmarked by corruption. After Theodore Roosevelt ascended to the presidency in September 1901, Pinchot fared better. Roosevelt called him "my most trusted lieutenant." With Roosevelt's backing, Pinchot in 1905 captured the reserve forests from Interior and got them for Agriculture, where the Forest Service could administer them.

Pinchot represented the moderate wing of the conservation movement. The Forest Service permits logging in the National Forests, as the reserves came to be called. The aim is to regulate the logging so that growth balances cut. But, even at best, such logging changes the character of the forest as cultivation changes a meadow. Around the turn of the century there appeared a group that advocated preserving much of the Olympic National Forest as a park, so that future generations could enjoy true wilderness.

Leaders of the total-preservation conservationists were particularly anxious to save the herds of Olympic elk, the largest and most stately members of the deer family. These were then being killed in large numbers by professional hunters, who sold their teeth as watchfobs to members of the Benevolent and Protective Order of Elks.

Representative Francis Cushman of Tacoma sponsored legislation in Congress to establish Elk National Park. It failed. The state legislature in 1905 barred elk-hunting, but a bootleg supply of teeth continued to flow off the peninsula for some years. Representative William Humphrey of Seattle introduced bills in 1906 and 1908 to create a game refuge, but neither passed.

In March 1909 Humphrey called on Roosevelt at the White House and talked to him, nature-lover to nature-lover, about the elk. That evening, just two days before leaving office, the President wrote out an executive order proclaiming Mount Olympus National Monument. It was a bully monument—620,000 acres, half of it forested, all of it closed to hunters and to loggers and miners.

Throughout the Taft administration there was agitation in Congress to get the monument reduced in size, or to have the regulations changed to permit mining and selective logging. Nothing came of it. For one thing, there was too much uproar going on about Richard Achilles Ballinger.

Taft had named Ballinger, a Seattle businessman, as his Secretary of the Interior. Ballinger's attitude toward conservation was that it was nice of past generations to have saved something for this generation to use. Louis R. Glavis, a special agent of the Land Office, which had been cleaned out and was in better odor, announced that Ballinger had told him to call off an investigation of a very large and very odd coal claim in Alaska. Ballinger fired Glavis. Taft backed Ballinger. Pinchot called Taft's actions "unprincipled." Taft fired Pinchot. Roosevelt broke with Taft, tried to beat him for the Republican nomination in 1912, and, failing that, formed the Progressive party, which opened the way for the election of Wilson.

Pinchot's successor as head of the Forest Service advised Wilson to reduce the size of the Olympic National Monument to permit prospectors to find needed manganese for the armament program. Wilson in three separate orders issued in 1915 cut the monument almost in half. Of the 328,000 acres left in the monument, 259,000 were above the timber line.

Precious little manganese was found in the liberated portion of the monument. But the lumbermen mined some fine spruce and fir.

vii

One spring day not long after the Forest Service had won control of the Olympic National Forest, a ranger was hiring a crew to pack supplies to a station deep in the mountains. A burly man, all shoulders and chest and beard, came up, eyed the hundred-pound supply sacks, and asked, "Would a man get double pay if he carried two of those at a time?"

"Yes," said the ranger, "as long as he lasted, which would probably be about twenty steps."

John Huelsdonk shouldered the two supply sacks and strolled off. He earned double pay that way whenever there was back-packing to be done. He needed the money to put his daughters through college.

The land around Spruce, where the Huelsdonks lived, did not lend itself well to general agriculture, so he raised cattle— beef cattle, since there was no market for milk. In the early days wolves often slashed the young stock, and bears ripped chunks from calves and sheep without first killing their prey; some of the animals recovered. When the cattle herds had increased to the point where they could be sold they were driven over elk trails to Pysht. The drive from the Huelsdonk place took four days.

The federal government did not seem a good neighbor to the settlers along the Hoh. They wanted roads. But before there could be roads there would have to be more farms, and settlers were scared away, rather than attracted, by the shifting policies with regard to the federal land.

When the Huelsdonk girls were growing up they went to school in a one-room cabin. It wasn't much of a school. There was only one teacher, who taught all grades, and sometimes the school district was so broke that the pupils worked out their problems on flat rocks, writing with bits of natural clay.

A generation later there was only one child of school age in the district. The district commissioners hired a school-teacher for Elsa Schmidt, and the teacher lived at the Schmidt ranch. Elsa graduated from high school without ever having had a classmate.

During the 1930s a road was pushed up the Hoh, past the Huelsdonk and Schmidt ranches. A reporter who had heard of Elsa's lonely childhood visited her. He was thinking about writing a tear-jerker, the story of a girl who grew up without a playmate. But Elsa didn't see it that way at all. She said she hadn't missed other children. She'd had plenty of play-mates. "I had squirrels to play with," she said, "and every spring a baby elk."

The ranchers on the Hoh had elk the way some people have mice. The Forest Service had eliminated the tooth hunters, and the ranchers had killed off the timber wolves and most of the cougars. The herd grew steadily, and by the mid-twenties game biologists were beginning to worry that it would over-graze the winter range. The climax bunch grass had almost disappeared; the huckleberry and elderberry were being eaten faster than they reproduced; and the elk were browsing on young spruce, a poor diet. They wouldn't starve, said the biologists, but they might suffer from malnutrition and, weakened, pick up diseases from the settlers' cattle.

The Huelsdonk girls tried to solve the problem by catching baby elk for shipment to other ranges and to zoos. Doris wrote about it for a mountaineers' magazine:

There is a sort of desperation in the gun hunt, a quiet lure in the camera hunt, but a deep fascination lies in the hunt for young elk, a veritable kidnaping process. Our weapon is a mere rope. . . .

The baby elk puts great faith in his protective coloring and will lie perfectly quiet as long as he thinks there is the slightest possibility of being unobserved.

When we grab him he is usually very quiet. He plays that he is tame or crippled. Once home, he tames very easily.

When our elk are about three months old we drive them over twenty miles of trail and then they are shipped to Seattle by truck and boat and from there distributed.

This thinning of the herd by the girl hunters was more than offset by their father's cougar hunting. A cougar will kill a hundred or more deer and elk a year. Even after the elk herd grew so large that it was a nuisance to the ranchers, Huelsdonk went after the big cats. Stalking cougar had come to mean more than bounty to him. He looked on a cougar as a living bit of pure destructiveness.

The best season for hunting cougar is winter, when they follow the elk and deer down from the high mountains, and their tracks are more easily followed in the snow. But the rain forest, rugged enough in summer, is doubly dangerous when the tangle of undergrowth is shrouded with snow and the rocks are sheathed with ice. A slide can mean a cold death.

Huelsdonk loved winter hunting. "His happiest moments," according to his daughter Lena, "were roaming the woods with dog and gun. Sometimes he ran out of food, but regular meals did not concern him much. The older he grew the less he demanded of ease and comfort. If the ground was too wet and he had no shelter, he was perfectly capable of roosting on a log beside his fire, like an owl, sleeping sitting up, entirely unsupported. He would camp for weeks in the snow of high Olympic ridges, trapping marten and cougar, with nothing except a six-foot square of light canvas for shelter and bedding."

viii

The State Game Commission, giving as its reason the danger of overbrowsing, opened a four-day season on elk in 1933. One hundred and fifty were killed, mostly big bulls. A national authority estimated that the strength of the herd had been depleted 20 per cent. The season remained closed until 1936, when, having modified the law so as to permit a selective season, the legislature opened one range for a limited hunt. The uproar over that was limited too. But in 1937 the commission announced that the season would be open for eight days in October and November in Clallam and Jefferson counties, outside the monument. You could shoot bulls, cows, and calves, though not more than one to a hunter. A license cost five dollars, and you didn't even have to have your eyes examined. Some Hoh ranchers took out from the hills for the duration.

The impulse to kill something big must be very strong. Sportsmen came from as far away as Florida for the hunt on the Hoh. Hundreds of big-game hunters drove up from California. Men who had never hunted before came to get in on the kill. I was working in Hoquiam at the time, and I remember being in a hardware store, talking to a city policeman, when a man came in and told the clerk he wanted to buy a gun.

"What kind of gun?" the clerk asked.

"Well, I'm going elk-hunting," he said, and he showed his elk tag. "How big a gun do I need?"

The clerk just looked at him for a moment, his mouth slightly open.

"Would a .22 be big enough?" the hunter asked.

"No," said the clerk, and brought him a 30-30. "You'll need this heavy at least."

"Wonderful," said the hunter. "Now show me how to put the bullets in."

The policeman showed him how to load and told him about the safety. The hunter was very grateful. We watched him drive away toward the mountains, and the policeman said, "I feel like an accessory before the fact."

That was the year the sporting-goods stores sold out on red hats—red shirts too. I remember men went into the woods wearing hats trimmed with red tissue paper, and some wore raincoats with red stripes. One old-timer came through town in the gaudiest get-up I ever saw. He had a red shirt and red pants and red hat, and he had painted his shoes red and the stock of his gun red. He had a donkey in the back of his pick-up truck, and he'd painted stripes on the donkey. I heard later he was shot on the first day of the hunt. They loaded him on the donkey to bring him out, and somebody shot the donkey.[1]

The hunters came with tents and trailers and boards for building lean-tos. A party of ten men from Elma had a big truck with a striped canvas top, and the truck bed was filled with hay to sleep in. That first weekend there were more than three thousand hunters in a thirteen-mile stretch along the Hoh. Cars were parked bumper to bumper in long areas near the stream.

Minnie Peterson, a pack-train guide, was in the sub-alpine country above the Hoh on the morning the season opened. "It was like a battle," she said, "or a Western. You'd hear a shot, then a burst of shots, and then shot after shot after shot

[1] I can find no confirmation of this in old newspaper files. Lena Huelsdonk Fletcher tells me that she is familiar with the story, but that it did not happen on the Hoh.

for minutes on end. There was drifting fog and it seemed like gunsmoke, though there wasn't that much shooting really."

The elk were badly confused when the hunt began. They were far from tame, but they had grown accustomed to seeing men. Most of them had never heard a rifle. The herds would stand stupidly for a moment after the firing began, looking around slowly, staring at whichever members fell; then they would break away and race, single file, for the hills, the tawny patches on their rumps flouncing ridiculously. If a cow elk was killed, the calf would often stand by, bleating, while the hunters butchered her—or until someone remembered it was open season on calves too.

Carl Fisher, a rancher in the valley, counted 160 shots fired at one small band of elk that was spotted crossing a stream. The hunters missed the elk, but one of them shot Mrs. Fisher's pet dog. The Fishers had put bells on their horses, but they hadn't thought to bell the dog. It might not have helped anyway. A guide from Port Angeles had belled his horses and put white blankets on them, but the middle horse in the train was shot.

Sometimes hunters quarreled over whose bullet had felled an elk. Game Protector Fred Rice was called to a willow-bottom area where a woman from Centralia and a man from Seattle were in dispute. The man said he had wounded a bull and started to follow it. The woman said she had been standing in the willow bottom when the elk staggered into sight and she shot it. Rice ruled the kill belonged to the woman, since she had fired the shot that felled it.

The Seattle man was a good sport. He said his party would help her pack the kill out. It was a nice gesture, marred a bit when one of the men disappeared with a quarter of the elk, and the game protectors at the check-out had to arrest the woman hunter for not having a license. Later she explained that she wasn't really guilty of illegal hunting, because the elk had already been dead when she fired that shot into its head.

On the fourth day of the hunt it began to rain, a real Hoh Valley rain with weight behind it. The sort of rain where the sky leans on the back of your neck. The wind rose, and the great trees creaked and moaned, and the streamers of moss hung clotted like seaweed when the tide is out. Thousands of seagulls rode in on the storm and began to feast off the entrails of the elk.

The rain fell harder and harder, and the river began to rise. Many hunters started back for town. Under the sound of the rain and the trees they could hear the grinding mutter of the Hoh, rolling the boulders on its bed. The first to leave got out safely, though at some points the river was already over the road. Those who delayed were trapped.

Bucking the outgoing traffic was a truckful of hunters who were returning to pick up four elk they had killed in a swale across the Hoh from the Jackson ranger station. They were very eager, and when they reached the ripple where they had forded the river previously the driver stepped on the gas to get a good run. The truck just disappeared. Three man got out alive and made shore, but the driver drowned. He left a wife and six children. His body and the truck were recovered in the spring.

The Hoh continued to rise. Hunters who had cached elk beside the stream returned to find them swept away. Those who had crossed the river came back to find it impassable. They stood on the bank and watched the water come up over their cars parked on the far shore.

Some Indians with canoes were brought up by truck to retrieve the stranded hunters from the far bank. The rescue went well until one of the Indians noticed a raft of late-running salmon stranded in a pool that had formed in a campsite. Rescue work stopped until the fish were taken.

It rained for twenty-four hours; about ten inches of rain fell at the Huelsdonk ranch, where there were measuring devices. Then the sky cleared. The Hoh, which is very swift, drained quickly. The hunters who wanted to quit were able to go home. Others showed up to take their places. They brought word of a tragedy down at Forks. The state liquor store, the only one for miles, was out of whisky. A hunter could still get gin, though.

When the season ended, 5280 hunters had killed 811 elk, which was about two hundred more than the game commission has anticipated. No one knew how many were wounded. Two professional hunters were hired to track down the cripples and dispatch them. The hunters had paid $26,400 in license fees, and they had spent an estimated quarter-million dollars on food, liquor, guns, equipment, and towing charges.

The hunt attracted some adverse publicity. A state game commissioner who had visited the valley was asked if he thought the regulations should be changed. Yes, he said, he thought it would be a good idea if everyone who went into the woods after elk had a gun of sufficient caliber to kill big game.[2]

One night some weeks after the season I met an old settler whose ranch had been in the line of fire during the battle of the Hoh. We were in a tavern. I bought him a beer and expressed sympathy. He bought me a beer and assured me I was wrong. The elk season had been the most wonderful thing

[2] There is still a season on the Olympic elk, but no subsequent kill has created controversy comparable to that of 1937. The animals are much more shy now, and during the season they stick to the deep woods, where it is very difficult for hunters to find them. There is general, though not unanimous, agreement among game biologists that a season is necessary to prevent overpopulation in the ranges where predators other than man have been thinned out.

that had happened since Social Security. You see, he'd had a cow—old sick cow. Poor damn cow. And when the season opened he took that poor old critter out in the woods and tied her to a stake, and then he climbed a tree. Some danger, but not much. Pretty soon—bang! But she didn't suffer at all. That hunter was a good shot. Right smack between the eyes. Fellow from Seattle, he was, and pretty rich. He was most terribly sorry about killing a cow that had won all those ribbons at the Grays Harbor county fair. He paid $135 right there, and he wrote out a check for $200. Didn't bounce, either.

The old settler dipped his beak into another beer. After that feller from Seattle was gone, he allowed, the old woman and him, they propped that poor damn cow up and got her leaning against a tree, and that week she earned $1425.37, three rifles, a spare tire off a pick-up truck, and she had twelve elk tags on her.

After the season he melted her down for the lead.

ix

The elk hunt of 1937 became part of a controversy then in progress over the proposal to turn the Olympic Monument into a National Park. The dispute, however, was not really about elk. It was about stumpage. The sawmills had begun to run out of trees.

The Olympic National Park dispute was very bitter, and it was complicated by side issues, ranging from elk to Henry Wallace, but the root question was simply how many trees of those remaining would be fed to the saws and how many would be saved for future generations.

Since the day in 1881 when the schooner *Kate and Ann* picked up a cargo of planks for Portland, the mills on Grays

Harbor had shipped more than twenty-five billion board-feet. Lumber from Grays Harbor was in houses and docks and mines all over the world. The mills had reached their peak in 1926, when they cut 1.6 billion board-feet. Most of the Grays Harbor mills had been built when there were plenty of large Douglas fir logs available. They were geared to handle large material. But the big trees were almost all gone. Only two of the operators controlled an appreciable stumpage of their own. The others had to buy on the open market. They expected to buy timber in the rain forest when the Forest Service put it on sale. There were enough big trees there to keep the old mills running another six to ten years.

That was the situation when an organization that called itself the Emergency Conservation Committee published a pamphlet entitled *The Proposed Olympic National Park* and sent it to newspapers, congressmen, state legislators, and conservation enthusiasts. The proposal was that the Olympic National Monument which Theodore Roosevelt had proclaimed be enlarged to cover a thousand square miles and, by Act of Congress, be made into a National Park. The proposed extensions would place most of the big trees under control of the Park Service instead of the Forest Service. Trees in the National Forests can be logged, though under strict supervision, but a National Park cannot be logged commercially.

The chairman of the Emergency Committee was Mrs. Rosalie Edge, a New York society woman long active in the conservation movement. The secretary was Irving Brant, a reporter for the St. Louis *Globe-Democrat*. And in the background was Harold L. Ickes.

President Roosevelt in 1933 had transferred administration of the National Monuments from the Forest Service, which was under Secretary of Agriculture Henry Wallace, to the Park Service, which was under Secretary of the Interior Ickes.

The two services enjoyed a vendetta of long standing, and the new cabinet members had entered wholeheartedly into the feuding of their respective bureaucracies. Ickes, as his recently published diaries show, worked and schemed vigorously to win back for Interior the forests that had been captured by Pinchot for Agriculture in 1905. His passion for conservation was undoubtedly sincere, and to it was added a nagging determination to win the National Forests from Wallace, bit by bit if necessary. (Ickes' tactics were not gentle. At one point in his diaries he remarks, "Rex [Tugwell] told the President that morale in the National Forest Service was at its lowest ebb. This proves that my onslaughts have not been without some effect.")

In 1935 Representative Mon C. Wallgren, a New Deal Democrat from Everett, Washington, introduced legislation to create a park of 728,360 acres. The House Committee on Public Lands held a public hearing on the bill the following year. Little was said against changing the National Monument into a National Park. But should it remain, like the monument, an area of meadows and glaciers, largely above the line of heavy timber? Or should it be enlarged to include the lower slopes and preserve—or, as some said, "lock up"— thirteen billion feet of timber?

Testimony was lively. Secretary Ickes paid his respects to the Forest Service by calling it the "Forest Lobby" and saying, "The ultimate purpose of the National Forest Service is to grow and develop trees so they may be available for use in the lumber industry."

Gifford Pinchot said of Ickes and his plans, "Ambition for power is no good reason for upsetting a layout that works superbly where it is."

Ickes said of the lumbermen, "If the exploiters are permitted to have their way with the Olympic Peninsula, all that will be left will be the outraged squeal of future generations over the loss of another national treasure."

Personalities aside, the main lines of argument centered on the following points:

Size. The lumbermen said the proposed park was much too big, that there was no need or demand for a park of such dimensions. Park advocates replied that it had to be big to preserve a true wilderness pattern, that it was no more possible to have a small wilderness than it was to have a small ocean.

Rain. Opponents pointed out that most of the additions proposed for the park were on the west side, which is the area of greatest rainfall. A Forest Service ranger said the forest was so thick in places that it was hard to walk half a mile in a day. Advocates replied the rain was what made the trees grow so big and beautiful. Besides, the rain falls mainly between October and April; most tourists would come in the summer. And a man making only half a mile in a day's hike might enjoy it anyway.

Taxes. Opponents said county governments got 25 per cent of the stumpage fee when National Forest timber was sold, and the counties needed the money. Advocates said the tourist dollar would make up for the loss.

Ripeness. Lumbermen said the Olympic forest was already overripe. The trees were mature and needed cutting. Otherwise they might be destroyed by disease, wind, or fire. Conservationists replied that a ripe tree is a beautiful tree. If trees died new trees grew out of them. Things had been going on that way for thousands of years, and the conservationists wanted to share with the people of the future the experience of such a forest.

Economic loss. Grays Harbor spokesmen said that if the timber were locked up the sawmills and pulp mills on the harbor would have to close, and men would be thrown out of work. Two billion dollars' worth of resources were being "dedicated to waste." Conservationists replied that there was plenty of pulpwood available outside the park to keep the mills on the harbor going forever. They admitted the sawmills needed logs if they were to keep running, but argued that the Grays Harbor mills could go through the remaining logs in from four to ten years. Was staving off their inevitable shutdown by so short a period worth this last old forest?

Sustained yield. Opponents said the forest would not disappear if it were logged under Forest Service regulations. Park advocates replied, "To a lumberman a forest is preserved when trees six hundred years old are cut down and followed by pulpwood saplings cropped every forty years."

The House Committee, after listening to the arguments, reported favorably on the bill to create the park, but Congress did not get around to voting on it.

In 1937 President Roosevelt visited the peninsula. He was brought to Port Angeles from Seattle on a destroyer and was driven to a lodge on Lake Crescent, under the shadow of Storm King Mountain, which the pioneers used as a weather-vane—if clouds formed on the summit a storm was coming in. Roosevelt spent a long evening talking to politicians, editors, Forest Service officials, Park Service officials; afterward the politically weatherwise said there was a storm ahead for the sawmill operators.

The next day the President was driven around the western half of the Olympic Loop highway. It was raining gently when he started. The party drove swiftly along the arc of the lake, with the mountains across the water shoulder-deep in clouds; then up through the Soleduck country, where Surveyor Rixon had met Carrie Jones in the deep forest—the old trees gone now, drained off to Port Angeles along the Spruce line, and the land bare and scarred; into second-growth, hemlock mostly, which covered the scars. South into the flatland of Forks, where the fleets of lumber trucks were parked, and then suddenly into the unlogged forest of great trees, the air sweet with the scent of wet cedar and sharp with the iodine smell of the beaches beyond; across the gentle Bogachiel and the charging Hoh to break for a few miles into view of the heavy gray waves falling onto the gray beach, and the wind-tortured trees straining against the sky. Back into the forest now, across the Queets, with the big Indian canoes on the widening river, and, in the village across the bridge, the dark-eyed children waving solemnly at the big cars. Through more forest, the road a tunnel under the meeting branches; onto the reservation of the Quinaults—and a pause for lunch at a big lodge with formal gardens and a view of the lake, where Quinaults in plaid shirts and blue dungarees raced the outboard motors on the shallow, white-water dugouts. And away again, out of the big trees and into the burned, slashed stumplands running down to Grays Harbor, sweet in spots with new growth, but ugly mostly, raw and ugly, so ugly that at one stretch the President turned to the congressman and said through clenched teeth, "I hope the son-of-a-bitch who logged that is roasting in hell!"; past the ranches with unpainted farmhouses and the great stumps showing gray in the fields, and the stump ranchers and their wives and children standing proud beside little stands piled with potatoes and beets and cabbages, under signs that said "See What This Land Will Grow, Mr. President." On through Hoquiam and Aberdeen, slowly, so the loggers and millhands waiting quietly on the rain-shiny streets could see the congressman with the President; across the Wishkah and the Wynooche, through Montesano, where the Wobblies had been tried and found guilty after the Centralia massacre;

through Elma and the moribund company town of McCleary and the long miles of second growth that opened suddenly onto an arm of Puget Sound and Olympia—the Olympics behind now, blurred and dim in the rain.

The President had seen nothing to change his mind about the park. He told reporters he was for it.

In Congress there was more maneuvering. Representative Wallgren introduced a new bill, this one calling for a park of 910,000 acres, including a 50,000-acre strip along the coast. Washington's governor, Clarence Martin, flew back East to protest to Congress and the President. Wallgren told Ickes that Martin was a reactionary and should be ignored. Ickes talked to Roosevelt and said Wallgren was naïve, that the way to handle things was to work for a smaller park but to include in the bill an amendment that would give the President the right to expand the park by proclamation. This worked.

On June 29, 1938, Roosevelt signed the bill creating a park of 680,000 acres. The fine print added that he could enlarge it by proclamation to 892,000 acres after consultation with Forest Service and Park Service officials and with the governor of Washington. Nothing said they had to agree.

In 1940, after consulting with the officials and noting the governor's protests, the President proclaimed an addition of 187,411 acres to the park proper. In addition he authorized the Public Works Administration to acquire a corridor two miles wide down the length of the Queets Valley, so there would be one river preserved in its entirety; and also to acquire a strip north from the Queets to Cape Flattery, thus keeping the coastal area as public land. The corridor and the strip were to be administered by the Park Service.

The protests over the proclamation were vigorous. The area included billions of board-feet of timber. And it stretched down the Hoh and the Bogachiel into the ranchlands. It did not include the Huelsdonk ranch, but it took in those of some of the Huelsdonks' neighbors. On the first day of spring that year John Huelsdonk appeared at Olympia to protest against the enlargement. He carried a sign that said "THIS ISN'T RUSSIA—Secretary Ickes Has No Right to Take Our Homes Away from Us." He saw the governor and said he was against having the rules changed again, against enlarging the amount of land controlled by government officials. He hated to see people who had given their lives to a wilderness ranch lose it to the government under the right of eminent domain. All very well to say that the forests belonged to all the people; Huelsdonk felt the forests should belong to those who knew how to live with them.

There were few who did not sympathize with Huelsdonk personally. The old man represented a fading tradition of self-sufficiency and resoluteness—that of the bare-handed conqueror of the wilderness. But many felt that his role was that of innocent bystander. If government regulations didn't change the pattern of life in the deep woods, the sawmill operators would. The real fight was over the question of whether the wilderness should be a wilderness of virgin forest or of slash and second growth.

The Iron Man asked the governor to call out the National Guard to keep the federal government from taking the land. The governor said he couldn't. The old man went back to his ranch, which the government did not try to condemn.

The day before he left office in January 1953, President Truman by proclamation brought the Queets Corridor and the Coastal Strip into the park. That raised the total to within a few acres of the 892,000 authorized by Congress.

There she stands, big and beautiful. As long as the great trees remain in the park there will be men willing to cut them down, saw them up, and ship them away to all parts of the country. And there will be others—I suspect a majority—who would rather come to see them than have them sent.

x

In the fall of 1945 a party of young hunters from California were camped on the Hoh. They had shot an elk, and, like many another tenderfoot party, they were faced with the problem of what to do next. One remembered seeing a ranchhouse down the stream and suggested they hike back and ask advice.

It was a big, solid old house in a wide clearing. A gray-bearded man came to meet them. He nodded as they explained their problem.

"I'll go back with you," said John Huelsdonk.

"It's a couple miles," said one of the young hunters.

Huelsdonk, they say, looked at the youngster good-naturedly and remarked that he thought he could walk that far. So they led him back to the scene of their kill, stopping a few times to let him rest. He told them how to skin the animal and quarter it. When they were through, Huelsdonk picked up the heaviest piece, shouldered it, and said, "I'll show you a shortcut."

He went straight up over a ridge, through a tangle of fallen trees, trotting easily along the steep, slippery path. For a little way the hunters kept him in sight. Then he was gone. They gave up and turned back to the gentler trail. John Huelsdonk had steaks frying for them at the homestead when the weary Californians finally staggered in.

A year later he was dead, and, in the words of one editorial writer, "buried in a country made richer by his deeds and his legend."

8

Shelton and the Hundred-Year Cycle

i

A good highway runs from Port Ludlow to Shelton. The road through Ludlow runs beside the empty harbor, where not even the ferries call now, past the site of the abandoned mill with the great stack rising like a tombstone, and off into the land of slash and second growth and burn—the country of *The Egg and I*. Betty MacDonald has described it:

> . . . Like a pestilence-struck village, the burn was covered with the gaunt dying bodies of the sick, the fallen rotting bodies of the dead, and over everything crawled the marauding blackberry vines, nettles and fireweed. A few low-class squatters, like alder, slalal, wild raspberry and blackcaps had made some half-hearted attempts at reclamation but only in the earliest spring were these even noticeable. . . . In summer it was parched and dry and ugly, and in winter it was gray and soggy and ugly. Mists haunted it day and night and winds came roaring up its entire length and crashed headlong into the house or came crawling from under the vines and logs on their bellies up through the orchard to snivel and whine at the doors and windows. The skyline of the burn was

189

so bleak and hopeless it made me want to run home, light all the lamps and huddle by Stove.[1]

At Quilcene, where the tracks of the Port Townsend & Southern stopped, the Port Ludlow road meets the eastern section of the Olympic Loop highway. The land here too has been logged, but the second growth has fared better and is beautiful. The road runs beside the canal and crosses the Indian rivers—the Quilcene, the Dosewallips, the Ducka-bush, the Hamma Hamma, the Lilliwaup, and the Skokomish. It burrows through the eastern edge of the National Forest and in places skirts the National Park.

Where Hood Canal bends east, the highway branches. One section goes through Annas Bay, where the railroad did not reach, and on to Bremerton. The other branch rises over a logged-off hill now again green with new forest, and slants down into Shelton, where great rafts of hemlock and fir float in the Big Skookum, as the pioneers called Ham-mersley Inlet, and where the stack of the pulp mill sends a white plume steadily skyward.

It takes an hour and a half to drive from Port Ludlow to Shelton, from the old days of logging to the new.

ii

The first lumber was cut in Mason County in 1853, the year logging began at Port Ludlow. But the first lumberman in Mason County was Mike Simmons, the big, unlettered Kentucky pioneer who had led the first American settlers to the Puget Sound country eight years earlier. Simmons built a water-driven mill on a creek emptying into the Big Skookum inlet, but a flood washed it away. He built another, and

[1] *The Egg and I.* Philadelphia: Lippincott, 1945.

sure enough, another flood banged into it. Big Mike figured there must be more floods where those came from. He gave up logging and became an Indian agent.

A successful water-driven mill was built on Oakland Bay at the head of Hammersley Inlet during the 1860s, but serious logging didn't start until the 1880s. The first steam mill was built back in the hills by W. H. Kneeland, who sent his finished lumber down to dockside on a long flume. Then, with the start of steam logging, several operators decided to push steel from the upper sound across the base of the Olympic Peninsula toward Grays Harbor. Three logging lines were started. Two of them quickly got into trouble financially, and the one that survived was the Puget Sound & Grays Harbor Railroad, which everyone called the Blakely because it was built to bring out logs for the big Port Blakely mill on Bainbridge Island across from Seattle.

As builder of the logging railroad the Blakely people sent down forty-three-year-old Sol Simpson. He turned out to be quite a lumberman. Within a few years he had taken over the Blakely line, under the name of S. G. Simpson & Company, and he was supplying logs to a number of major mills around the sound.

Simpson did a number of things, loggingwise, that people said couldn't be done. For one thing, he used horse teams instead of bull teams on his skid roads. It was agreed by all right-thinking operators that this was a superb way to go broke. The theory was that horses weren't strong enough and cost too much to maintain, but the fact was that Simpson's horses got out logs faster and more economically than bull teams—not as fast, though, as the donkey engine, which came along before Sol's horse-team revolution had had a chance to spread far.

Simpson's real heresy was that he did not get rid of his

land after logging it. Most lumbermen peddled what they could to stump ranchers or town-builders and gave the rest back to the county in lieu of taxes. Lumbermen considered holding cut-over land in the same light as retaining old mistresses—sentimental and damned uneconomical.

No one knows why Sol Simpson held onto his land. The idea of a second harvest was foreign to his time (which is not to say he didn't have it). But hold it he did, and so did his successors, the Reed family. They cut the trees and they sold the logs to mills all over the sound, and they saved the useless acres of brush and stumps.

One man who, across the years, bought a lot of Simpson logs was Henry McCleary, who ran the Henry McCleary Timber Company in a town he called McCleary. McCleary made doors—138,000 doors a month—and he also ran his town. He made all the decisions about things that would cost money in his town, and otherwise he left his people alone. They could hardly have been freer to do what they liked—off duty—had they lived at Home Colony. Henry McCleary didn't believe in anyone's interfering with anyone else, except in line of business, where the stronger enforced their will on the weaker for the general good of all, since the stronger were obviously better fitted to make decisions.

Among the families that came to McCleary to help the boss make good fir doors was the Pellegrini family, fresh from Italy. Their son, Angelo, now a professor of literature at the University of Washington, has written of the impression the town made on him as a boy in 1913: [2]

> The houses were rectangular insecurities of wood, unpainted, in various stages of dilapidation. From their appearance one could not easily decide whether they were old or just simply neglected. They were all alike in size and design; and

[2] *Immigrant's Return.* New York: Macmillan, 1951.

although there was vast space they leaned against one another in grotesque rows. From the steep, shingled roofs
tubular chimneys of tin, each covered with a conical hood,
stretched precariously upward. The stoops, littered with
wood, tubs, and various odds and ends, slanted perilously
away from the front door. They gave an impression of pov-
erty even worse than we had known.

That impression, Pellegrini learned, was wrong. The
natives of McCleary were not lazy. Their lives were centered
on the forest and the mill:

> They identified work with the crackle and swish of falling
> Douglas firs, or with the screech and hum of steam-driven
> saws that ripped the forest giants into huge timbers and thick
> planks, some a yard wide and fifty feet long. Such men could
> see little relevance in turning the garden sod, planting beets
> and carrots, or buttressing the stoops which threatened to
> give way under their weight.

The thing that made the greatest impression on the young
immigrant newly arrived from a country where every scrap
of building was cherished, was the conveyor, which carried
waste from the mill to a fire dump:

> The conveyor was an impressive sight. It was a V-shaped
> trough, a foot wide at the base, about four feet wide at the
> top, and some two hundred feet in length. It was cradled on
> a frame-work of steel which, starting close to ground level at
> a point in the mill near the sawyer's carriage, gradually in-
> creased in altitude to about seventy-five feet at the terminal
> end. That height was the necessary margin of safety between
> the end of the conveyor and the burning heap below. In
> the trough revolved an endless chain made of massive links
> to which foot lengths of four by four were bolted at intervals
> of ten feet.
>   Into that conveyor, for ten hours a day, six days a week,
> for years and years, was dumped all the lumber that was
> deemed unfit for the market. One who stood at the dump

end for an entire day, as my brother and I did many times, might have seen samples of all dimensions that were cut in the mill. The bulk of the refuse consisted of the massive outer slabs of the log, with bark several inches thick and studded with knots. But there were also girders, beams and planks of various dimensions. At a point on the conveyor where it paralleled the mill's power plant a man was stationed with a grappling hook. He pulled out the four-foot lengths intended for the mill's furnaces and slid them down a chute into the fireroom. All else went to the fire—a roaring fire which burned continuously, day and night, for at least ten years.

The Simpson people, who owned stumpage near McCleary, worked in neighborly cooperation with the old tycoon and his sons for thirty years. When the Henry McCleary Timber Company ran out of timber in 1941, the Simpson Logging Company bought the plant, the town, and about six thousand acres of stumps the McClearys had accumulated.

The Simpson interests, after years of supplying other operators with the makings, had begun to saw lumber themselves. In 1925 Mark Reed, who was in turn Sol Simpson's foreman, confidant, son-in-law, and successor, built the first Simpson mill at Shelton to cut logs, *hemlock* logs.

Hemlock is the Cinderella tree of the Olympic Peninsula. For more than half a century it was considered a weed and a menace; hemlock seedlings thrive in deep shade, and they tend to crowd out Douglas fir, which needs a bit of sun on its plume. During the lifetime of the first loggers in the West hemlock was ignored. Almost no one sawed it. This was partly because it was heavier than Douglas fir, which created shipping problems, and partly because the tree is smaller than fir. The first loggers could afford to be choosy, though hemlock was pretty hard to overlook. Theodore

Rixon, who cruised the Olympic Reserve, described it as "not a large tree either in height or diameter, and the amount of clear trunk is not great"; but he estimated that 42 per cent of the trees in the reserve were hemlock. That's a lot of weeds.

The research chemist was the fairy godfather who liberated the Cinderella tree from the scullery. In 1909 the sulphate process was discovered for making newsprint out of wood. Hemlock wouldn't work at first, but scientists intensified their study of the structure of the tree. By the 1920s they had learned ways to take a hemlock apart and put some of it together again as paper or as cellulose for scores of purposes.

It was like finding a whole new forest. Today thirty-two pulp mills in the coastal forests employ directly about twenty thousand persons, pay them approximately eighty million dollars a year, and produce more than three million tons of pulp and paper products.

The first pulp mills on the peninsula were built at Port Angeles. They were brought there largely through the promotional efforts of a pioneer named Thomas Aldwell, who as a young man took a homestead on a natural damsite on the Elwha, acquired title to other nearby land, organized a power company, and spent years rounding up customers.

The Crescent Boxboard Company, a subsidiary of Paraffin Companies Inc., built a boxboard mill at Port Angeles in 1918, and in 1920 the Washington Pulp and Paper Corporation started turning out newsprint in a huge plant on Ediz Hook. In 1927 the corporation, now operating under the name Crown Zellerbach, built a big mill in Port Townsend —the first major industry the town has had.

One of the financial backers of Zellerbach was the Chicago investment firm of Peabody, Houghteling and Company. It was represented in its pulp and paper dealings by E. M. Mills. Mills was so enthusiastic about the industry that he led in the organization of another pulp concern, Olympic Forest Products Corporation, now known as Rayonier, Inc., which built its first mill in Shelton. It now has other plants on the peninsula at Port Angeles and Hoquiam.

Rayonier was for many years a steady market for Simpson logs, particularly hemlock logs. The sawmill that Mark Reed built for Simpson in 1925, and the pulp mill that E. M. Mills put up for Rayonier in 1927, stand side by side on the Shelton waterfront. Logs from the sawmill are pulled onto a moving lift that raises them to the pulp-mill log deck. They move along a chute to the debarking chamber, where steel skewers grip and turn them while an operator behind shatterproof glass peels off the bark with a stream of water that strikes with a force of 1400 pounds to the square inch, sending clouds of shredded bark spraying against the walls of the chamber. The log, naked and yellow-brown, leaves the chamber and is carried by rollers to a chute. Down it slides into the mouth of the chipper, a machine with knifed teeth that quickly and loudly chews it into wafers about the size of potato chips. These the machine spits out over a series of screens that sort the chips by width and weight. The chips are dropped into vats of chemicals, where they cook under pressure. Then the bottom valve is opened and they are pushed out and blown against a target, a steel plate; the force of impact breaks the chips into individual fibers. They are now pulp. This is washed, then mechanically screened to get rid of unbroken pieces, usually parts of knots. This mush is then bleached and chemically refined into a pure white slurry of fibers, which is fed into a machine that squeezes out the water and flattens the remaining fibers into blotter-like sheets. Rolled or baled, these sheets are shipped to other mills, where they are finished into any of a number of cellulose products—mostly into cellophane.

The Rayonier laboratories are in a small building in the shadow of the pulp mill. There a team of scientists from leading American and European universities continues the study of the structure of wood. Out of this research will come the forests of the future. It seems probable that the next great discoveries will come from the study of lignin, which, with cellulose, makes up the woody tissue of the tree.

The pulp industry has already revolutionized the harvesting of the peninsula forest. Pulpwood grows fast and can be cut when young—forty years is often old enough. The mills use trees formerly considered weeds, and they use hunks of wood that formerly would have been left to burn or rot. The burning dumps, such as the one that marked McCleary, have long since burned out. The mill incinerators, whose glowing domes were the symbol of a successful lumber town, are now cold and rusted. The materials that formerly went into them, the bark, slabs, edgings, mill ends, and sawdust, are ground up, pressed, glued, or somehow reassembled into new forms ranging from Presto logs to gunpowder. Lumbermen no longer think of a tree as something to be cut up into squares of lumber, but rather as a bundle of fibers, wrapped in bark, to be taken apart and put back together again in many different forms.

A forest can be stretched farther that way.

iii

Men have been making plywood for more centuries than anthropologists can determine, but they have been making it well for, at most, three decades. Across the ages veneers have developed more blisters than loggers' hands, and it is probable that Babylonians as well as Brooklynites have cursed plywood panels that rolled back at the edges like dandelion stems.

It was in 1905 that the first wood from the rain forest went into plywood. A Portland concern specializing in wooden drums tried gluing together panels of fir and cottonwood. The operation was simple. The workers peeled off thin sheets of the two woods, laid them flat, spread on some starch glue, pressed the sheets together, and hoped they would find a buyer before the sheets came apart.

The first improvements in process came with the introduction of a mechanical glue-spreader and casein glue, made from dried skim milk; plywood made this way was a bit more water-resistant than that stuck with the old animal glues. The First World War brought about an increased use of plywood. The material was used in airplanes, though some pilots never got over uneasiness at the possibility that the sheets would divorce in time of crisis. After the war plywood was ready to challenge natural woods in fields where water-resistance was not a factor. But there was a shortage of casein glue. Farmers had trouble meeting the demand for skim milk. This led to increased importations of soybeans, which were becoming popular as cattle food. A Seattle chemist, I. F. Laucks, is said to have been down at a dock when a shipment of soybeans was unloaded in the rain. He stood on some wet beans and noticed they made his shoes sticky. He became interested in the adhesiveness of soybeans and developed a soybean glue, cheaper and tougher than casein.

Among the mills that benefited by the stickiness of soybeans was the Olympia Veneer Company of Olympia, one of the most influential mills in the history of the northwest lumber industry. Olympia Veneer was a cooperative. It was founded in 1921 by 125 men, who put up a thousand dollars each (they had expected to get by with five hundred apiece) and then worked in the mill for more than six months without pay until they had perfected their process and built up an inventory.

Then, abruptly, plywood found a market. Automobile engineers used it for runningboards, dashboards, floorboards. Construction engineers experimented with plywood forms for concrete; contractors used plywood for interior walls. The stockholder-laborers began to pay one another salaries. They began to pay dividends. In time many of the owner-workers dropped out of the cooperative to found private plywood companies. Finally Olympia Veneer sold its plant and migrated to Oregon, where there was a larger supply of peeler logs. The company remained technically a cooperative, though only fifty of its more than 1100 workers were stockholders. In 1955 it merged with United States Plywood.

Meanwhile the scientists continued to improve the product. In 1934 Harbor Plywood Company on Grays Harbor announced that its lab people had perfected a process that made waterproof plywood waterproof. Similar announcements had been made in the past, and there was deep skepticism. But it was waterproof, all right. You could make boats out of it, or put it on the side wall of a station wagon, or the outer wall of a house.

The Second World War sent demand for plywood soaring above plant capacity. Among those who benefited were 250 men who had started a mill at Anacortes—another cooperative. The plans for the mill had been born five years before while the men patrolled a picket line before a struck plant. It had taken them five years to raise enough to build the plant and, like the men of Olympia Veneer before them, the worker-bosses found themselves unable to pay themselves a living wage. But once they got going they were able to pay themselves much more than union scale. By 1943 a stockholder's job in Anacortes Plywood could not be bought for ten thousand dollars.

Well, if you couldn't buy into Anacortes Plywood you could help found your own cooperative. All over the peninsula, all through the Douglas-fir country, plywood workers were talking about the bonanza at Anacortes. More cooperatives were formed. Some bought out private mills; others built new ones. The biggest of the cooperatives went up at Port Angeles.

By the end of the Second World War 15 per cent of the nation's plywood, and 25 per cent of the State of Washington's total, was being glued in worker-owned mills. Cooperatives turn out about 15 per cent more plywood per employee than the privately owned mills. This is hardly surprising, since every worker knows that increased production will show up almost immediately on his paycheck. The worker-stockholders usually vote themselves high wages rather than dividends, thus minimizing corporation taxes. The cooperative wage rate averages about a dollar above top union scale. There is very little differential among the employees; skilled and unskilled shareholders draw the same pay.

The future does not appear as green with banknotes as the past for the cooperatives. The market is getting steadily more competitive. The big private mills have elaborate sales organizations; the cooperatives don't. But the most serious problem is that of log supply. Plywood plants need thick logs. The question of how many plywood peeler logs are available in the rain forest is in dispute. The most optimistic estimate says there are enough for thirty years. This seems high. Even if correct, it does not solve the cooperatives' problem. As newcomers to the lumber business, they have little stumpage of their own. A few big companies control more than half of the remaining peeler logs—not only own them, but acquired them when the price was low, and still carry them on their books at $4.50 per thousand board-feet. A cooperative buying peelers on the competitive market must pay between twenty-five and forty dollars a thousand. At millside a log may cost a hundred dollars per thousand feet. In a buyer's market this differential could more than offset the cooperatives' advantages in productivity per man.

For the plywood cooperatives, then, prosperity is a race against time. They have to pay off their investment before they run out of peelers. Science may save them. The silviculturists are seeking to speed the growth of trees for peeler logs. Technologists are working out ways to use smaller trees in the plywood industry. And there is always the possibility that some new process will revolutionize the whole business.

The plywood mill at Shelton is not a cooperative. It is part of the Simpson operation. It was built in 1941.

iv

When Forest Survey figures for 1940 were published they added up to trouble for the Simpson Logging Company, Mason County, the town of Shelton, and, to a lesser extent, the National Forest in the Shelton area.

Mason County is mostly trees. There are 612,250 acres in the county, and the Forest Survey found that 582,030 were timbered. A little more than half of this forest land was held by private owners, but it contained only 11 per cent of the merchantable timber; the rest was second growth. Eighty-nine per cent of the timber ready for harvest was owned by the government.

The county in 1940 had 3701 persons gainfully employed. Slightly less than half were engaged directly in forestry, logging, and wood-processing industries; two-thirds of the other workers in the county were providing services for those working in the woods and mills.

Mason County came quite close to living by lumber alone. But the supply of trees was running out. The stands owned by the Simpson Logging Company would not carry the mills for more than ten years. The company had a major asset—all the acres that Sol Simpson and Mark Reed had held onto after logging. Without much assistance from anyone, this land had started to grow new trees. The forest's recuperative powers are tremendous. For mile after mile the cut-over had sprouted new hemlock and fir and spruce. Much of it was "thirty years high." But between the time this second growth would be ready to harvest and the time when Simpson's ran out of mature lumber there would be a gap of many years without saw logs.

In the watershed back of the privately owned lands stood those of the National Forest that Cleveland had set aside for the future. The Forest Service would make these forests available to lumbermen, to be logged on a sustained-yield basis. If you figured a hundred-year-cycle for regrowth, the Shelton unit of the National Forest would yield a cut of about forty million board-feet a year. Shelton and McCleary needed a hundred million feet a year to keep the mills going without drastic curtailment. There was no assurance that the Shelton mills would get all or most of the timber from the nearby unit. It would be sold on the basis of competitive bids, and in amounts less than those needed to keep Shelton and McCleary running at capacity.

Out of these joint needs came a unique experiment in forestry. The private company agreed to pool its forest lands with those of the National Forest and to manage the whole area on a sustained-yield basis under the direction of the Forest Service.

The Cooperative Agreement for the Management of the Participating Forest Properties in the Shelton Cooperative Sustained-Yield Unit was signed December 1946 and went into effect on January 1, 1947. It covers operation of 158,760 acres of company land in Mason, Grays Harbor, and Thurston Counties, and 111,466 acres of National Forest land. There were 5,329,892,000 board-feet of merchantable timber, four-fifths of it on government lands. Slightly more than half was Douglas fir, the rest largely hemlock. When the agreement expires, on New Year's Eve in the year 2046, our grandchildren will have standing on these acres as much timber as we do now. It is a cheering thought.

The Shelton Working Cycle was not established without opposition. Shelton and McCleary's gain was Grays Harbor's loss. Sawmill operators in Hoquiam and Aberdeen had expected to bid on the stumpage, much of which was in their county. They objected to Simpson's being used as a chosen instrument for logging it. After a series of hearings, the Forest Service officials decided that the benefits of the plan, which would largely stabilize the forest industry in Mason and eastern Grays Harbor Counties, outweighed the losses to the tidewater mill towns in western Grays Harbor.

The Forest Service and the company have worked out methods for logging the Shelton unit. In the recreation areas along lakes and streams they take only selected trees. This is an expensive way to log, but it leaves the beauty spots relatively unchanged. On the main part of the operating area the policy is to clearcut in staggered settings. This leaves a patch-work pattern of growing timber to scatter seed over the cut areas. The size of a setting to be clearcut ranges from a few acres to as much as eighty acres, the size depending a great deal on the topography as it affects logging operations.

To a layman a clearcut patch is not as beautiful as one logged selectively, but to a silviculturist it has the beauty of efficiency: the clearcut land restocks itself more easily with desirable species from the surrounding forest; it produces a greater volume of growth per acre over the rotation period; and it is more easily protected from fire.

During the first ten years the harvest in the working unit is being maintained at a hundred million feet of logs a year. Beginning in 1957 the allowable cut will be revised to whatever figure a recently completed free census shows to be feasible for continuing on a sustained-yield basis.

The Forest Service ranger in the Shelton unit, William Bryan, inspects all phases of the logging operation to see that the specifications are met. The Forest Service gives its men on the scene a great deal of authority. As one Simpson man smilingly put it, "West of Shelton, Bryan is the law of the land."

The unit ranger and the company each submit thick annual reports to Forest Service district headquarters in Portland. These go into all phases of the operation. Some of the minor items illuminate the complexities of modern logging. Here are some examples.

In an average year it took 5.9 man-hours of logging employment to produce a thousand feet of log scale. Another twenty-one hours were needed to turn the thousand feet of logs into products the company sold.

The fast streams of the logging area presented problems in erosion. So a cottonwood nursery was established, and cottonwood seedlings were planted on the gravel bars and lowlands. They proved effective.

Animals, small and large, can menace the growth of the

forest. Mice ate incredible amounts of seed. Experiments are being conducted in the use of poisoned seed in restocking. Bears presented a bulkier problem. They have a taste for the cambium, or growing layer, of the young fir and hemlock trees. In some areas of second growth bears chewed off the bark on from 70 to 80 per cent of the young trees, killing them. So a bear-control project was started in cooperation with the Washington State Game Department and the United States Fish and Wildlife Service. The agencies furnished two hunters, a trapper, dogs, traps, and experience; Simpson put up the land and the bears. In three years they reduced the bear population by about five hundred, and the trees were growing again on schedule.

Logging always has been largely a matter of transportation. To get the logs to the mill the company has built 178 miles of truck roads and is extending the network about forty miles a year.

Fire losses on the 269,000 acres have averaged less than twenty-five acres a year, the lowest average for any forest in the nation.

After the Simpson interests bought McCleary, they offered the residents of the former company town the opportunity to buy their own homes. Nine out of ten did so. In Shelton 75 per cent of the residents are home-owners.

v

The base for current logging operations in the Shelton Working Circle is Camp Grisdale on the Wynooche River. Old-timers still call this the Turnow Country, in reference to a paranoid Tarzan named John Turnow who terrorized the southern Olympics a generation ago.

Turnow, a contemporary of Billy Gohl, was a giant who was

born of a good family in the Wynooche Valley. He was big
and strong and simple. He was an excellent woodsman, and
he liked to live alone. He was full grown—excessively so,
about six feet four, and 240 pounds—before anyone realized
he was insane. He was sent first to a private sanitarium, and
when he became restive there was transferred in 1909 to a
state institution in Oregon. He escaped immediately by jump-
ing over a ten-foot wall and disappearing into a neighboring
forest.

A few months later loggers on Grays Harbor began to talk
of seeing a wild man in the woods, a bearded giant who moved
through the forest as quietly as a cougar. He didn't harm anyone, but the loggers confessed it made them uneasy to look up
and see the big fellow standing there, bearded, sometimes
barefoot, watching them with the quivering curiosity of a
deer. Usually Turnow disappeared if they spoke, just faded
out of sight in the underbrush. It was enough to give a man
a turn. The only words he is reported to have uttered were
hardly reassuring. A timber-cruiser who encountered Turnow
on a trail quoted him as saying, "Tell everybody none of them
better come out to get me. I'll kill anyone who comes after
me. These are my woods."

The next year the bodies of twin brothers who had gone
hunting along the Satsop were found under a pile of brush.
Each had been shot between the eyes. It was assumed that
they had encountered Turnow. A great manhunt started, but
no one found him—not that year. In 1912 a hunter reported
seeing a camp near the headwaters of the Satsop. The deputy
sheriff and a game warden went to investigate. Two weeks
later their bodies were found in a shallow ditch. They too
had been shot between the eyes.

It was a nervous time in the woods. Every creaking bough,
every animal sound might be Turnow. He was rumored to be

everywhere, but not once was he actually sighted. On some weekends there were as many as a thousand men in the hunting parties looking for him. His elusiveness and woodsmanship became legend. Headline-writers called him the Cougar Man, the Wild Man of the Olympics, a Mad Daniel Boone, a Thoreau without Brains. It was said he swung through the trees like Tarzan.

In April 1913 three deputy sheriffs located Turnow's cabin by a small lake on a branch of the Satsop. They were old hands in the woods and competent shots. Quietly they spread out, then moved in on the shack from three sides. Turnow was in the woods watching them. He had been warned of their approach by an old Indian trick: he had tethered frogs at some distance from the cabin, and when they stopped croaking he took to the woods—or so it is believed. All that is known for sure is that he was in ambush, and as the deputies approached his shack he got in the first shot, from behind a tree. It killed one of the posse. The others returned Turnow's fire. His next shot killed a second deputy, which left it between Turnow and Deputy Sheriff Giles Quimby.

Quimby, crouched behind a log, saw Turnow peer from behind a tree. He took a quick shot at the bearded head, and it disappeared. There was no answering shot. Quimby waited. The wind rustled the needles; after a time the frog chorus swelled full. He slipped away through the woods and went to the nearest Simpson camp to recruit help. It was a wise but unnecessary precaution. Turnow was dead.

I thought of Turnow as I drove past his lake on my way to Camp Grisdale one day in the fall of 1954. The wilderness that hid him from searchers for three years, a wilderness of ancient Douglas fir, is gone; the great trees that Turnow and the deputies hid behind while battling for their lives were logged off years ago. Now the lake is surrounded by a stand of plumy second growth, already thick enough to offer concealment. No one lives by the lake. The frogs were chirping steadily.

Camp Grisdale is about fifty miles from Shelton, halfway between Puget Sound and the Pacific. It is a deep-woods camp, as deep as they come, but it bears about the same relation to the old wilderness camps that nurtured the Wobblies that a Diesel caterpillar does to a bull team or a chain saw to a cross-cut. Mark Reed, after he became president of the logging company, used to reminisce about the first logging camp where he had worked. As was the custom of the time, he brought his own blankets. The foreman said he could put them in the bunkhouse but would have to build his own bunk. He asked for lumber, and the foreman told him he might find some at the hog lot. Reed scraped the planks and built a bed and rustled some straw from the barn, where the bull teams were comfortably housed.

"That night," Reed recalled, "the hard boards and the odor of hogs kept me awake for a long time, and I vowed then that if I ever had charge of a real camp I'd provide decent furnishings for the men who worked in the woods." At Grisdale the loggers sleep on Beautyrest mattresses, and a male chambermaid makes the beds daily and changes the linen each week.

It's a big camp, perhaps the biggest logging camp in the world, some people say; it houses about three hundred men. In the old days there were no women in the woods; a Shelton lass of easy virtue not so long ago disrupted things at one Simpson camp by pitching a tent nearby in April and announcing she was ready to pick blackberries. Now Grisdale is a bit of suburbia. There are accommodations for fifty families in a spread of neat clapboard houses. There is a grade school for the children. There is a general store with everything from tin pants to lipstick, at city prices. There are a library, a bowling alley, a rec hall where movies are shown.

Some things don't change. A man can still build up a considerable appetite swinging an ax, guiding a chain saw, setting choker, or piloting a Diesel cat. Loggers are still prodigious trenchermen. When the cook bangs the steel triangle hanging outside the cookhouse door the men file into a dining room that is almost too shiny and spotless; the scrubbed tables reflect light. The men eat with the air of skilled workmen doing an important rush job—little talk, little waste motion, and no time out until the task is complete. Dinner on the night I was in camp consisted of two salads, bread and rolls, fried ham, boiled beef, pork chops, fried potatoes, mashed potatoes, asparagus, beans, peas, carrots, fruit, two kinds of cake, three kinds of pie, Jello, cookies, and milk, chocolate milk, tea, coffee, and fruit juice. Most of the men went through two helpings of the main dishes. I saw one go through four platefuls of meat and vegetables, two pieces of pie, two pieces of cake, and a quart of milk. He usually did, his friends said. Twenty minutes after the dinner gong rang the last man had finished eating and the waitresses were swamping out.

When I was talking to the cook I asked if he enjoyed watching the men take to the table. "Sometimes," he said. "But take that bald fellow at your table, the one in the plaid shirt. Did you see him with that cream pie? Real whipped cream on top. So he scrapes it off, pours on sugar, sloshes on half a can of Carnation, stirs it up, and eats it with a spoon. If I had a gun I'd shoot him."

After dinner I dropped in at the headquarters, where a number of loggers were discussing the plans for the next day with Clarence Lockwood, the camp superintendent, and Max Schmidt, the logging manager. Lockwood, a gaunt, taciturn man, sat on his shoulders in a tilted chair. He wore whipcord pants, a white shirt, and a metal safety hat. Somebody mentioned the hat, and he said, "Makes me feel less like a chair logger." But he took it off.

Schmidt, the logging manager, is an enormous young man, six feet, seven inches tall, with a quick, shy smile that flashes down from the heights. He is a second-generation Simpson logger. He was born in Camp Three, where his father was a high climber and his mother (one of the first women to work in a Simpson camp) was head flunky. He went to the University of Washington School of Forestry.

"I don't think we'll be logging tomorrow," he said. "Just too damned much rain. Two and eight-tenths inches so far today, and still coming."

"Those roads would bog a goose," somebody said.

"There's a washout at the big gully," Schmidt said. "That's going to take some fixing."

He went to the map and showed me where the road had gone out. The map was crisscrossed with logging roads radiating from the camp. Other lines showed where new roads were being built. Each logging road must be built according to the rigid specifications laid down by the Forest Service. Surveying, bulldozing, grading, surfacing, and maintaining these roads is the greatest single expense in the logging operation. The roads must stand up to the tremendous beating given them by heavily loaded trucks traveling through the rain.

"We're building the roads now that we'll be using in two or three years," Schmidt said. "We're planning those we'll be using in twenty or thirty years. When you're in the logging business you're in the transportation business."

It's mostly the trucking business. Logging railroads no longer climb the hills to the yarding areas. The logs are brought from the wood patch to Grisdale on trucks, then loaded on the company railroad for the haul to dump grounds in Shelton Bay.

There have been other changes in method in recent years. In big spreads, and especially in rough terrain, the high-lead system is still used, but in smaller spreads the logs are yarded by Diesel cats. And in the last few years the cross-cut saw has virtually disappeared. Trees are now felled by men with chain saws. They can cut five times faster and leave shorter stumps.

"You get more mileage from the fellers and more mileage from the trees," said Lockwood.

I asked how the old-timers took to the changeover from cross-cuts.

"Love it," he said dryly. "Except those who quit. Some old Finns just said they couldn't stand the smell of gasoline."

Turnover at the camp is much lower than it was in the old days. At the turn of the century most logging camps were said to have three crews—one coming in, one on the job, one going out. Now it's not unusual for a man to work a lifetime with one company. Quite a few of the loggers at Grisdale can remember Mark Reed, who died in 1933. And there are more than a score of second-generation loggers working in the woods for Simpson's.

Long shutdowns are the main reason for men's leaving the job. Deep snow will close a logging show, and so will prolonged dry weather. A number of old-time families moved out of Grisdale in 1954, when an industry-wide strike for higher wages kept the woods closed most of the summer, but some have since returned.

Chokermen tend to be the most migratory of loggers. The camp superintendent estimated that there was a 50-per-cent turnover among the chokermen every three months. "They come and they go," he said. "No beef. They don't leave sore.

They just work a while and they quit. It's the same in everybody's camp. It's the old pattern. Some loggers always did like to move around. You don't change that overnight."

On leaving Camp Grisdale the next day, I drove to the headquarters of the South Olympic Tree Farm, a few miles south. A tree farm is a place where trees are grown as a crop. The trees have not necessarily been planted; most of the timber on the nation's thousands of certified tree farms seeds itself. The growing timber is tended by specialists who guard it against disease, plant seedlings in bald patches, gather seeds for future forests, and police the area against fire.

A tree farm is a growing forest under private management. It is not to be confused with State Forests or National Forests, which are called forests, not having had the benefit of a public-relations man. The tree-farm movement started in 1941. South Olympic was the fifteenth to be organized in the nation. At first it was made up mainly of the acres of cut-over that Sol Simpson and Mark Reed had hung onto; within a few months, however, the Weyerhauser Timber Company and the Milwaukee Land Company, which had extensive holdings in the area, put their forest lands under common protection. Smaller units have been added, and there are now 176,000 acres under supervision.

Oscar Levin, a big, quiet Scandinavian with experience on both public and private forest lands, came out from Minnesota to manage South Olympic. Since 1948 he has been assisted by Bill Looney, a Northwest product. Scratch a forester, and you find a fireman. Levin and Looney had developed 160 miles of roads from which fire-suppression crews could approach any danger spot on their vast farm. Most of these protection roads were made by converting old logging railroad grades into truck roads. As a source of water supply during the "fire months"—May through September—the tree farmers developed seventy water holes at springs and small streams and in swamps. They planted beavers in remote spots to make natural water holes. Lookout towers were built.

In the eleven years since the tree farm was organized only fourteen fires have burned on the acres under management. The total burn has been sixty-four acres. Seven of the fires were started by lightning; seven were caused by man. The largest, which did exactly half the total damage, originated in a house and spread through thirty-two acres of Douglas fir. The average annual loss on the tree farm has been less than ½₀₀ per cent.

Tree farmers plant trees in areas where natural restocking has failed. Levin and Looney have supervised the spudding-in of about twelve million seedlings. The little trees come from the Nisqually Forest Industry Nursery, which is supported by private lumber companies. The nursery lies on forty acres of land just east of the Pacific Coast Highway (U. S. 99) between Tacoma and Olympia. It is a tree farm in the strictest sense of the word. Ten million trees are started from seed each year. To a motorist driving past, the lines of young fir and spruce and cedar and hemlock look like rows of corn. The crop is harvested in dead winter, December and January, when the trees are five or six inches high. They are sorted, swathed in moss, wrapped in waxed paper, and packed in crates, six thousand to a crate. Forestry crews plant them, about seven hundred to an acre, in areas where the terrain did not encourage natural reseeding, or which have been swept by fire. It is an expensive process—costs in 1954 averaged twenty-two dollars an acre—but it strengthens the entire forest.

The seedlings are hardy, and most of them survive transplanting. (At the nursery they were subjected to dry periods to weed out weak stock.) Except for fire, their greatest enemies are animals. The young trees may be nipped by grouse, pruned by rabbits, rolled on by itchy elk, chewed off clean by the omnivorous mountain beavers, browsed on by deer, or girdled by bears. But most will grow to be two hundred feet tall or more.

Seedlings do best when planted on land at the same height and with the same climate pattern as the parent tree. Most of the stock planted on South Olympic comes from seeds gathered on the tree farm. The seed-gathering program started in 1949, and fifteen thousand bushels of cones have been threshed for seed.

Cones are gathered in the fall by seasonal pickers, who are paid by the bushel. A cone contains from twenty to eighty seeds; a bushel of cones, when dried and threshed, will yield from four ounces to a pound of seed. Each pound of threshed Douglas fir seed contains forty thousand potential trees.

The cone season was just drawing to a close on the day of my visit. The cones had been warmed in the kiln until they opened, then run through the thresher, a machine which shakes and blows and sorts chaff from seed. I watched as Bill Looney poured a stream of gold-brown Douglas fir seed into a small sack. Before he drew the strings I dipped my hands in the seed. It felt cool as dawn. I walked with Looney to the little office, where several large canvas sacks of seed were leaning against a bookcase, awaiting shipment to the nursery —Sitka spruce, western hemlock, Douglas fir, red cedar. I hefted the sack of fir seeds.

"Fifty pounds," said Looney.

For a moment I will never forget, I stood in the dim office, with the rain beating on the roof, and I held in my hands the seed of two million Douglas firs—the forest that our children's children's children will see growing on the slopes of the Olympics.

9

Gersh's Damned Paradise

i

A Coast Guard air station occupies the tip of Ediz Hook, a narrow finger of land two miles long that points into the Strait of Juan de Fuca from Port Angeles. The station consists of a landing strip, a scattering of hangars and personnel buildings, and a small dock. It is the only land still belonging to the federal government from the military reservation President Lincoln established on the suggestion of Victor Smith.

From the windows of the air-station wardroom on the second floor of the headquarters building, you can look across the harbor to Port Angeles, a lumber and fishing town with a population of eleven thousand. Behind the town loom the Olympics, abrupt and knuckled, obtrusive as a fist. Ediz Hook points east, toward the San Juan Islands and the more distant snow peaks of the Cascade Range. Across the strait, eighteen miles to the north, lies Vancouver Island, dark, big, mountainous, foreign. The strait stretches west for sixty miles.

Most of this you can see from the wardroom, but the service area of the Coast Guard air station is much wider. It reaches south to the Oregon-California border, north almost to Alaska, and east and west to the cruising limits of the Grumman amphibians and the ancient Flying Fortresses.

There are eighteen officers at the air station, all but two of them pilots. Since there is relatively little turnover in Coast Guard pilot personnel, most of these men are veterans of several years' service and have done tours at some of the ten other stations scattered around the continental United States. Wardroom bull sessions often touch on the wide differences in activities at the various bases. In New York most of the work concerns small boats. In San Francisco a majority of the missions are intercepts, flights in which the Coast Guard goes to meet planes that have run into trouble between Hawaii and the mainland. But at Port Angeles there is no way of guessing who will need help next.

The personnel now at the station have given aid to commercial fishermen, sports fishermen, duck-hunters, skiers, loggers, motorists, construction workers, pregnant women, bear-hunters, cougar-hunters, elk-hunters, rabbit-hunters, goeduck-hunters, geologists, fire-fighters, mountain-climbers, oyster-scowmen, prospectors, F. B. I. agents, military planes, Rh-factor babies, flooded-out farmers, an ulcerated army sergeant, passengers from Pacific transports, and a photographer stormbound on a lonely island.

"The trouble with this country," a Coast Guard pilot remarked to me one day in January of 1955, "is that it's a damned paradise. It's a standing invitation for people to go out and do something healthy and get deep in trouble."

The speaker was Commander David Gershowitz, a helicopter pilot from Brooklyn. He went to the wardroom window and pointed across the harbor to the Port Angeles boat haven, where a congregation of gill-netters and purse-seine boats stirred gently in their pews.

"Some of the best salmon-fishing in the world around here,"

he said. "Beautiful fish. A good man can make a fortune catching them. So all summer long we're ferrying injured fishermen to the hospital or lowering doctors to them out on the boats. Commercial fishermen! once they're out of sight of land they cut their fingers, they bust their appendix, they have heart attacks, they come down with every complaint known to mankind, except maybe pregnancy. But they're professionals. Most of them know what the weather's all about and what their boats can do.

"That's where they differ from the sports fishermen and the pleasure-boat people. We have, I think, more pleasure boats registered in the Puget Sound district than in any other district except New York. And that doesn't count the flimsies, the little jobs under sixteen feet, run by outboards. They aren't registered. Nobody knows how many of those there are, and I hate even to think—just little boats, nice for running around in good weather, but no good in real weather. Manned by unprofessionals. Where there is a sandbar, they can find it.

"When the weather is good they manage to get back, even if they break down. Somebody comes along and gives them a tow. But when the weather is bad and the wind is rough and nobody has any business out, when the ability to apply the seamanship they haven't got becomes important, then there's nobody else to tow them in, and the Coast Guard gets involved.

"We have the same problem with unprofessional pilots. Guy owns a plane. Guy owns a lake. He says, 'Who the hell's trying to tell me I can't fly my plane to my lake?' So he tries it. They're forever clobbering themselves with those hills. Why, in the Search and Rescue Room in Seattle there's a big map showing where planes have been reported smashed up in the Olympics and Cascades. Red dot for each site, so whenever a pilot sees something on the side of a mountain and calls in, they can check to see if it's been previously reported. Three hundred little red dots."

Gershowitz paused a moment, then raised his green eyes to look at the mountains that hulk up five thousand feet directly behind the town. They were dusted with new snow and very beautiful.

"Just a damned paradise," he said. "Some of the best skiing in the world, right up there. Skiers! broken legs! That's not our problem. Some guy goes skiing and tries to take down a spruce with his shin—what's that got to do with the Coast Guard? Well, he's lying there with broken bones, maybe bleeding, maybe freezing. No mechanical equipment can get to him, and it's a hell of a long climb. So we go.

"Same with loggers. The forest out there is pretty hairy—big trees, and lots of them. The guys who work in the woods are forever getting themselves under falling trees, or a log rolls off a truck and pushes them halfway to China. They get all smashed up inside, and they're way to hell an' gone at the end of some splendid specimen of mud and rut. The private pilots say they can't get in to carry a guy out—we're always careful, you know, not to compete with private enterprise in this rescue business; we don't want to take away some guy's bread and butter. But if they can't make it we take the eggbeater and fly him to a hospital.

"And, on top of everything, there are families living out there in those mountains. I guess you'd call them pioneers. It used to be, anything go wrong with a pregnancy out there and the woman was dead—the kid too. Now we can usually get them to the hospital within a couple hours at most."

Gershowitz looked at the mountains again. "They sure make a hell of a lot of trouble," he said. "But they make things interesting."

ii

The Olympics rise sheer on all four sides of the peninsula. The mountains reach five and six thousand feet, drop off, and rise again. No single peak crowns the range. Most residents of Seattle, Tacoma, and Olympia, familiar as they are with the long line of mountains, cannot identify the individual peaks. In the era before men in large numbers took to climbing mountains simply because they were there, pioneers sometimes speculated about the land behind the visible barrier. Since the central area didn't seem to rise, perhaps it went down. There were rumors of an enchanted valley, warmed by hot springs and redolent of palm trees. A New York newspaper peopled the valley with cannibals.

From time to time there were attempts at exploration. In 1882 a party of hikers in the foothills of the southern slope came back from an all-day outing to announce that they had climbed Mount Olympus—all thirteen of them, seven men and six women. They might as well have claimed Mount Whitney or the Matterhorn: they could not possibly have even approached Olympus.

That same summer the commanding officer at Fort Townsend casually assigned a detail to build a trail from one end of the peninsula to the other. It took them five months to get into the foothills, and the project was allowed to fade away.

In 1885 the commanding general of the Department of the Columbia dispatched four enlisted men and two civilians under Lieutenant Joseph O'Neil with instructions to explore the interior. They landed at Port Townsend, where O'Neil chanced to meet Victor Smith's persuasive boy, Norman. Smith assured the lieutenant that Port Angeles was a logical starting point for the trip, which it was; and also that he,

Smith, was indispensable to the project, which was doubtful. O'Neil signed him on, and Smith escorted the party in triumph to Port Angeles.

The trip to the interior was not quite what they had anticipated. The party had had in mind a climb of two or three days up the mountains, then a descent into the land of the warm springs and the deep lakes formed by the interior drainage. Instead they took ten days to climb to the top of the first line of foothills, dragging their mules behind them. Over the foothills were more foothills, and, beyond them, mountains.

Lieutenant O'Neil went back for more mules and an Indian guide. The guide disappeared. O'Neil sent a party of three off with instructions to reach the Pacific, while he led the others along the eastern slope. The Pacific group lost a pack from a mule and turned back. O'Neil fell off a cliff. He escaped injury, but he lost the enlisted man in his party. The man simply disappeared. O'Neil was still looking for him when a message came from the general, transferring him to Kansas.

The next big party to take to the hills behind Port Angeles was made up of civilians, and it was a dilly. In 1889 the Seattle *Press* gave big play to a statement by Governor Elisha Ferry that the Olympics needed exploring, a point of view which the newspaper endorsed. "Here is an opportunity for someone to acquire fame by unveiling the mystery which wraps the land encircled by the snow-capped Olympic range."

Some days later the publisher of the *Press*, W. E. Bailey, fresh on the frontier from his native Philadelphia, found himself closeted with one of the world's most intrepid explorers—or so the visitor said. To take one look at him was to realize this was no ordinary man. What ordinary man would appear in a newspaper office in a leatherstocking outfit of buckskin, wearing his curly hair in a shoulder-deep mane, carrying a Winchester, and leading two brindle mastiffs?

James Halbold Christie was the man's name, and he described himself as "no ambitious, untried youth . . . but a man tried in all the vicissitudes of mountain, forest, and plain." The rest of the cast wasn't bad either. As companions on his proposed exploration of the darkest Olympics he had brought along Christopher O'Connell Hayes, twenty-two, billed as a lineal descendant of Daniel O'Connell, known to Irish Catholics as the Liberator; John Henry Crumback, a Canadian who claimed to be an old Indian-stalker; and Johnny Sims, an Englishman who claimed to be an old Boer-stalker. They all looked good to Bailey, who agreed to finance the expedition in return for an exclusive report for the *Press*.

Christie went right out and hired two more explorers, one of them a physician. He bought a short ton of supplies and caught the packet for Port Angeles, where he encountered Mayor Norman Smith, full of advice.

Christie didn't take advice from everyone. There were plenty of pioneer-type people around to tell him December was hardly the best time to start exploring the Olympics, but he brushed off their objections, saying that he wanted to be over the mountains and into the interior valley with the spring run-off. Experienced packers thought that two thousand pounds of supplies might be more than six men could haul through a wilderness, but Christie explained they'd go by boat —up the rivers, like Lewis and Clark.

If it was rivers they wanted, Norman Smith could oblige. He suggested the Elwha, a beautiful deep stream, navigable for thirty miles, he said, and opening, he was sure, onto the warm central valley. So they bought lumber for a boat, hired a wagon, and started for the Elwha.

The wagon couldn't get within a mile of the river. The men got out and began to build a trail. It took two weeks. They bought two mules and began to haul the supplies along their trail, but the mules got mired and the men wound up back-packing or sledge-hauling everything, including the lumber to build the boat that was to float them to glory—upstream.

The Elwha was swift, dirty-gray, and cold. The weather was cold. It snowed. Carpentry was difficult, and the men got sick and drank their full trip's supply of whisky and banged their thumbs and blistered their hands, but by the end of December their boat was ready. She was thirty feet long and, if not beautiful, sturdy. They named her *Gertie,* and they launched her, and she sank.

They bailed out *Gertie* and wrestled her ashore and turned her over. They spent two weeks drying her out and calking her. In mid-January *Gertie* took to the water and floated like a boat. They loaded in the supplies and began poling her upstream. *Gertie* wouldn't pole. She had to be pushed or pulled, each of which involved wading. It was enough to discourage an average man, and five miles and ten days later the *Press* party admitted discouragement. They abandoned *Gertie* and prepared to load the mules. Then a blizzard began.

The explorers were still within range of civilization. They holed up with an old settler until the storm cleared. They spent their time building sledges of unusual design, but none of them worked. The group physician got word that his wife was sick and went home to Puyallup. The other five, though hardly undaunted, loaded the mules, Jenny and Dolly, and pushed on. Jenny went over a cliff. The men kept going. They were not without determination.

They came into a valley where elk and deer and other game abounded. They regained strength on the venison. Then on again, into truly unexplored land, up along a river they named the Lillian, up and out of the winter grazing range and into a land of thin grass and sparse brush. Their pemmican griped them; their dogs ate the last of their bacon; and Dolly just lay down and refused to move. They freed her; she staggered down the slope, and they struggled up. They were reduced to taking supplies they could pack on their own backs, but they kept going. For weeks they ate little but flour.

For nearly two months Christie and his companions rummaged around the Elwha basin, bestowing upon the mountains and valleys and streams and lakes the names of their sponsors, their wives, friends, sweethearts, and the animals they killed. In May they crossed from the headwaters of the Elwha, through the Low Divide, to the upper reaches of the Quinault River. There, where the waters flowed west, they encountered a bear, shot it, and ate it in two days.

Descending the Quinault, they met a white hunter and some Indians. The Indians told them there was a trail leading south to Grays Harbor; the hunter said they could raft down the Quinault. Forgetting *Gertie*, they made a raft, loaded it with their camping equipment, and pushed off. They immediately ran into a natural dam, turned over, lost most of their supplies, and nearly lost one of the party. The hunter retrieved them, fed them, escorted them to a trail, and started them off for Aberdeen.

So, early in June, six months after leaving Seattle, they came out of the woods and learned that a pair of Minnesotans, C. S. Gilman and S. C. Gilman, father and son, had some months earlier, in November, gone up the Quinault, through the Enchanted Valley, across the divide, and onto the foothills rising to Mount Constance. Not only that, but they had made a north-south crossing from the Pysht to the Quinault while the *Press* party was building *Gertie* and wrestling her up the Elwha. But the Gilmans had not been sponsored by a newspaper. Their explorations attracted little attention.

Christie and his men wrote a full account of their adventures for the *Press*. They were not efficient explorers, but they saw a number of places first, and to them must go the credit for publicizing the fact that the Olympic Mountains were really mountains.

Among those unimpressed by the *Press* party performance was Lieutenant O'Neil, who had won a new detail of enlisted men from the Army and was going back into the mountains. He thought he could do better than Christie. As a matter of fact, he could, though he antagonized a considerable number of people in the process. The lieutenant was on his way to becoming a general, and he dearly loved to give orders.

O'Neil's party consisted of ten enlisted men, two packers, a doctor, and three scientists—a naturalist, a botanist, and a mineralogist—who had been recruited from the Oregon Alpine Club. The party approached the Olympics from the southeast. They moved slowly up the Skokomish, building a trail as they went. O'Neil detailed men to explore the Duckabush and the Dosewallips. The main party went up the North Fork of the Skokomish, crossed the divide, and traced the rivers that ran west and south—the Quinault, the Humptulips and the Hoquiam; the Satsop, the Wynooche, and the Wishkah. Then, having made the crossing on foot, O'Neil, at the request of the Hoquiam Board of Trade, made the east-west trip again with a mule train. This was to encourage prospectors.

It was on this pack trip that O'Neil detailed N. E. Linsley and B. J. Bretherton, the naturalist and the mineralogist, to go with some soldiers and climb Mount Olympus. (The third alpinist, Louis Henderson, had given up some time previously, complaining of an aching back. There are those who attribute his departure to his distaste for O'Neil's military approach to mountaineering. Anyway, he packed up his botanical specimens, shook hands all around, and left.)

Linsley and Bretherton and five enlisted men worked up the Quinault and to the Elwha, then west to the Queets River (where one man got lost, but made the trip out unassisted) and on into sight of the Hoh glacier, which, later parties have found, offers the easiest approach to the summit. They circled the mountain until, on September 22, 1890, they made an assault on the peak from the south.

Bretherton, Linsley, and a Private Danton reached the top, they said later, and, finding no place to build a cairn, they climbed down a little way and deposited a copper box among some rocks. In the box they stuffed such souvenirs as they could spare: buttons, old shoelaces, playing cards, and a beer check, among other things. Then they struggled down the Queets and eventually caught up with O'Neil at Port Townsend. He pronounced himself dissatisfied with their work.

The copper box has never been found, but experienced mountaineers are inclined to think Linsley, Bretherton, and Danton did reach the top of one of Olympus's three peaks.

After 1890 there were casual expeditions by small parties almost every year, and there was also the timber cruise by Dodwell and Rixon, but no more organized attempts were made on Olympus until 1907. In that year a Port Angeles banker, W. R. Delabarra, agreed to raise funds to build a trail into the interior so that a Seattle alpine club, the Mountaineers, could make a large-scale assault on the peak in August.

The old *Press* party trail up the Elwha was tidied up. Horses were sent into the interior. The Humes brothers, who had built a cabin in the valley where Christie and his party feasted off elk, were hired to pack food and clothing into the interior.

Then, a few days before the Seattle group was to catch the steamer for Port Angeles, along came three eastern climbers, Hershell Parker, Belmore Browne, and Walter Clark. They breezed up the improved trail, hired one of the Humes boys as a guide, crossed into the Queets Basin, and on the afternoon of July 17 reached the summit of the middle peak.

The Mountaineers were most unhappy. They were particularly displeased with Humes for showing the interlopers the way. Humes couldn't understand what all the fuss was about. Why worry who was first? The mountain was still there. If they liked to climb mountains they still could.

Climb it they did, and in considerable numbers. On August 12 a party of three reached the summit of the east peak, only to have their view spoiled by the little cairn that had been left by Jack McGlone, the Rixon-Dodwell packer, eight years before.

The next day a dozen of the party made it to the top of the middle peak—and found the marker raised by Parker, Browne, and Clark only a month earlier. There was still time to go to the west summit, which, though lower, was probably virgin. As they approached the west peak the cloud cover parted, and they saw a new pinnacle gleaming above what they had thought was the summit. They climbed it and found they could look down on the middle peak and the east peak. This was the ultimate pinnacle of the range, 7954 feet above sea level, and on it they found no mark of previous ascent.

iii

With regard to sports fishing in the Olympics, the people of Port Angeles are inclined to paraphrase Izaak Walton's remarks on the wild strawberry. "Doubtless God could have

made a better fishing area," they say, "but doubtless God
never did."

The strait offers salmon, and the streams and lakes offer
trout. There are the rainbows, which drew a lyrical description from David Starr Jordan:

> . . . a thing of beauty, a joy forever, beyond dispute; its
> back was well sprinkled with ocelot-like spots; the color a
> deep green, the lower surface silver, while all over seemed
> drawn a filmy gauze of some old-rose fabric, of inexpressible
> delicacy and beauty, which was intensified along the median
> line on a band of pink and rose and other tints that produced
> all the colors of the rainbow and gave this radiant creature
> rank among the birds of brilliant plumage.

For those who relish a fight, there are the steelheads, trout
that spawn in the sea. And in Lake Crescent there is a unique
species of trout, which in 1898 Professors Carl Akeley and
D. G. Elliott of the Field Museum in Chicago named the
Beardslee, in honor of Rear Admiral Leslie A. Beardslee, who
had caught some on a visit to the peninsula. (The naturalists
also named the elk herd the Roosevelt elk, after Colonel
Theodore Roosevelt of the Rough Riders.)

E. B. Webster of Port Angeles, in a pleasant book entitled
Fishing in the Olympics, estimates that the Beardslee is
traveling twenty-five miles an hour when it strikes; the trout
takes about a hundred feet of line, then breaks the water in a
series of leaps that carry the fish six or seven feet. Webster
says the longest known fight with a Beardslee lasted three
hours and forty-five minutes, after which a Tacoma angler
landed an eleven-pounder with a four-and-three-quarter-
ounce rod and the lightest of lines.

Another of Webster's stories concerns a Port Angeles en-
thusiast known as Doc White, whose practice it was never to
be near water without fishing tackle. White was on the steamer

Sol Duc en route to Victoria one day when the boat broke down. Soon he had a line over the side, and while the other passengers gritted their teeth against the roll of the boat he happily told them of the fish he'd catch for dinner—fish to fry, fish to bake, fish to boil.

One seasick listener retreated to the mizzendeck rather than listen to more. Just as he came opposite the galley the steamer gave a heavy lurch. White's spinner came out of the water and swung inboard. The passenger grabbed it and backed into the galley.

From above came the shout, "Got one!" The passenger yanked the line.

"Must be a whale," shouted White.

People began giving advice. For a quarter-hour White played his catch and the passenger played White.

Then, the *Sol Duc*'s cook having proved helpful, the passenger released the line. Doc White carefully reeled in his catch. Over the rail came a kippered herring.

For a moment there was silence. Then the fisherman turned to a friend. "Take that fish off the hook, boy," he said grandly. "It's not as large as I thought, but nobody ever caught a fish that was older." [1]

iv

It has been said that Port Angeles was made by spruce, scenery, salmon, and the Smiths.

There are five species of salmon on the Pacific Coast. They go by different names in different sections, but along the strait they are known as kings, silvers, sockeyes, pinks, and chums. The kings, which are huge—up to a hundred pounds—and

[1] From *The Story of Port Angeles and Clallam County, Washington,* by Lauridsen and Smith (Seattle: Lowman & Hanford, 1937).

the silvers, which are numerous, draw the sports fishermen; but the sockeyes built the fishing fleet.

The sockeye gets its name from the Indian word *suk-kegh*. It is a small fish as Pacific salmon go, averaging about six pounds in weight, but it is rich in protein, standard in size, abundant in number, and regular in habit—an ideal fish on which to base a canning industry.

Sockeyes are born in mountain streams. They hatch in the spring from eggs laid in the spawning beds the previous autumn. The fry move into the mountain lakes that summer; most of them migrate to sea the next April or May, though a few stay in fresh water for another year. When in their fourth year, they return to the river of their birth, and in the very tributary where they were born they spawn and die.

The first sockeyes show up off the coast in June. The run continues into October. The fish move in great schools, tens of thousands of them, close to the surface. For as long as men have lived along the strait there have been fishermen awaiting the summer run.

Commercial fishing of the Pacific salmon started in 1827, when the Hudson's Bay Company shipped some smoked sockeye to Hawaii, but it did not become intensive until the 1880s. Then the development of steam boxes and quick soldering processes made commercial canning possible.

When their spawning urge starts them back toward their native stream, sockeyes stop feeding.[2] Only a few will rise to strike at lures, so they must be caught in nets. Fishermen have devised an assortment of nets with which to harvest the run: fish traps (now illegal in the United States except for those operated by Indians, and obsolete in Canada) made of chicken-wire and built on the principle of a maze; soft gill-

[2] In Alaska sports fishermen catch sockeyes on flies at the start of the spawning run.

nets into which the salmon thrust their heads and, caught by the gills, cannot back out; purse-seines, which are lowered to encircle a school, then drawn shut at the bottom; reef nets, which are spread horizontally between two boats, then raised when the salmon run over them.

Sockeyes live in any mountain stream that widens to a lake during its course, but the great sockeye stream of the early days was the Fraser River. Most of the sockeyes migrating through the strait were on their way to the Fraser, which flows into the sea just north of the Canadian border. No one knows the size of the old runs. Counting fish—like estimating the size of the ones that get away—is no exact science. Biologists guess that two hundred million sockeyes went up the Fraser or were caught out of the run during a ten-year period ending in 1913. Certainly they were abundant.

As the size of the fish pack increased, so did the complaints of conservationists. The fishers and the canners replied that the very fact the pack was increasing showed that there were still plenty of fish; the conservationists said it only showed that the fishermen were killing a higher percentage of the run.

Every fourth year is a big year for sockeyes. It is called the dominant fourth. The biggest fourth in memory was the run of 1913. Thirty million sockeyes were pulled from the strait, the sound and the river. The catch at 1955 prices would be worth $90,000,000; even at the time it represented a bonanza of $25,000,000.

Fishermen in Port Angeles and other fishing centers in the area could hardly wait for the 1917 run, the next dominant fourth. Their anticipating was whetted by the increased demand for canned foods, especially those rich in proteins, brought on by the war in Europe. When the long-awaited season approached the fishermen were ready. Many had new boats and new gear and big new debts. They jockeyed fiercely for the best locations at the island passages and river mouths where the sockeyes congregate. The packers were ready with new equipment and a backlog of orders. Everything awaited the run, but there was almost no run.

Day after day that summer watchmen waited by the chicken-wire fish traps, anticipating the run that would fill the pens and pay in a day for the new wire stretched between the pilings. It didn't come. The lookouts on the ladders of the reef-net boats stared across the lovely, empty water between the San Juan Islands and thought of the mortgage. Purse-seiners and gill-netters lowered their expensive webs and raised them again, nearly empty.

The 1913 sockeye pack from the area of the Puget Sound and the Gulf of Georgia had been 2,392,895 cases. In 1917 it was less than one-quarter as large—785,651 cases. In 1921 the catch came to only 142,593 cases. A few years later an economist wrote, "The Fraser is no longer a factor in the salmon fishery." Sadly the fishermen at Port Angeles and other ports turned to the other species.

In 1937 Canada and the United States signed a treaty establishing the International Pacific Salmon Fisheries Commission, and empowered it to build up the salmon run through research, regulation, and construction. They asked Dr. William F. Thompson, director of the University of Washington school of fisheries and a well-known tracer of lost fish runs, to find out where the sockeyes had gone.

Thompson assembled an international team of fish biologists, ten Canadians and six Americans. They began an inquest into the death of the sockeye run. From the material his investigators uncovered, Thompson worked out a theory.

The sockeyes, he reasoned, were not merely a species of salmon, but a species that is divided into a number of races. Each race has its own home stream and its own optimum spawning period. So most members of a race would start back to their home stream within a few days of one another. Case histories of tagged fish indicate that any sockeye that was held up as much as two weeks on its way to spawn would fail to complete its journey. Therefore it was possible that changing river conditions had delayed whole races for a fortnight or more, virtually sterilizing their home streams.

This theory was checked against the history of the flow of the Fraser River. It was found that in 1913 and 1914 slides, triggered by railroad construction, had clogged the Fraser in the Hell's Gate area. This obstruction raised the height of the flood and increased its force. Thompson theorized that when the flow reached a certain height it slammed Hell's Gate shut against the migrating sockeye.

Figures showed that while the roughest rocks had been blasted away or dredged out in 1915, there was still enough slide material in the gorge to push the river at flood several feet above its pre-1913 levels.

The Salmon Fisheries Commission called on a Port Angeles man for advice. He was Milo Bell, a fisheries expert who specialized in the design of devices to help fish swim upstream.

Bell had a model of Hell's Gate constructed by University of Washington engineering students. He spent weeks and months running water through it, approximating the varying stages of river flow. He finally proposed a unique fishway— a pair of outsize flumes, like big bathtubs forty feet deep and four hundred feet long, fastened to the walls of the canyon. They could be set so as not to complicate further the flow of the river through Hell's Gate. The downstream ends would be placed so as to create a natural eddy that would draw the fish into the bypass. Bell made a model, and it worked.

But the real thing would cost nine hundred thousand dollars.

The commission, which had a budget of $74,000, asked the United States and Canada to put up money to cover the cost of construction. The two countries agreed. The first salmon passed through the fishway in 1945.

A veteran fish counter, peering into the murky waters above Hell's Gate in 1946, pronounced the run at that point the largest since 1912. Indians on the upper tributaries joyfully welcomed the arrival of "many fish, green and strong," whereas for years they had seen only a straggle of weak, gashed creatures.

The sockeye runs built steadily but not spectacularly until 1954. That summer the fishermen saw the waters of the strait alive with migrating sockeyes. It was a run such as no one along the peninsula had seen for a generation. During ten days in August sockeye fishermen caught fish worth fifteen times the cost of the fishways. In the brief summer season they took 9,500,000 sockeyes, worth an average of two dollars each to the fishermen. The value of the catch when packed was $33,000,000.

Purse-seine boats from Port Angeles and the other American fishing towns averaged $35,187 on the year's salmon season. The high seine boat, *Sea Master,* marketed $87,000. Crew members in the seine fleet averaged something over $2500 for the season. Most boats fished one hundred days but landed three-fourths of their catch in the ten rich days of late August when the sockeyes were sweeping north.

The commission is sure the Fraser runs will not only continue but build up. The fishermen think so too. For the first time in years there seems agreement that fishing has a future, even for the little fellow. Barney Olson, a bald, blue-eyed man who has been with the fleet for twenty-three seasons, summed it up when he said, "Last year I told my son to go find a job in a defense plant. I figured there was a future in bombers if nothing else. This year he's going out with me. Next year too, I hope. If a man can make a living gathering food, he ought to."

10

This Veritable Breed

i

One of my first assignments as a reporter back in the thirties was to cover a Pioneer Picnic. The principal speaker, an ancient minister of the Gospel, of imposing dimensions, concluded his peroration something like this: "No longer are there men and pioneer ladies capable of meeting the challenge imposed by the wilderness, for in truth this rarest of humans, the true pioneer, this veritable breed, has perished from the face of the earth."

This statement was no more accurate than many others one hears at old-time picnics, political rallies, or annual banquets. Perished, indeed! There are roads and electric lights on the peninsula now, and some toilets flush, but it remains a wild and lonely place and as such exerts an odd attraction for the self-sufficient and the eccentric, two strains of the veritable breed. As a friend of mine who pirates logs for a living once remarked, "This is one place you can make a buck without a boss."

Though a majority of the 150,000 residents of the Olympic area depend on the lumber industry for a living and work for companies, big or small, others depend directly on the bounty of forest and beach. On the peninsula are shake-froers and brush-pickers, clammers and log pirates, basket-weavers, and a professional octopus trapper. There are a woman who guides pack trains, and a couple who for years migrated with an elk herd. There are a man reputed to breed cougars for bounty and a Chamber of Commerce secretary who bottles snow-worms from the glaciers of Mount Olympus. A local judge has told me of a family that has lived thirty years in a remote and beautiful valley where there are some manganese deposits: they are waiting hopefully for a railroad company to lay track to their hideout and make them "rich enough to get the hell back to Kansas."

There are those whose way of life is wild, and others, like L. J. Wyckoff, whose way is mild almost beyond compare. Wyckoff, a lean, tanned man, more content than most human beings, raises lavender. He's a sweet-scented pioneer, the first—and for many years the only—commercial lavender-grower in the United States.

Another botanical pioneer is Joseph Eberhardt, who grows blueberries. Eberhardt's thirteen-acre spread on Hunter's Point, near Shelton, has drawn world attention. More than a hundred thousand blueberry bushes are shipped from the ranch each year. They go to every state and a dozen foreign countries. His hybrid from New Jersey and Alaska strains is the biggest thing in the blueberry business today, and he is raising a plant that produces berries the size of plums.

It takes years to become an Eberhardt or a Wyckoff, but any latter-day pioneer with good legs and tough skin can become a brush-picker. Brush-picking is sometimes called "forest-combing" by its practitioners, and is usually referred to as robbery, banditry, or vandalism by outraged property-owners. It may be a million-dollar business, but precise figures are not available—hardly surprising for an enterprise founded on trespass and theft.

The underbrush taken by brush-pickers is mainly huckle-berry and salal and sword-fern, all of which grow in the lush forest lowlands and are purchased with no questions asked by most companies that specialize in supplying greenery to florists about the nation. At least three hundred freight-car loads move east and south each year, and few are the funerals or formal weddings that take place in America unattended by some of this hijacked undergrowth.

To become a brush-picker you have only to go into the woods and start picking. A child can do it, and many children do, as brush-pickers tend to work in family groups. Some pickers operate legally, paying the owners of forest property for the right to roam their land looking for sword-ferns the required two feet in length, or huckleberries and salal grow-ing in deep shade, which makes the leaves glossy. Other pickers rely on the fact that the peninsula is big and thinly populated.

A good brush-picker on a good day in a good location can make up to fifty dollars, but few do, and none for many days a month. The people drawn to brush-picking are not often of a type given to sustained effort. They like to knock off for a day or a week, to drop a hook where the salmon are lying, or try out a sandspit for goeducks if there is a minus tide, or help a friend saw the brand off a rustled log. Brush-picking aver-ages out as subsistence living, but it has its charm: few tasks can be performed amid greater beauty. Among brush-pickers I have encountered there were vacationing college profes-sors, retired timber-cruisers, one poet, a bootlegger, beached towboat men, clerks who had talked back to the boss, and one boss who got tired of back talk. The basic ingredient of the profession is a fine, wild assortment of old folks who can be found stretching their pension checks wherever the price of waterfront property is still low.

Along the shores of the sound and the canal and the strait, and a few places on the ocean side of the peninsula, in houses of hand-froed cedar or driftwood planks, live the old rebels: free-thinkers of assorted kidney, Wobblies, crusaders for free silver and other dead causes, Technocrats—determined believers one and all, men of one book; the men who once peopled places like Home Colony and Burley, rebels, now drawing their rocking-chair pay from the government, and very unrepentant. Some are silent and morose, and an evening with them is an evening of monosyllables, of wondering in what cemetery of hope your companion's mind is buried; but others are great talkers, widely read, gaily bitter about the society that defeated their causes and now supports them; and an evening spent with such men in a cabin of sweet-smelling cedar set in second growth on a high bank looking across the sound is to step back a generation, to a simpler time. The soft line from the kerosene lamp plays on the worn backs of *Looking Backward* and the works of Jack London and Frank Norris. There may be an I. W. W. songbook or the collected *Speeches and Editorials* of Daniel de Leon. The collected poems of Robert Service are almost sure to be there. For these are the old days, and Alaska still gleams bright and golden as the land of the lucky strike, where even a social rebel might get rich quick, finding honest money in beach or stream. The conversational tide flows from injustice in the woods to the arrival of the *Portland* in Seattle with her million-dollar cargo in dust; from the free-speech fight in Spokane to the perils of Stampede Pass; from the castration of Wesley Everest to the caddish way in which Alexander Pantages, the Greek showman, done wrong to Klondike Kate after she staked him. On such an evening your host may suggest a midnight stroll along the beach, not just for the beauty, which is great, but for treasure. Beach dwellers take everlasting delight in going out to see what the tide has brought them. It may be a green float pulled from the net of a Japanese fisherman five thousand miles away; an empty wine bottle from the Greek freighter that passed during the afternoon, outbound for India with a load of wheat; a bit of frayed rope; a serviceable broom; a three-sided picture frame; or a lily-pad, the butt end trimmed from a peeler log at some plywood mill. Sometimes there is a log rolled up on the beach like a stranded whale.

A log can mean a night's work, for although anyone who lives on a beach considers anything that washes up on the beach to be his, by the divine right of beach dwellers—and anything that washes on a neighbor's beach to be his too, if the neighbor is not home—the law holds that a log belongs to the man whose brand is upon it. So the very least a beach dweller can do with a gift from the tidal gods is to deface the brand with a few strokes of an ax. It is wiser to get out the cross-cut and saw the branded end clear off. Even after these elementary precautions have been taken, the log is still subject to seizure by the log patrol, so it is best to float it to some nearby cove where it can be hidden for later delivery to a friendly millowner, who will pay half the going rate, log scale.

If the log is red cedar a beach man can handle it himself with wedge and saw and froe. He drives the wedges into the log until it splits along the grain. When the log is broken into bolts, the bolts are cut into two-foot lengths. Then, using the froe, a heavy blade fourteen to twenty inches long and about three inches wide, he splits the bolts down the grain into heavy, rough shingles, known as shakes. They last forever, and there is always a market for them.

Most log-pirating on the peninsula is carried on in this casual way—but not all. Millowners and towboat people don't object much to losing an occasional log, but they are opposed loudly and earnestly and in every session of the state legislature to losing logs by the raftful. A boom of logs is worth tens of thousands of dollars. Rough water may cause a few logs to leap over the boom-sticks, but the real danger is that a chain will break, spilling a whole section.

Back in the 1920s, when log-pirating was best organized, the rustlers were not content with picking up stray sticks. They made certain that spills would occur. Sometimes they sawed a boom-stick almost in two, or filed the link chains so that rough water, or even a change in the tide, assured a break-up. Tug skippers were bribed to spill their loads in convenient spots. Log piracy reached its peak when an off-duty bootlegger got a Canadian watchman drunk in a rafting cove on Vancouver Island, hitched a towboat to a huge boom, and headed south into American waters.

Soon after that the Washington State legislature passed "an act to protect the title of the owners of floating logs, timber, and lumber." It established the branding system for logs; they are branded with a stamping ax. It also gave log owners the right to pursue their logs onto private property, and it established the legal basis for the operation of the log patrol.

The patrol began in 1928 as a sort of floating vigilance committee, organized and financed by some of the bigger companies to discourage pirating. W. E. (Ed) Craw, a former Everett police captain, was the chief of the patrol. He was deputized in a half-dozen counties and rode his range in a fast motorboat. He sent a number of pirates to jail, but it was probably the depression that broke up the pirates' operations. Nobody could sell logs in those days.

During the early 1930s the log-patrol men took on the duties of aquatic cowboys. They rounded up strays and

herded them back to their owners. With the coming of the
war logs became valuable again. A few waterfront men had
noted that there was nothing in the law to prevent a private
citizen from organizing his own log patrol, even if he had no
logs to patrol. Soon a dozen or more log patrols were scouting
for other people's logs. Lumbermen complained that it was
hard to tell a patrolman from a pirate. A spokesman for the
big companies complained to the state legislature that "it has
become a case of every pirate being his own watchman." The
private log-patrol operators hired a lobbyist, and he told the
legislators that logs were needed for the war effort, that the
sale of salvaged logs was conducted under state regulations,
and that brand-owners got part of the money paid for their
logs. The patrols continue to operate.

My favorite log-patrol man was Frank Butts, the carefree
captain of the *Brant*. When I knew Butts, in 1949, he was
living aboard a patrol boat with his wife and their two young
children. It was a good life. When the *Brant* left her moorage
on the Duwamish River in Seattle and glided past Harbor
Island into Puget Sound, Butts seldom knew where he was
headed. "We just follow the logs," he said. But as often as
not he wound up coasting the shore of the peninsula.

Butts cruised close to the beach, watching for logs on the
sand. When he saw one, if the tide was high, he nosed the boat
ashore. The *Brant* barely drew a glass of water forward,
though she needed five feet astern. When the prow hit sand
Butts would jump ashore while his wife, Margaret, took over
the controls. Margaret's job was to see that the boat did not
get "in irons"—that is, drift sideways to the shore. Butts
would dig a hole under the inshore end of the log and slip
a choker around it. Back in the cabin, he would throw the
Brant into reverse. The line snapped taut, and the log charged
across the beach and into the water.

At the end of a day's search for sticks Butts ran the *Brant* into one of the tiny coves that pocket the peninsula. He had no favorite among them. "You always think the one you're in is the best place on earth." If he got as far north as the San Juans, where there are few logs but wonderful swimming beaches and fine people, Butts was likely to knock off for a week. Then, to make up for lost log-gathering time, he would visit the Dungeness spit, which catches more logs per frontal foot than any other stretch of shore known to beachcombers.

After rounding up a satisfactory show of logs, Butts hauled them back to the patrol moorage in Seattle. The operator who owned the boat would pay him $17.50 a thousand feet for the logs he retrieved. He was a happy man. I've lost track of him, but I like to think of him, roaming the sound.

Log-patrolling is one thing, and log-poaching is quite another. A poacher steals trees. He goes into someone else's stumpage and starts cutting. Usually a poacher trucks the logs out to a mill, though some operators have been known to bring in portable sawmills and saw lumber on the spot. Lumber-poaching suits are frequent in superior court in western Washington.

The boldest poachers invade the National Forests. In the old days this activity was considered just part of the lumber business, but the old order changeth, and now the poacher must worry not only about the Forest Service rangers but about the F. B. I.

One night in January of 1954 a man noticed lights flickering on a hillside behind his home. It was in a National Forest, and he knew there was a fire-lookout station on the hill. But what was anyone doing watching for forest fires in January? He phoned a forest ranger friend to find out. The ranger said there was no one in the station as far as he knew, but he'd go check. He found that eleven trees had been cut, two of them within recent hours.

The rangers checked the back roads and came on a logging truck with two logs. The driver said the sticks had been taken on a pulp-company tract near the National Forest. The rangers let the driver go on, but they followed the road to the pulp-company land and found it blocked with a windfall. The rangers called the F. B. I.

Special Agent Will Ralston was assigned to the case. It was a bit out of his line, but he decided to follow the usual procedures. He went with the rangers to the scene of the crime. There he singled out the two freshest cuts and had rounds sawed from the stumps. These rounds, each about a foot thick and four feet in diameter, were tagged and taken to the Tacoma F. B. I. office.

Ralston and the rangers went to the log dump where the truck-driver sold his logs. They asked the scaler to locate the two the driver had brought in. The logs were hauled from the water, and the butt ends were cut off.

Then the driver was picked up. He denied everything. Ralston showed him how the butt ends of his logs fitted the rounds from the stumps taken in the National Forest. The driver confessed and later pleaded guilty in federal court to stealing government property. He was fined one thousand dollars and ordered to pay four thousand dollars in restitution for the stolen logs.

In the old days on Puget Sound a similar bit of detective work might have disrupted an industry.

ii

It is in the high hills that you encounter the real pioneers, the people of almost excessive competence, who make you feel the slackness of your own muscles and the softness of your own life.

There's Ignar Olson, the packer and cougar-hunter, well into his sixties and quite capable of going anywhere in the mountains, with or without horses, and getting there in less time and better shape than men half his age.

There's Minnie Peterson, born on the Hoko River near the tip of the peninsula about the time that John Huelsdonk came to the Hoh. She married the Forest Service ranger at Forks and raised a family of four and, when she was a grandmother, took to operating a pack train out of Sol Duc. The commander of a Coast and Geodetic Survey party in the Olympics said, "My men had some doubts about asking a woman to go to some of those mountains. She convinced them. In fact she scared 'em half to death. She can get those horses anywhere." In her spare time Minnie helps her husband, Oscar, run two ranches, one at Forks, the other on the Hoh.

And there are the Crislers, Herb and Lois, who were not to the mountains born. Crisler, a Carolinian, first saw the Olympics as an aerial photographer during the First World War, when he was assigned to map the forest for the Spruce Division. After the war he spent his vacations there. In 1930, as a stunt sponsored by a Seattle newspaper, he went into the Olympics at the Elwha River with no provisions and no camping equipment except a hatchet and a pocket knife. Thirty days later he appeared on the Quinault River. He had lost twenty pounds. The notes he kept for the newspaper were laconic:

> August 23—Had only few berries to eat all day.
> August 24—Went to Hoh after fish but caught none. Heavy rain. Nothing to eat today. Storm is brewing. Heavy rain. Clouds. Very hungry.

August 25—Nothing to eat today. Weather is bad. Fog. Saw deer and bear but got no pictures. Am terribly hungry.

August 26—Happy day. Killed two grouse [by throwing rocks]. Cooked livers and hearts first. They cook faster. Then cooked birds and ate ravenously. No pictures today. Saw band of elk at a distance. Have hiked seventy-five miles including side trips.

In spite of the hardships, Crisler loved the Olympics more than ever. He returned to the old Humes cabin on the Elwha, and there in 1942 he brought his bride, Lois, whom he had rescued from the life of a freshman composition teacher.

The teacher and the photographer gave themselves a difficult assignment: to make a complete photographic record of a year in the life of their nearest neighbors, the elk herd. The Crislers packed supplies into the high mountains so they could live through the summer within sight of the herd. They followed the migration down into the valleys in the fall. During winters they left the Olympics and went lecturing to earn money for more film, but they were back by the river when the cows dropped their calves in spring. They followed the herd for years. During the war they served as lookouts in remote stations. Eventually their record was complete. They sold the film to Disney. It was released as *The Olympic Elk*, a lovely picture and, unlike others in the Disney nature series, not in the least coy.

When I think about pioneers, and especially about pioneer women, who gave up the familiar and the certain to cross the fever-ridden plains and take up their lives in rude houses at the edge of the dark forest, I like to think too of Lois Brown Crisler, reading at freshmen one year, and the next following the elk on the alpine meadows.

11

Land's End

It was raining, of course. It rained nearly all that summer and fall on the Northwest Coast. The wind from the south, strong and steady and cold, fanned across the swell, kicking up a nasty chop around our lifeboat. There were no white-caps. The water was heavy green. Four miles to the east we could see the hulk of the mainland, its cliff green-black under the claylike clouds. To the west the ocean stretched unbroken for four thousand miles. The thirty-six-foot boat seemed small.

We were making the once-every-three-weeks run from LaPush, the Quillayute fishing village where the Coast Guard maintains a life-saving station, to Destruction Island, the bleak rock which many Coast Guardsmen consider the most remote and forlorn spot in the United States.

The boy from Los Angeles ducked out of the forward compartment. He was nineteen years old, just a few weeks out of Coast Guard boot camp. This was his first trip to Destruction, where he was to be stationed. He held his lips carefully against his teeth. "Pretty rough," he said, gulping.

"I didn't think you'd stay in that compartment long," said

the bos'n. His name was Roberts. He had a rugged, uncomplicated face and looked, I thought, rather like Wallace Beery. "You feel the weather down in there plenty." He pointed ahead. "See your new home?"

The boy turned and looked. Some miles ahead, low and bleak and ominous, lay Destruction Island. He stared at it for a long time, and then he said, "Well, it's only eighteen months."

The bos'n grinned. "You know the difference between Destruction and Alcatraz?"

"What's the difference?"

"On Alcatraz you get time off for good behavior."

"Very funny." The boy tried to light a cigarette. The wind blew out the matches as he raised them toward his face. He gave up and tossed the cigarette overboard.

"Actually," said the bos'n, "most guys get transferred after a year."

"No time at all," said the boy. "Well, I asked for it. Forty-two on, nineteen off. In nineteen days I can drive home and have a couple weeks with my folks. I couldn't do that on shore with just weekends."

He turned and studied the mainland. The waves broke lacy-white and dangerous at the base of a cliff crested with dark evergreens. The tops of the firs and cedars scraped the bottom of the leaden clouds. Somewhere behind the clouds lay the mountains.

"Some country," said the boy.

"It's not bad," said the bos'n. "It's one place you can still get away from people."

"I'll say," the boy replied, not without bitterness.

"I've fished places in there no one ever fished before, far as I could tell," said the bos'n. "There are spots where you can limit on trout in fifteen minutes." He spun the wheel delicately, and the boat curved westward. "You can't beat that, being first to see a piece of your own country. It's a privilege."

"I'll settle for L. A."

"Don't fight it, kid. Relax and enjoy it."

The lifeboat droned southward through the chop.

The landing on Destruction, on a narrow channel known as The Hole, is on the southeast tip of the island. Roberts made his approach along the western shore. Since the highway around the peninsula skirts the shore opposite Destruction, I had often seen the island from the east—a long, low, black rock lying in the breakers like some enormous and menacing whale. But the western shore was as unfamiliar as the far side of the moon.

Half a century ago a visiting naturalist rowed out to the island to study the rhinoceros auklets, small birds that nest in burrows on the island during the summer. He wrote:

Destruction Island, unlike most of the Olympiades, is not a stubborn remnant of some ancient rocky headland, but rather is a detached fragment of a valley floor—in fact, a chip of the prosy mainland block four miles distant. It owes its preservation to a series of outlying reefs, grim bones from which the sea has stripped the flesh, and is itself a phase of dissolution. On this account its top is level, while its sides are fresh-cut and steep, although a brave luxuriance of vegetation serves to retard, as it disguises, the progress of decay.

About this island of sixty acres gather a few memories of the human, a tragedy of discovery, a shipwreck or two, and latterly the brave, lonesome life of lightkeepers. But these are matters of two centuries, a mere yesterday. Drop down behind the sea-wall, out of sight of the friendly lighthouse, and you could forget that man ever lived. Nor would you suspect what is the real interest, the historically continuous interest of this spot. It is the home of ten thousand rhinoceros auklets. They are the cave dwellers of Destruction.

Most other visitors to the island have agreed with the naturalist: it is strictly for the auklets. There is hardly a soft word about the long rock in log or journal. Time after time it is referred to as "dreary," "forlorn," "barren," "god-forsaken."

It was here the Spaniards first landed on the Washington coast, and they named the island "Isla de Dolores"—the Isle of Sorrows. No one actually christened the island with its present name. In 1787 Captain Barkley named the Hoh River, which empties into the Pacific a few miles north, Destruction River, because the Quillayutes had wiped out a landing party from the *Imperial Eagle*. The name just drifted out to sea and stuck on the island. The early settlers and the skippers of coastal vessels called the Hoh "Hoh" and the island "Destruction." Mapmakers finally made it official. "After all," Bos'n Roberts remarked, "the damn place *looks* like Destruction."

For all its sullen appearance and sinister name, Destruction has been the scene of few marine disasters. Some small fishing vessels have been blown to grief against the island, but there is no record of a major wreck there. However, forty-two vessels have been broken against the mainland cliffs or have foundered in gales within sight of the island. There have been no wrecks on this stretch of the coast since 1943, when a Russian freighter blundered onto the rocks near LaPush in a heavy fog. The present run of eleven years without a major wreck is the longest since regular shipping began along the coast a century ago.

Bos'n Roberts stopped our lifeboat just off the Hole. "Pretty quiet in there today," he remarked, studying the narrow channel between the rock cliffs. "You should see it when there's a good wind from the south. We get a real surge. Kill a boat in a minute in there."

An outboard nosed out of the Hole and worked toward us through a bed of iodine-colored kelp streamers. "Thought you were coming all the way in," the seaman in the outboard said to Roberts as he came alongside. He was a slight, brown-haired young man with a fluffy mustache.

"Thought I was nuts," said Roberts. "This rig costs forty thousand dollars. It'd take all my pay for a year to buy the Uncle a new one."

The boy from Los Angeles and I clambered down into the outboard. "See you this evening," said Roberts to me. "If the wind holds, that is." The boats moved apart.

"If that wind does shift," the young seaman said, "you've found a home. You could be with us quite a while."

The outboard took us up the Hole to a cove barely fifteen feet across. The cliff rose forty or fifty feet, then folded into a steep, brush-covered hill. Three men stood on the break of the cliff, working the boom arm of a derrick. A square box at the end of a cable came swinging down; we got in and were hauled up, spinning slowly. Opening my eyes, I could see the lifeboat, very white against the dull green water, moving away. The box came to rest gently on the platform.

A lean man in green fatigues came from the winch and stuck out his hand. "I'm Hagen," he said. "I'm in charge here."

We climbed a long flight of gray steps up the hill and came out on an oval of tableland. The island is overgrown with a shoulder-high tangle of salmonberry and salal, impossible to walk through. A path tunnels through the brush to a clearing in which are clustered the quarters, the oil house, and the blunt pillar of the lighthouse. Near the quarters we passed a concrete tennis court, netless, the slabs awry, grass bunched in the cracks.

"Play much tennis?" I asked.

Hagen shook his head. "No time," he said. "We're busy as hell out here—painting, keeping the place up, fighting the bushes. Besides, we get rain half the year, and when it isn't raining it's foggy or the wind is blowing. Get a good wind in winter, and it blows the tops of the waves clear over the island. I've seen spray hit the top of the lighthouse. This place isn't set up to be any Forest Hills."

We went into the quarters, a big, solid house stemming straight from New England. The boy from Los Angeles disappeared into his room to break out his gear. Hagen and I settled at the kitchen table, and over the coffee he told me about the island.

The lighthouse was built in 1891, and some of the older Indians at LaPush still talk about the difficulty of landing the stones for the ninety-four-foot tower. In the old days the light burned lard oil, ten gallons a night, and there were five wicks, which had to be hand-wiped each morning. Now it is all electric, with direct current supplied by Diesel generators. The Lighthouse Service of the Department of Commerce operated the station from the time of its dedication until 1937, when the Coast Guard took over all lighthouses.

In the old days a family was planted on the island and left to flourish or wither. For months on end the lightkeeper and his family were confined to the island, their only visitors the birds, their work perpetual. Supplies came once a year. Months might pass without their even sighting a boat, for during the winter the lumber schooners held far to the west. No small boat could survive the surf of the winter storms. A bad appendix was a death sentence.

"Still," said Hagen, "a lot of fellows think the old system was the right one. Know why? Women. The lightkeepers had their wives out here, so the place was home. They *lived* here, didn't just put in days. They had a garden and even kept cows. Way it is now, we're just a bunch of guys doing time. Come on, I'll show you what's real rough about this place."

He led the way to the lighthouse, up the circular stairs, and out a door to the catwalk. To the west lay the gray ocean, unbroken to the horizon except for a scattering of trollers. They were fishing; their working poles were slanted at forty-five degree angles. Across the channel to the east lay the mainland.

"There's Ruby Beach," said Hagen, pointing to a break in the cliffs. "The highway's right on the beach there. At night you can see the lights of the cars going by. That's the roughest thing of all, watching those lights—people going somewhere. You just sit and look and look, and you grow older all the time."

The strength of the complement on Destruction varies between five and eight. The men theoretically serve up to eighteen months, but the terms actually average little more than a year. The men are on duty eight hours, off for sixteen hours. During weekends the work is held to a minimum, so they have a chance to fish, wash clothes, or "stack up some sack hours." Only one man has served two terms on Destruction since the Coast Guard took over the island. He inexplicably asked for and got a second hitch, but did not request a third. Most of those sent to Destruction have put in for isolated duty, but that may mean either an all-male outpost like Destruction or a station like Tatoosh, the next lighthouse to the north.

Tatoosh Island, at the entrance to the strait, is smaller,

higher, windier, and wetter than Destruction. Its lighthouse, recommended by George Davidson after his survey in 1852, was dedicated in 1857. The Tatoosh light is brighter, its radio beam stronger, its foghorn louder than Destruction's, but the big difference is that on Tatoosh there are women. Tricycles stand on the lawn before the lighthouse; diapers flap in the same winds that snap the storm signals.

A telephone circuit connects Destruction and Tatoosh, and the noncoms in charge often talk over their problems. "Women can make a lot of problems on an island," Hagen told me, "but it's the sort of trouble I wouldn't mind having."

ii

Five women were living with their husbands on Tatoosh when I visited the island—three Coast Guard wives and two Weather Bureau wives. They ranged in age from eighteen to twenty-nine. None had ever thought of herself as a pioneer.

There were seven children, six of them under school age. The seventh was being taught by his father, Clyde Melenthe of the Weather Bureau, who gave up schoolteaching as a profession some years ago "because I wanted to earn a living." The other parents have hinted they'd like to have Melenthe set up a kindergarten, but he has held firm. "I came out here to get away from that."

The Tatoosh Island families work hard at not getting bored. They team up to rent movies. They buy paperback books "by the drugstoreful." Some of the men fish for king and silver salmon. The N. C. O. of the Coast Guard station and his wife, Norm and Rina Barto, have taken up painting "by the numbers"; they order painting charts from a store in Port Angeles and dutifully fill them in as instructed.

Recently a TV set was installed in the living room of the N. C. O.'s house. A Canadian station brings Liberace to the wilderness.

"It's a healthy place," Rina Barto told me. "We don't even have colds unless some newcomer brings one to the island. My boys don't seem to mind the rain at all. It's a bit lonely for them, but they don't seem to mind, at least not as much as the grown-ups do. They love to watch the weather balloons go up in the morning and evening, and to play on the beach and gather shells and chase birds and—well, you know, boys on an island. But for us grown-ups it's not so easy.

"You know what I miss? I miss the dime store. And I miss being able to get milkshakes. When I get off the island—I've been off twice this year—when I do I get a chocolate shake and a chocolate sundae and a side order of french fries, all at the same time.

"And I miss the Fuller Brush man. Never thought I would, but I sure do—somebody dropping around unexpectedly.

"You know, it's hard, shopping by phone. I don't mean rugged or anything, not like the old days out here. It's just that when you don't go to the store you forget. Gee, how you forget. And anyway, any woman likes to pick out her own vegetables and maybe pass the time of day. You miss that out here, ordering by phone the way we do.

"I thought we'd save a lot of money out here, but you can't cut corners, shopping by phone. And besides, there are ways to spend money on an island. Don't let anybody tell you. Sears! That catalogue! We call it the wish book. You can sure build up a lot of longing for something just looking at the pictures in a catalogue.

"And—I suppose I shouldn't say this, but I guess most of all I miss a chance to get away from the kids, just for an hour or so. You know, when you go out to see people of an evening and you get in a baby sitter and all at once you're younger again, just for an hour or so. I miss that."

iii

Down on Destruction the Coast Guardsmen envy the Tatoosh crew their TV nearly as much as they do the women. It's a link with home. As it is, they look forward most to the mail, which comes once every three weeks, and to their once-in-six-weeks trips off the island.

Men due for relief sweat out the weather. If the wind is blowing when their leave time comes the outboard may not be able to make it out of the Hole, or the lifeboat may not be able to fight across the bar of the Quillayute at La-Push. When the trip is delayed the man due to be rotated simply loses his time.

"Back in 1950," Hagen told me, "our refrigeration plant broke down, and the O. I. C. telephoned for help. Fellow came out from Port Angeles, Art Hassel, and he fixed it up in a hurry, but while he was working the wind was rising, and by afternoon the Hole was plugged up. He was out here nearly two weeks, right in the middle of December. Guess he almost went nuts. Then the wind died down a bit, and a couple of the fellows come out in the lifeboat and picked him up—Christmas morning. They started to tell him how sorry they were not to get him off sooner, and you know what the first thing he said was? 'Those poor damn bastards who got to stay—why, they're making Christmas tree balls out of old light bulbs.'"

The wind seemed to be rising. I licked my finger and raised it to the wind, and my finger felt cold. Hagen grinned at me. "Don't worry. You'll be able to get off."

"What happens if a boat is in trouble and the lifeboat is stuck behind the bar at Quillayute?" I asked.

"Oh, if they really have to get out they get out. A mail run's one thing, and business is another. Take the time Frankie Johnson drowned."

Johnson, I learned, had been a Quillayute Indian, and he had drowned in February 1953. The day had been cold, very cold, and the wind strong from the south. A heavy surge crashed over the outer wall of the jetty at LaPush and fought with the outgoing tide for domination of the channel. The bar was turbulent. The commercial fishing vessels that operate out of LaPush during summer and fall had long since returned to their home ports. But the Quillayutes have special treaty rights permitting them to fish year-round. (One woman in the village remembers seeing the treaty signed by Michael Simmons on the beach in 1855.) So it was that at three P.M. Frankie Johnson went out in his lean black dugout to inspect the set nets at the mouth of the river. The canoe was of the type the Indians used when the Spaniards came, but it was driven by an outboard motor. As Johnson approached the nets the motor conked out. The canoe was swept down the narrow channel toward the bar.

The Coast Guardsman on watch in the lookout tower spotted Johnson and called the boathouse. Bos'n Roberts and Carl Jones were working there. They launched a canoe and started after Johnson—too late. The dugout was already in the waves that broke over the south jetty. Johnson stood, ready to jump.

From the lookout tower the man on watch shouted, "Don't jump! Don't jump!"

It is doubtful that his words carried through the crash of the waves. Johnson jumped. The empty canoe shot across the bar, bounced wildly in the breakers, and then, taken by some freak current, was thrown over the north jetty into comparatively calm water, still upright.

After diving from the canoe, Johnson swam for a moment against the tide. Then he too was carried over the jetty and into the heaving surf on the outside. He was not seen again, either by the man on the tower or by Roberts and Jones, who had approached the jetty in their canoe. The two Coast Guardsmen saw no chance to get across the bar in the small boat. They paddled back to the boathouse. When they arrived Roderick Dowell, the noncom then in charge of the station, was launching the thirty-six-foot lifeboat. They jumped in and started for the bar.

The lifeboat fought its way out into the ocean through water described officially as "extremely rough"—one of the rare times the phrase appears in the station log, an impeccably conservative document. Waves broke completely over the boat. The crew was drenched. Roberts and Jones, who were wearing cotton fatigues and oxfords and were without storm clothes, felt the cold miserably. For an hour the lifeboat wallowed along just outside the surf line, the men scanning the breakers and the tangle of bleached driftwood spread white on the dark sands. They did not see Johnson.

The radio crackled, telling them to give up the search and get back before dark. They started for the station. As they approached the bar the lifeboat began to surf; waves from behind lifted the stern clear of the water so that the rudder failed to catch and the propeller fluffed air. "We were," Roberts said later, "at the mercy of the sea."

They fought clear of the bar and, still outside, radioed headquarters. Group Commander told them to run north around Flattery and take refuge at Neah Bay. They started, but the motor began to cough. Air was in the fuel line. They turned and struggled toward Destruction, hoping to lie in the lee of the island until the motor could be repaired. They came around behind the island and dropped anchor, a hundred-pounder on seventy fathoms of three-inch line.

Night closed in. The wind rose to a full gale. Waves hit the face of the island with the sound of rockets. Spray streamed in sheets across the island. The lifeboat was thrown around like a celluloid ball in a washing machine. The crystal flew out of the radio set; the compass bounced out of the binnacle; the fire-extinguishers were torn from their brackets; and Dowell, although strapped to the wheel, was thrown against the control lever with such force that three ribs on his right side caved in.

The men struggled to get the motor started.

"We were all sick," Roberts said afterward. "Oh, were we sick! We were going down into the engine room, sucking oil out of the tanks, and spitting it onto the filter, trying to get it going. I can still taste it, that oil. Talk about sick.

"When I wasn't down in the engine room I kept taking bearings. They kept changing. I couldn't figure it out at first. Then I realized we were dragging that damn anchor. We dragged it from six miles one side of the light to six miles the other, twelve miles in four hours, anchored. There've been times we couldn't make that much speed without an anchor.

"We finally got the engine going, but we couldn't raise the anchor, not in that sea, being weak the way we were from heaving. The only thing to do was cut loose. But if we cut it and the engine gave out again, it meant the rocks. So we radioed for help. Neah Bay dispatched the forty-footer to escort us, but the storm was too big and she turned back. So they sent the eighty-three-footer, and she nosed out and turned around and went back to bed—too much weather. So they assigned an old thirty-six-footer, same as us, and she made it. She escorted us to Neah Bay, and we waited there until we could get back to the station. Believe me, that was no milk run."

Frankie Johnson's body was washed ashore three days later.

I asked Hagen whether the men on Destruction ever went out on rescue parties.

"No. Our job is running the light station. We don't have equipment out here for working in the ocean. That's up to Quillayute. We keep the light burning and the radio going, and when there is fog we sound the horn. That's plenty."

The light on Destruction is a 500-watt bulb raised by prisms and reflectors to 90,000 candlepower. On clear nights it can be seen eighteen miles at sea. It blinks in a rhythm of ten seconds on, two and a half seconds off.

The radio beacon too pulses out a regular signal (dot-dash-dot-dash) on 300 kilocycles. The signal, when related to those from other stations, or to the boom of Destruction's diaphonic foghorn, enables a navigator to determine his position. Destruction also monitors the signals of two other Coast Guard stations to make sure all the strands are in place in the electronic safety net that is spread over ships in the Pacific.

Hagen went down the stairs to the garage-like ground floor and turned on the foghorn. Its throbbing bellow beat at us. The air trembled with it. Gulls rose, their screams of protest silent against the voice of the machine.

"Some guys can sleep through this," said Hagen, throwing the switches that subdued the horn. "Me, I just lie there and hate the fog. Last August I had to run the horn three days steady."

It was raining hard as we walked back to the quarters. Hagen leaned into the wind, an angular man, competent and hard-bitten. "I don't like it out here," he said. "None of us do. But don't get the idea we feel abused. There are a lot worse places. We could be out on some chunk of coral where everything that bites raises bumps. This is a job, same as any other. Somebody's got to do it, and we're it. That's all."

He paused a moment and looked out at the trollers. They had raised their poles and were headed back to LaPush, running before the rising wind. "Somebody's got to be here," Hagen said softly.

As we started into the quarters we met the boy from Los Angeles, who was being shown around the island by the seaman who had run the outboard.

"How you doing?" I asked.

"Swell," he said. "Forty-one days, twenty-two hours, and fifteen minutes to go."

iv

I was able to get off the island that afternoon. The sky had lowered, and the rain beat down hard. Destruction disappeared in the mist, and the shore of the mainland swelled and faded as the low clouds drifted across the face of the forest.

I thought of the Spaniards approaching the beach where the Indians lay hidden, afraid and armed. I thought of Lieutenant Vancouver and Mr. Gray cruising side by side along this coast and arguing about the existence of the Columbia River. I thought of Frankie Johnson, tending his nets, and Bos'n Roberts, doing his job.

The shoreline that I could see from the lifeboat was part of the Olympic National Park. It is dedicated to remaining a wilderness, as it probably would have remained in any case, for the trees are too wind-tortured to make logging them worth while. Like the glaciers and the alpine meadows, its beauty is protected by its worthlessness.

Can beauty be worthless?

I thought: This is the last bit of the country, the farthest reach. It looks now as it did when Captain Gray saw it. It is unchanged since Lewis and Clark started west. It is the last wilderness, and will remain so. And I was glad.

INDEX

Index

265